Understanding the European Union

A concise introduction

John McCormick

palgrave

First published 1999 by
PALGRAVE
Houndmills, Basingstoke, Hampshire RG21 6XS and
175 Fifth Avenue, New York, N.Y. 10010
Companies and representatives throughout the world

PALGRAVE is the new global academic imprint of
St. Martin's Press LLC Scholarly and Reference Division and
Palgrave Publishers Ltd (formerly Macmillan Press Ltd).

ISBN 0-333-73898-5 hardback
ISBN 0-333-73899-3 paperback

This book is printed on paper suitable for recycling and
made from fully managed and sustained forest sources.

A catalogue record for this book is available
from the British Library.

Cataloging-in-Publication Data is available from the Library of Congress

ISBN 0-312-22165-7 hardback
ISBN 0-312-22166-5 paperback

10   9   8   7   6   5
08 07 06 05 04 03 02 01

Copy-edited and typeset by Povey-Edmondson
Tavistock and Rochdale, England

Printed and bound in Great Britain by
Creative Print & Design (Wales), Ebbw Vale

Contents

List of Boxes, Tables, Figures and Maps

Boxes

Tables

Figures

Maps

List of Abbreviations

ACP	African, Caribbean, Pacific
CAP	Common Agricultural Policy
CFSP	Common Foreign and Security Policy
CoR	Committee of the Regions
COREPER	Committee of Permanent Representatives
DG	directorate-general
EAGGF	European Agricultural Guidance and Guarantee Fund
EC	European Community
ECSC	European Coal and Steel Community
ecu	European Currency Unit
EDC	European Defence Community
EEA	European Economic Area
EEC	European Economic Community
EFTA	European Free Trade Association
EMS	European Monetary System
EMU	economic and monetary union
EP	European Parliament
EPC	European Political Cooperation
ERDF	European Regional Development Fund
ERM	exchange rate mechanism
ESF	European Social Fund
EU	European Union
G7	Group of Seven industrialized countries
GAC	General Affairs Council
GDP	gross domestic product
GNP	gross national product
IGC	intergovernmental conference
IGO	intergovernmental organization
IO	international organization
MEP	member of the European Parliament
NAFTA	North American Free Trade Agreement
NATO	North Atlantic Treaty Organization
OECD	Organization for Economic Cooperation and Development
OEEC	Organization for European Economic Cooperation
PR	proportional representation
SAP	Social Action Programme
SEA	Single European Act
TEN	trans-European network
VAT	value-added tax
WEU	Western European Union

Introduction

The creation of the European Union will go down in history as one of the most remarkable achievements of the twentieth century. In the space of just forty years – less than two generations – Europeans fought two appalling wars among themselves, finally appreciated the dangers of nationalism and the futility of violence, and sat down to design a system that would make it inconceivable that they would ever take up arms against each other again.

The results have been substantial. A body of treaties and laws has been agreed and a set of institutions has been created that have altered the political, economic and social landscape of western Europe, changed the way Europeans relate to each other, redefined the balance of power in the world by creating a new economic superpower, and helped bring to Europe the longest uninterrupted spell of peace in its recorded history. The European Union is the world's biggest economic power, is one of the two largest markets in the world, expresses itself ever more forcefully in global trade negotiations, and has planted the seeds of a common foreign and defence policy.

Of course not everyone agrees that European integration is a positive development, nor is everyone ready to credit Brussels with bringing peace to Europe. Europeans have mixed opinions about the wisdom of shifting powers from the member states to a new level of government, and while opinion polls show that about half the population approves of the European Union, the other half either disapproves or is not yet sure what to think. Eurosceptic politicians and media are more than willing to point to the more extreme examples of 'interfering Eurocrats', and of the costs of giving up sovereignty to institutions that they like to describe as secretive and unaccountable. They also question the extent to which integration can be credited with the economic growth and prosperity that has come to much of Europe since 1945.

But whether we like it or not, the European Union is here to stay. The changes it has brought have spun a web of links among the state of western Europe that would be difficult to unravel. Free trade and the free movement of EU citizens have steadily dissolved the barriers that for so long reminded Europeans of their differences, and while national and regional identities are still alive and well, they no longer contain the seeds of the kinds of competition and conflict that have so often brought war and destruction to Europe. If the single market has taken Europe to the brink of economic union, then the projected completion of the single currency in 2002 will push it over the brink, and will take the region closer to political union.

Under the circumstances, Europeans are going to have to become more familiar with the nature and the structure of the European Union. Ten years ago it was only a peripheral factor in most of their lives, but with the completion of the single market and moves towards a common foreign policy and a single currency it is becoming increasingly difficult to ignore. We are all having to learn more about the powers of the European Commission, the content of the Maastricht and Amsterdam treaties and the meaning of concepts such as structural funds, cohesion and the democratic deficit.

This is an introductory book about the European Union, written for anyone who is confused about how it works and about what it means for the 373 million people who live under its jurisdiction. Unfortunately confusion seems to be the order of the day – Europe has been busy integrating itself for nearly fifty years, but three in four of its inhabitants confess to a poor understanding of the EU, its policies and its institutions, and about one in eight admit that they know nothing at all about how it works (see Box 6.1 on page 154).

This is a worrying state of affairs. As long as the confusion persists, Europeans will keep their distance from the EU, the process of integration will continue to be driven by the elites who have made most of the major decisions since the outset, and the values and priorities of the European people may not be reflected in those decisions. A common criticism of the EU is that it is not very democratic, and that bureaucrats have too much power and too little accountability – but little will change unless Europeans learn how this remarkable and controversial entity works, and increase the pressure for accountability.

From my vantage point as a British citizen living in the United States, I have watched with fascination as my fellow Europeans have strengthened their bonds, and with concern as so many have admitted their uncertainty about the consequences. My annual trips back to Europe have allowed me to compare public and media responses to the EU on both sides of the Atlantic, and to gain the kind of perspective that distance often allows. At the same time my students at Indiana University have presented me with the challenge of convincing them why they should care about something that is happening 4000 miles away.

Part of that challenge involved finding a textbook that explained the EU in terms that were real and approachable, but while there has been dramatic growth in the literature on the EU in recent years, there are remarkably few introductory texts on the market, and even fewer that successfully convey the significance of the EU. Too many authors have allowed themselves to become bogged down in treaty articles and Eurojargon, and – the worst sin of all – they often make one of the most fascinating developments in European history sound rather dull and bureaucratic.

These problems prompted me to write *The European Union: Politics and Policies*, which was published in 1996 by Westview Press primarily for a North American audience and designed mainly for upper-level classes in European politics. The present book is more introductory in purpose and broad-ranging in scope. I have tried to write it in a way that will make it equally accessible to readers in Europe, North America, and anywhere else in the world where the EU is studied. Its central purpose is to demystify the European Union, to help readers come to grips with this strange new economic and political entity, and to do this all as clearly and as succinctly as possible.

To this end it includes all the important details about how the EU works and what it does, but it also sets out to provide context by introducing, explaining and assessing the history of the EU, the goals and motives behind European integration, the impact of integration on the member states, the changes the EU has made to the lives of Europeans and the long-term implications of the European experiment. It also provides critical analysis of the EU, offering thoughts on where it has done well and not so well, and improvements that need to be made.

Chapter 1 provides a survey of the theoretical background to regional integration, explaining the motives behind international cooperation, showing how the EU is different from conventional international organizations, and placing it in context by briefly describing several other exercises in regional integration around the world.

Chapter 2 provides historical background of the EU by discussing the evolution of the idea of Europe, and showing how the terms 'Europe' and 'European' have changed and evolved. The chapter also provides a political, economic and social survey of Europe today, which serves as a foundation for the discussions about integration in later chapters.

Chapter 3 consists of a short history of European integration since 1945. It describes and explains the different steps in the process, from the creation of the European Coal and Steel Community, through the treaties of Rome, Maastricht and Amsterdam, to the completion of the single market and plans for a single European currency.

Chapter 4 looks at the five major European institutions – the Commission, the Council of Ministers, the European Parliament, the Court of Justice and the European Council – and explains how they are structured, how they function, how they relate to one another and how they fit into the broader process of making European law and policy.

Chapter 5 assesses the relationship between the EU and its member states, and the changing character of the EU. It looks at the constitutional issues raised by integration, and illustrates the effects of integration by looking at developments in regional and environmental policy, explaining what they have meant for the member states.

Chapter 6 does much the same for the relationship between the EU and its citizens. It looks at the problem of the democratic deficit and examines the impact that EU policies on citizenship, culture, workers' rights, unemployment and worker mobility have on the lives of Europeans, ending with a discussion of the need for democratic reform.

Chapter 7 focuses on the economic impact of European integration, with particular emphasis on the changes that have resulted from the single market programme. It looks at the ups and downs of the Common Agricultural Policy, and finishes with an assessment of the implications of the plan to introduce a single European currency.

Chapter 8 assesses the European Union in a global context. The chapter begins with a survey of the attempts that have been made to develop a European foreign and defence policy, then assesses the role of the EU as the world's newest economic superpower and looks at the EU's relations with different regions of the world.

In order to help readers keep up with the constant and rapid evolution of the EU, the publishers are creating a World Wide Web page for this book and other introductory texts in the European Union series which will provide information on key developments – such as changes in the composition of the European Parliament following the 1999 elections and of the Commission – and links to selected other internet resources. The address will be:

http://www.palgrave.com/politics/EU

Acknowledgements

The students in my classes have been the most important influence on this book because it was written mainly with the needs of students in mind. So I want to thank them for providing the points of reference that helped me decide what to include, what to leave out and what questions to address. I also want to thank Steven Kennedy, who – more than any other publisher I have worked with – helped shape its outline and provide a sense of what readers would need. My thanks also go to the anonymous reviewers who provided comments on the idea and the manuscript, to Neill Nugent, Willie Paterson and Vincent Wright for their work as series editors, to Stephen Heathorn for his help with Chapters 2 and 3, to Keith Povey for his good work as editor, and to all the production staff. Finally and most importantly, my thanks and love to Leanne for her moral support, and for not minding my antisocial attachment to my PC.

JOHN McCORMICK

Map 1 *The EU*

EU member states

Chapter 1

Regional Integration

When we think of the way the global system functions, and of our place in that system, most of us think in terms of states, and of ourselves as citizens of one or other of those states. Maps of the world show continents and regions divided by state frontiers, demarcating areas that come under the administration of different governments and separate systems of law. When we travel from one state to another, we usually have to present passports or other documents, and are reminded that we are in transit until we return to the state to which we 'belong'.

States have been the primary actors in the global system for more than 200 years, and students of international relations have for decades devoted their time and energy to the study of alliances, changing patterns of cooperation and conflict, and fluctuations in the balance of power between and among states. However, the state is not the only kind of administrative community, nor is it even necessarily the best. In fact there are many who argue that the modern state system is declining, undermined by several fatal flaws, and that the world may be moving steadily towards broader regional groupings that will help us set aside our national differences, avoid conflict and concentrate instead on the benefits of cooperation.

The most serious challenges to the idea of the state came during the first half of the twentieth century with two devastating world wars, each of which brought fundamental changes in attitudes towards the relationship among states, and each of which led to urgent debates about the dangers of nationalism and the threat of war that seemed perpetually to hang over the state system. The pressures and desires to build peace through cooperation rather than competition reached a new level of intensity after the Second World War, when plans to build a new global order dominated by Europe and North America were disrupted first by the cold war and then by the emergence of an increasingly demanding and influential bloc of Asian, Latin American and African states.

1

For many, the cold war – a war of ideas and ideologies rather than of direct conflict between the major protagonists – exemplified all the doubts about the value of the modern state, which was forged out of violence and seemed unable to guarantee the safety of its citizens except through a balance of terror with other states, and over which hung the constant threat of nuclear annihilation. A successful state must keep most of its people happy most of the time, but many theorists asked whether the modern state could ever do this given its ties with nationalism, and its potential for misunderstanding and conflict. Such doubts led to growing support for the idea of peace through international cooperation, which led to an explosion in the number of international organizations, spearheaded by the creation of the United Nations in 1945.

The search for peace has also led to experiments in regional integration, the argument being that economic, social and political integration can reduce or remove the causes of conflict. The European Union is just one of those experiments, but the one that has evolved the furthest and brought the greatest changes for its citizens. Regional integration has also been tried in Latin America, the Caribbean, southeast Asia, parts of Africa and – since 1989 – in North America, but so far on a more modest scale (see later in this chapter). The European Union could provide a model that might eventually lead to the breakdown of the state system as we know it, and to its replacement by a new community of political and economic units and networks.

Despite the impact it has already had on the lives of more than 370 million Europeans, we are still some way from really understanding the dynamics of the EU. It is more than a conventional international organization, but it is neither a state nor a superstate. So what is it? In an attempt to provide some answers, this chapter looks at the nature of international cooperation, and describes and assesses competing ideas about how the EU has evolved, and what it has become. It also looks at other experiments in regional integration in an attempt to put the EU into a broader perspective.

International cooperation

International cooperation has taken many different forms, from the narrowly focused to the broadly idealistic, and has resulted in the development of many different methods and systems for promoting cooperation. The most common has been the creation of international organizations (Box 1.1), within which multiple national groups, corporations and governments cooperate on matters of mutual interest. The

---

Box 1.1 International organizations

Most of the standard definitions of an international organization (IO) describe a body that promotes voluntary cooperation and coordination between or among its members, but has neither autonomous powers nor the authority to impose its rulings on its members. IOs are a relatively recent phenomenon, their creation having been prompted in large part by the lessons learned from two world wars. In 1900 the world had just 220 IOs; by 1969 the number had grown to about 2000, by 1981 it had reached 15 000 and it now stands at about 38 000 (Union of International Associations Homepage, 1998).

There are different kinds of IO that have developed for different reasons and with different structures, methods and goals. Most fit broadly into one of two main categories:

- *Intergovernmental organizations* (IGOs) consist of representatives of national governments and promote voluntary cooperation among those governments. IGOs have little or no autonomy in decision making and little or no coercive power over their members. Examples include the United Nations, the World Trade Organization, the Organization for Economic Cooperation and Development (OECD) and the North Atlantic Treaty Organization (NATO).
- *International non-governmental organizations* (INGOs) are bodies that work internationally, or consist of groups of national non-governmental organizations. They include multinational corporations such as Royal Dutch-Shell and General Motors, but most are non-profit-making interest groups that cooperate in order to pursue the collective goals of their members, or to bring pressure on governments for policy change. Examples are the International Red Cross, Amnesty International and Friends of the Earth.

In terms of scope, IOs can be regional, universal, specialized or multipurpose. In terms of structure and strategy, they can involve cooperation (working together on policy without making major commitments or structural changes), association (reaching formal agreements that might bring structural changes) or harmonization (making adjustments to policies in order to bring them into alignment).

European Union is an international organization in the sense that its members are nation-states, but it has moved well beyond conventional ideas about international cooperation.

International cooperation rarely involves the surrender of significant sovereignty or independence by the participants, although no state has ever been truly independent because none has ever been wholly self-sufficient. However, if cooperation does lead to the surrender of sovereignty, we begin moving into the realms of what is known as supranationalism, a process of cooperation that results in a shift of authority to a new level of organization that is autonomous, above the state and has powers of coercion that are independent of the state. Supranationalism can take at least three different forms: Confederalism, consociationalism and federalism.

Confederalism

Confederalism is a system of administration in which two or more organizational units retain their separate identities but give specified powers to a higher authority for reasons of convenience, mutual security or efficiency. The component units are sovereign and the higher authority is relatively weak, existing solely at the discretion of the units and doing only what they allow it to do. Federalism is different in the sense that it involves the local units surrendering some of their sovereignty and giving up power over joint interests to a new and permanent national level of authority. Both are in turn distinct from the unitary system of administration used in countries such as Britain, France, Japan and Italy, where sovereignty rests almost entirely with the national government, which can abolish or amend local units at will.

Among the few examples of countries that have practiced confederalism are the United States in 1776–89 and – to some extent – Switzerland today. In the case of the United States, the founders were equally worried about anarchy (too little government) and tyranny (too much government), and until 1789 the original colonies related to each other as a loose confederation. The assumption was that they might cooperate enough to form a common system of government, but they did not; the 1781 Articles of Confederation created little more than a 'league of friendship' that could not levy taxes or regulate commerce, and national defence was founded on state militias. It was only in 1787 that work began on developing an entirely new federal system of government, redefining the idea of federalism in the process.

For its part Switzerland was almost entirely confederal until 1798, and although it is now technically a federation, it has given up fewer powers to the national government than has been the case with other federations, such as Germany, the United States and Russia. The Swiss encourage direct democracy by holding national referenda, have a Federal Assembly elected by proportional representation and are governed by a Federal Council elected by the Assembly. One of the members of the Council is appointed to a one-year term as head of state and head of government.

The European Union is confederal in several ways:

- Decisions taken by the leaders of the member states have resulted in a transfer of some authority to the European Commission and a cluster of specialized EU agencies (see Box 4.3), but the member states still have the upper hand through their powers of appointment to the EU institutions, and through their powers to make decisions in the Council of Ministers, and the EU is governed as a whole through a process of negotiation and bargaining among national governments.
- The member states are still distinct units with separate identities, have their own systems of law, can sign bilateral treaties with other states, and can still (just) argue that the EU institutions exist at their discretion.
- There is no European government in the sense that the EU has obvious leaders – such as a president, a foreign minister or a cabinet – with sole power to make policy for the EU member states. This is changing however; the Commission represents the EU as a whole in international trade negotiations, and the Treaty of Amsterdam includes a provision for a single member of the European Commission to represent the EU on foreign policy matters (see Chapter 8).
- The EU may have its own flag and anthem, but most citizens still have a much greater sense of allegiance to their own national flags, anthems and other symbols, and progress towards instilling a sense of a European identity has been mixed (see Chapter 6).

The waters have been further muddied by the fact that some EU institutions are more federal in nature than confederal, and by the fact that the EU has been building a body of law that is obliging the member states to fall into line with each other by changing national laws. The development of two bodies of law is one of the main characteristics of a federal system.

Consociationalism

Consociationalism is a concept that is unfamiliar to most Europeans, and despite its value in helping us to understand the EU, it is rarely mentioned in any discussions about European integration. It is a system sometimes proposed for societies with deep religious, racial or linguistic divisions, such as Belgium and Israel, and involves government by a coalition that represents the different groups in that society. As much decision making as possible is delegated to the groups, power and resources are divided in accordance with the size of each group, and minorities may be deliberately overrepresented and protected by the power of veto. The idea of consociationalism grew out of attempts in the 1960s to shed light on the means by which deeply divided societies went about governing themselves. While it is usually applied to the structures and processes of parties and governments in small western European states such as Austria and Belgium, it can also shed light on how regional integration has evolved and what it can become (Taylor, 1990).

Lijphart (1979) describes four preconditions for consociationalism, all of which are found in the EU:

- There must be several groups of people (the citizens of the member states) who are insulated from each other in the sense that their interests and associations are inwardly directed, but although they have a high degree of self-determination, they also come under a joint system of government (the European Union).
- The political elites of the different groups (the leaders of the member states) work together and share power with each other in the manner of a grand coalition or cartel (the European Council and the Council of Ministers), reaching decisions on matters of common interest as a result of agreements and coalitions among themselves. It helps if they are encouraged to do this by external threats.
- All the groups have power of veto, but government is based on consensus among the elites of each group.
- The different groups are represented proportionally in all the major institutions of their common government (see details in Chapter 4 on voting procedures in the Council of Ministers, and membership of the European Parliament), but the rights and interests of minorities are protected from dictatorship by the majority, and decision-making authority is delegated as much as possible to the different groups.

As Paul Taylor puts it (1990, p. 174), the leaders in a consociational system 'are faced continually with the dilemma of acting to preserve the general system whilst at the same time seeking to protect and further the interests of the groups which they represent'. There is also an element of selfishness involved, because the leaders tend to pursue their own definitions of the common interest while often overlooking the views of citizens. Ian Lustick (1979) argues that the leaders must be able to rise above the divisions among the groups, work with the elites of the other groups in a common effort, and be able to accommodate the different interests involved. Those interests tend to be defined by the elites, which usually express them vaguely in terms of the common welfare of the groups. The elites work with each other in a system of political or material exchanges, bargains and compromises, and bureaucracies and legal agencies act as umpires in helping to interpret the bargains that have been reached. A consociational system is like a set of delicately but securely balanced scales, but the stability of the whole system may occasionally oblige the leaders to use undemocratic methods to discipline the segments.

Federalism

A federal system is one in which general (or national) and local administrative units coexist with shared and independent powers, neither having supreme authority over the other. Unlike confederalism, federalism usually involves an elected national government with sole power over foreign and security policy. There is usually a single currency and a common defence force, both national and local bodies of law, a written constitution, a court that can arbitrate disputes between the different units of government, and at least two major levels of government, bureaucracy and taxation. The general government has independent powers that can be increased according to the interpretation of the federal constitution. The cumulative interests of the local units tend to define the joint interests of the whole, and the general government constantly couches its mission in terms of fulfilling the wishes of the people, describing itself as the servant of the people, functioning only for their convenience.

The United States is a good example. It has been a federal republic since 1789, when the original 13 colonies agreed to move from a confederal relationship to a federal union, voluntarily giving up power over areas such as common security but retaining their own sets of laws and a large measure of autonomy over local government; for example the states can raise their own taxes and have powers over education, the police and roads. According to the US constitution, federalism prohibits the states from making treaties with other states or foreign nations, having their own currencies and – without the consent of Congress – levying taxes on imports and exports, and maintaining a military in peacetime. The federal government for its part cannot unilaterally redraw the borders of a state, impose different levels of tax by state, give states different levels of representation in the US Senate (where every state has two representatives), or amend the constitution without the support of two thirds of the states. Meanwhile the states reserve all the powers not expressly delegated to the national government or prohibited to them by the national government. Another key feature of the US model is the common sense of identity of its citizens, most of whom put their loyalty to the United States above their loyalty to the states in which they live.

The EU member states can do almost everything that the states in the US model *cannot* do: they can make treaties, operate their own tax systems, maintain an independent military and so on. The EU institutions, meanwhile, have very few of the powers of the federal government in the US model: they cannot levy taxes, operate a common military, do not yet enjoy the undivided loyalty of most Europeans, and do not have sole power to negotiate all agreements on behalf of the member states with the rest of the world. The EU is not yet the kind of federal institution that the most ardent Europeanists would like, but it does have some of the features of a federal system of administration (Wallace, 1994, pp. 38–40):

- It has a complex system of treaties and laws that are uniformly applicable throughout the European Union, to which all the member states are subject, and that are interpreted and protected by the European Court of Justice.
- It has a directly elected European Parliament, which has limited but growing powers over the process by which European laws are made.
- The EU budget is the germ of a fiscally independent supranational level of government.
- The executive European Commission represents all the EU member states, and has the authority to oversee external trade negotiations on their behalf.

One way of looking at the practice of European federalism is to picture the EU as a network in which individual member states are increasingly defined not by themselves but in relation to their EU partners, and in which they prefer to interact with one another rather than third parties because those interactions create incentives for self-interested cooperation (Keohane and Hoffmann, 1991, pp. 13–14). It has been argued that the EU has become 'cooptive', meaning that its participants have more to gain by working within the system than by going it alone (Heisler and Kvavik, 1973). Once they are involved, they must take some of the responsibility for actions taken by the EU as a whole, and the governments of the member states are finding it increasingly difficult to get away with blaming the European institutions.

Federalism is not an absolute or a static concept, and it has taken on different forms in different situations according to the relative strength and nature of local political, economic, social, historical and cultural pressures. For example, the US model of federalism was in place long before that country began its westward expansion, explicitly includes a system of checks and balances and a separation of powers, and was adopted more to avoid the dangers of chaos and tyranny than to account for social divisions. In India, by contrast, federalism was seen as a possible solution to the difficulty of governing a state that was already in place, and that had deep ethnic and cultural divisions; the national government has a fused executive and legislature on the British model, but has a federal system of administration.

The most enthusiastic European integrationists would like to see a federal United States of Europe in which today's national governments would be little more than local governments, with the same kinds of powers as state governments in Germany or the United States. Before this could happen, the EU institutions would have to be able to act on behalf of all the member states in at least foreign relations, and there would need to be a single European currency. European federalism could eventually look very different from US, Indian or even German federalism. For example it already includes the peculiarly European idea of subsidiarity, where decisions are taken as closely as possible to the people.

Theories of integration

What are the motives behind regional integration, where did the European Union come from and how did it reach the point where it is today? Standard theories of political integration argue that people or states create alliances or common political units for one of three reasons: they may be forced together by a Napoleon or a Hitler, they may share common values and goals and reach agreement on how to govern themselves as a whole, or they may come together out of the need for security in the face of a common external threat. A fourth possible reason is convenience or efficiency: they may decide that they can promote peace and improve their quality of life more quickly and effectively by working together rather than separately.

International cooperation in western Europe was long influenced and driven by the first three motives, but a shift to the fourth since 1945 has encouraged Europeans to rethink their attitudes towards each other and to work more closely together. At least until the late 1970s, the focus was on integration in the interests of economic development: barriers to trade were pulled down, national monetary and fiscal policies were harmonized and the free movement of people, goods, money and services was promoted, all in the hope of bringing new levels of prosperity. The supporters of economic integration never saw it as an end in itself, however, and as the EU member states have built closer economic ties, so some of their leaders have flirted increasingly with the idea of political cooperation. Which came first is debatable; as Ernst Haas (1968, p. 12) argues, economic integration 'may be based on political motives and frequently begets political consequences'.

In *The Uniting of Europe*, his ground-breaking study of the European Coal and Steel Community (ECSC), Haas defined political integration as 'the process whereby political actors in several distinct national settings are persuaded to shift their loyalties, expectations and political activities toward a new center, whose institutions possess or demand jurisdiction over the pre-existing national states' (Haas, 1968, p. 16). Leon Lindberg, in his 1963 study of the European Economic Community (EEC), defined political integration as the process by which (a) nations forego the desire and ability to conduct foreign and key domestic policies independently of each other, instead making joint decisions or delegating the decision-making process to new central organs, and (b) political actors such as policy makers, bureaucrats, legislators and interest groups shift their political activities to a new centre (Lindberg, 1963, pp. 6–7).

The evolution of the European Union has been characterized by at least two major sets of conflicting views about the nature of integration.

Realism versus functionalism

Realists argue that states are the most important actors in international relations, that domestic policy can be clearly separated from foreign policy, and that rational self-interest and conflicting national objectives lead states to protect their interests relative to those of other states. Realists talk about an anarchic global system in which states use both conflict and cooperation to ensure their security through a balance of power among states. They see the EU as a gathering of sovereign states, believe that those states retain authority over their own affairs, give power to new cooperative bodies only when it suits them, and retain the right to take back that power at any time. In short, the EU exists only because the member states have decided that it is in their best interests. Realism dominated the study of international relations from the 1940s to the 1960s, and was taken a stage further in the 1970s and 1980s by neorealists, who argued that the structure of institutions mattered more than their intentions. For example, they studied the changing power of states and the effect of this on international relations.

A contrasting approach is offered by functionalists. While realists talk about competition and conflict, functionalists move away from self-interest and towards a common interest in cooperation (see Table 1.1). They argue that the process of integration has its own internal dynamic, and that if states cooperate in certain limited areas and create new bodies to oversee that cooperation, they will cooperate in other areas through a kind of 'invisible hand' of integration. In short, functionalism argues that European integration has its own logic that the EU member states find hard to resist. Although membership involves contracts that in theory could be broken, in reality they have an almost irresistible authority, and integration has now become so much a part of the fabric of western European society that secession would cost a state far more than continued integration.

Table 1.1 *Realism and functionalism compared*

	Realism	Functionalism
Dominant goals of actors	Military security	Peace and prosperity
Instruments of state policy	Military force and economic instruments	Economic instruments and political acts of will
Forces behind agenda formation	Potential shifts in the balance of power and security threats	Mutual convenience and the 'expansive logic of sector integration'
Policy issues	An emphasis on high politics, such as security and defence	An initial emphasis on low politics, such as economic and social issues
Role of international organization	Minor, limited by state power and the importance of military force	Substantial. New functional IOs will formulate policy and become increasingly responsible for implementation

Source: Adapted and expanded from a similar table in Robert O. Keohane and Joseph S. Nye, *Power and Interdependence: World Politics in Transition,* 2nd edn (Boston, Mass: Little, Brown, 1989).

Intergovernmentalism versus supranationalism

Debates have long raged about whether the EU is an organization controlled by governments working with each other as partners, or whether it has developed its own authority and autonomy. At the heart of this debate has been the question of how much power and sovereignty can or should be relinquished by national governments to bodies such as the European Commission and the European Parliament. Britons and Danes (and even the French at times) have balked at federalist or supranationalist tendencies, while Belgians and Luxembourgers have been more willing to give up sovereignty.

Some observers question the assumption that intergovernmentalism and supranationalism are the two extremes of a continuum (Keohane and Hoffman, 1990), that they are a zero-sum game (one balances or cancels out the other), that supranationalism involves the loss of sovereignty, or that the EU and its member states act autonomously of each other. It is argued, for example, that governments cooperate out of need, and that this is not a matter of surrendering sovereignty, but of pooling as much of it as is necessary for the joint performance of a particular task (Mitrany, 1970). The EU has been described as 'an experiment in pooling sovereignty, not in transferring it from states to supranational institutions' (Keohane and Hoffmann, 1990, p. 277).

Others have argued that it is wrong to assume that 'each gain in capability at the European level necessarily implies a loss of capability at the national level', and believe that the relationship between the EU and its member states is more symbiotic than competitive (Lindberg and Scheingold, 1970, pp. 94–5). Ernst Haas argues that supranationalism does not mean the exercise of authority over national governments by EU institutions, but rather that it is a process or a style of decision making in which 'the participants refrain from unconditionally vetoing proposals and instead seek to attain agreement by means of compromises upgrading common interests' (Haas, 1964, p. 66).

Explaining European integration

Functionalism has dominated the theoretical debates since the 1950s about how the EU has evolved. Jean Monnet and Robert Schuman – often described as the founders of the European Union – were functionalists in the sense that they opted for the integration of a specific area (the coal and steel industry) with the hope that this would encourage integration in other areas (Box 1.2). As Schuman put it, 'Europe will not be made all at once or according to a single plan. It will be built through concrete achievements which first create a de facto solidarity' (Schuman Declaration, reproduced in Weigall and Stirk, 1992, pp. 58–9).

Although some federalists have argued that 'the worst way to cross a chasm is by little steps' (Streit, 1961), functionalism is based on the idea of incrementally bridging the gaps between states by building functionally specific organizations. So instead of trying to coordinate big issues such as economic or defence policy, for example, functionalists believed they could 'sneak up on peace' (Lindberg and Scheingold, 1971, p. 6) by promoting integration in relatively non-controversial areas such as the postal service, or a particular sector of industry, or by harmonizing technical issues such as weights and measures.

Among the best-known exponents of this idea was the Romanian-born British social scientist David Mitrany, who defined the functional approach as an attempt to link 'authority to a specific activity, to break away from the traditional link between authority and a definite territory'. Mitrany felt that peace could not be achieved by regional unification, because this would replace international tensions with interregional

---

Box 1.2 Stages in the process of regional economic integration

Integration can be motivated by different needs and different goals – political, economic, social and so on. For its part, economic integration can take several forms, representing varying degrees of integration (Balassa, 1961, p. 2), but if a logical progression could be outlined along functionalist lines, it might look something like the following:

1. Two or more states create a free trade area by eliminating internal barriers to trade, such as tariffs and border restrictions, while keeping their own external tariffs against non-member states.

2. The growth of internal free trade increases the pressure on the member states to agree a common external tariff, otherwise all the goods coming in to the free trade area from abroad will come through those states with the lowest tariffs. Agreement on a common external tariff leads to the creation of a customs union.

3. The removal of internal trading barriers increases the market for agriculture, industry and services, which now expand their operations to other members of the customs union. This boosts investment in those states, and increases the demand for the reduction or removal of barriers to the movement of capital and labour, creating a common market (or a single market).

4. With citizens moving more freely among the member states of the common market, there is growing pressure for coordinated policies on education, retraining, unemployment benefits, pensions, health care and other services. This increases the demand for coordinated interest rates, stable exchange rates, common policies on inflation, and ultimately a single currency, thereby creating an economic and monetary union.

5. The demands of economic integration lead to growing political integration as the governments of the member states work ever more closely and frequently together. Pressure grows for common policies in almost every other sector, including foreign and defence policy, possibly leading to political union.

---

tensions. Neither did he support the idea of world government, which he felt would threaten human freedom. Writing in wartime London in 1943, he argued for the organisation of separate international bodies with authority over functionally specific fields, such as security, transport and communication. They should be executive bodies with autonomous tasks and powers, and do some of the same jobs as national governments, only at a different level. This focus on particular functions would, he argued, encourage international cooperation more quickly and effectively than grand gestures. The dimensions and structures of these international organizations would not have to be predetermined, but would instead be self-determined (Mitrany, 1966, pp. 27–31, 72).

Once these functional organizations were created, Mitrany argued, they would soon have to work with each other. Rail, road and air agencies would need to engage in technical coordination (with regard to timetables for example) and functional coordination (to deal with differing volumes of passenger and freight traffic, for example). Different groups of functional agencies might then have to work together, which would lead to coordinated international planning. This would result not so much in the creation of a new system as in the rationalization of existing systems through a process of natural selection and evolution. States could join or leave, drop out of some functions and stay in others, or try their own political and social experiments. In short, they would be allowed to share power only if they shared responsibility. This could eventually lead to 'a rounded political system... the functional arrangements might indeed be regarded as organic elements of federalism by installments' (ibid., pp. 73–84).

Haas's study of the ECSC in 1958 and Lindberg's of the EEC in 1963 led to the reconstitution of Mitrany's theories as neofunctionalism. This argues that certain prerequisites are needed before integration can proceed, including a switch in public attitudes away from nationalism and towards cooperation, a desire by elites to promote integration for pragmatic rather than altruistic reasons, and the delegation of real power to a new supranational authority. Once these changes take place there will be an expansion of integration caused by spillover, a phenomenon in which 'imbalances created by the functional interdependence or inherent linkages of tasks can press political actors to redefine their common tasks' (Nye, 1971a, p. 200). In other words, joint action in one area will create new needs, tensions and problems that will increase the pressure to take joint action in another. For example the integration of agriculture will only really work if other sectors – say transport and agricultural support services – are integrated as well.

Neofunctionalist ideas include the notion of an 'expansive logic of sector integration', which Haas saw as being inherent in the ECSC (Haas, 1968, pp. 283 ff). The ECSC was created partly for short-term goals such as the encouragement of Franco-German cooperation, but Monnet and Schuman also saw it as the first step in a process that would eventually lead to political integration (Urwin, 1995, pp. 44–6). Haas argued that the process of spillover was not automatic, and found during the course of his study that very few people supported the ECSC idea at the start. Once it had been working for a few years, however, trade unions and political parties became more enthusiastic because they began to see its benefits, and pressure grew for integration in other sectors. Urwin notes that the sectoral approach of the ECSC was handicapped because it 'was still trying to integrate only one part of complex industrial economies, and could not possibly pursue its aims in isolation from other economic segments' (ibid., p. 76). This was partly why it was not until six years after the creation of the ECSC that agreement was reached among its members to achieve broader economic integration within the European Economic Community.

Spillover is such an ambiguous term that it needs to be broken down into more specific subcategories, of which there are at least three:

- *Functional spillover* implies, for example, that if states integrate one sector of their economies, the impossibility of isolating one economic sector from another will lead to the integration of other sectors (George, 1996, p. 24). So many functional IGOs would have to be created to oversee this process, and so many bridges built across the chasm between states, that the relative power of national governmental institutions would decline and the chasm would no longer exist. There would eventually be complete economic and political union.
- *Technical spillover* implies that disparities in standards will lead different states to rise (or sink) to the level of the state with the strictest (or most lax) regulations. For example, while poorer EU states such as Greece and Portugal may argue that the imposition of environmental controls amount to a handicap, making it more difficult for them to catch up with their wealthier partners, the decision-making process in the EU still encourages those states with the strictest environmental laws, such as Germany and Sweden, to accelerate the adoption of tighter controls by the poorer states.
- *Political spillover* is based on the argument that once different functional sectors become integrated, interest groups such as corporate lobbies and trade unions will increasingly switch their attention from trying to influence national governments to trying to influence the new regional executive, which will encourage their attention in order to win new powers for itself. These groups will appreciate the benefits of integration and act as a barrier to a retreat from integration, and politics will increasingly be played out at the regional rather than the national level (ibid., pp. 25–6).

Neofunctionalist ideas dominated studies of European integration in the 1950s and 1960s, but briefly fell out of favour in the 1970s, which Haas (1975) put down to their weak predictive capacity. However their fall from grace was probably due to other reasons. First, the process of integrating Europe seemed to have ground to a halt in the mid-1970s. The prevailing sense of despondency is obvious in a 1975 European Commission report on economic and monetary union, which complained that experience had done nothing to support the validity of the functional approach (that is, that unity would 'come about in an almost imperceptible way') and that what was needed was 'a radical and almost instantaneous transformation' (Commission, 1975, p. 5). (Ironically, the Commission was not providing the kind of leadership that was vital to the idea of neofunctionalism.)

Second, the theory of spillover needed further elaboration. The most common criticism of neofunctionalism was that it was too linear, needed to be expanded or modified to take account of different pressures for integration, and needed to be seen in conjunction with other influences. Ten years after the publication of *The Uniting of Europe*, for example, Ernst Haas (1968, pp. xiv–xv) was arguing that functional theory had not paid enough attention to changes in attitude following the creation of the ECSC, the impact of nationalism on integration, the influence of external events such as changes in economic and military threats from outside, and social and political changes taking place separately from the process of integration. He later wrote about 'fragmented issue linkage', which he felt took place 'when older objectives are questioned, when new objectives clamor for satisfaction, and when the rationality accepted as adequate in the past ceases to be a legitimate guide to future action' (Haas, 1976, pp. 173–212).

New variations on the theme of spillover were described by Philippe Schmitter (1971), including the following:

- *Spillaround*: an increase in the scope of the functions carried out by an IO (breadth) without a corresponding increase in authority or power (depth). For example, governments of the EU member states have allowed the European Commission to become involved in new policy areas, but have worked to prevent it winning new powers over the policy process.
- *Buildup*: an increase in the authority or power of an IO (depth) without a corresponding increase in the number of areas in which it is involved (breadth). Nye has written about 'rising transactions' (or a growing workload) which 'need not lead to a significant widening of the scope (range of tasks) of integration, but to intensifying of the central institutional capacity to handle a particular task' (Nye, 1971b, p. 67). This, for example, would explain why the growing workload of the European Court of Justice led to the creation of a subsidiary Court of First Instance to deal with less important cases (see Chapter 4).
- *Retrenchment*: an increase in the level of joint arbitration between or among member states at the expense of the power and authority of the IO. This has happened at times of crisis in the EU, such as when member states pulled out of attempts to build exchange rate stability in

the 1980s and early 1990s as a prelude to establishing a single currency (see Chapter 7).

- *Spillback*: a reduction in both the breadth and depth of the authority of an IO. This has yet to happen in the case of the EU as a whole, although the powers of the European Commission over policy initiation have declined in relative terms as those of the European Parliament and the European Council have grown.

Joseph Nye (1971a, pp. 208–14) gave new impetus to neofunctionalist ideas by taking them out of the European context and looking at non-Western experiences as well. He concluded that experiments in regional integration involve an integrative potential that depends on several different conditions:

- The economic equality or compatibility of the states involved, which is partly why questions have long been raised about the wisdom of allowing poorer southern and eastern European states to join the EU. At the same time, differences in the size or wealth of the member states may be less important than the presence of a motivative force that helps bring them together. For the EU, that force was once the tension between France and Germany (see Chapter 3), and is now the economic dominance of Germany.
- The extent to which the elite groups that control economic policy in the member states think alike and hold the same values.
- The extent of interest group activity. Such groups play a key role in promoting integration if they see it as being in their interests.
- The capacity of the member states to adapt and respond to public demands, which in turn depends on the level of domestic stability and the capacity – or desire – of decision makers to respond.

On almost all these counts the EU has a relatively high integrative potential, in contrast to another key experiment in regional cooperation: the North American Free Trade Agreement (NAFTA) (see below). The United States may be a strong central force for integration, but it is much wealthier than Mexico in both per capita and absolute terms, elite groups in Mexico are more in favour of state intervention in the marketplace than those in the United States and Canada, trade unions in the United States have been highly critical of NAFTA, and public opinion in Mexico is much more tightly controlled and manipulated than in the United States and Canada. NAFTA may help close some of the gaps, leading to an improvement in integrative potential and removing some of the obstacles to a North American single market, but many obstacles remain.

New developments in integration theory

Many theorists have emphasized that integration must be understood as a multidimensional phenomenon. They argue that it is impossible to separate economic and social pressures for integration from political pressures, that EU governments have given up powers over technical, social and economic tasks, and that the EU experience has shown that integration often evolves because of political 'acts of will' rather than functional or technical pressures (Dougherty and Pfaltzgraff, 1990, p. 459). In the end the debate comes down to one basic question: to what extent is integration brought about by coercion, altruism or pragmatic considerations, to what extent is it voluntary, and to what extent does it have its own internal motivative pressures?

Robert Keohane and Stanley Hoffmann (1990; 1991, pp. 18–25) argue that spillover is an important concept, but cannot be seen in isolation from other broader influences and pressures. They raise at least three key arguments about the nature of integration:

- Spillover is not automatic, but depends for its success on prior intergovernmental bargaining. Once a bargain has been made, the work of the EU can expand in the way predicted by functionalist theory. They quote the 1986 Single European Act as an example, arguing that national governments took the final steps that led to its agreement.
- Institutional change in the EU must be seen as a form of adaptation to pressures from the global economy, such as growing economic competition from Japan and the United States, or Europe's response to the turbulence in global currency markets in the 1970s. They argue that the Single European Act was driven more by events in the global economy than it was by the internal logic of spillover. The underlying thrust of this 'political economy hypothesis' is that the EU has had to change in order to keep its businesses and economies competitive in the global economy. But the idea could also be applied to other policy areas; for example, greater EU foreign policy cooperation was encouraged by crises such as the Iraqi invasion of Kuwait in 1990 and the Bosnian civil war of the early 1990s, or the problem in Kosovo in 1998.
- They describe a 'preference-convergence hypothesis', based on the argument that large-scale social change is often a result of the conjunction of unrelated events, and that changes in EU policy and policy-making structures emerge from the convergence of national government preferences rather than internal or external pressure. It could be argued that the Single European Act and the Maastricht and Amsterdam treaties were a result of that kind of convergence, but it would be hard to isolate the different pressures that brought them about.

Box 1.3 The pros and cons of regional integration

Almost all Europeans have an opinion about the European Union, but their opinions are often based on a patchy grasp of how the EU has affected their lives, and are often coloured by the populist rhetoric of anti-European media, political parties and political leaders. In the debate over the merits of integration, so far it has been easier to point accusing fingers at the costs than to outline the benefits. The costs most often quoted by Eurosceptics include the following:

1. Loss of sovereignty, national independence and national identity.
2. A reduction in the powers of national governments, and the creation of a new level of 'big government' in Brussels removed from the grassroots interests and concerns of the people.
3. Increased competition, loss of jobs and other economic threats posed by the removal of market protection.
4. Concern about drug trafficking and crime arising from easier cross-border movement within the EU.
5. Problems related to some of the more controversial aspects of integration, such as the Common Agricultural Policy.
6. The imposition of uniform laws that take no account of national social, economic and cultural differences.

For pro-Europeans, the benefits of integration include the following:

1. The peace and security brought by cross-national ties make it less likely that member states will go to war.
2. The single market offers European businesses a larger pool of consumers and allows the creation of world-leading corporations to compete with the Americans and the Japanese.
3. There is greater freedom of cross-border movement within the EU.
4. The creation of a pan-European consciousness and the pooling of the economic and social resources of multiple member states.
5. There is a greater chance of building global power and influence when the member states act in concert rather than individually.
6. Political and economic pressures have encouraged member states to 'rise' to the standards maintained by more progressive states on issues such as environmental protection and social welfare.
7. States can work together to transfer funds, investments and opportunities to the poorer parts of the EU.
8. The strengthening of democracy and the promotion of economic development in some of the EU's weaker member states.

The European Union today is still far from the entity envisaged by federalists such as Monnet and Schuman, but it has come a long way in just two generations. The member states have not yet transferred as many powers as the federalists would have liked, the EU institutions do not yet have the kind of autonomy that federalists hoped they would, opinion is still divided about the wisdom of integration (Box 1.3) and no theories have yet fully explained the timetable of integration. As Ernst Haas (1958, p. 445) argued, the causes of integration cannot be pinned down unless we can be clear about whether the rise in the number of common tasks (or transactions) precedes, reinforces, results from or causes integration.

None of these problems detract from the value of neofunctionalist theory, which has yet to be replaced by theories that are better able to explain why and how the EU has evolved. Since 1950 – through a combination of political will on the part of elites, encouragement from the United States (at least in the early years), the need that Europeans felt to protect themselves both from each other and from external threats, and the need to rebuild the European economy to respond to competition from the United States and Japan – Europeans have built a complex web of economic, political and social ties among themselves. In their wake, governments in North, Central and South America, in south and southeast Asia, and parts of Africa and the Middle East have launched their own ventures in regional cooperation and integration.

Other exercises in regional integration

The success of the European Union tends to draw attention away from several other exercises in regional integration in other parts of the world (Table 1.2). Their motives are similar or the same – peace through cooperation, security from neighbouring and distant enemies, the creation of greater economic opportunities, shared values, convenience, efficiency, and the self-interest of elites – but their chances of success vary.

North American Free Trade Agreement (NAFTA)

The removal of barriers to trade has taken on a new significance for the United States, Canada, and Mexico, which are currently in the process of building a free trade area that – with a combined GNP of nearly $8 trillion and a population of nearly 400 million – is just as wealthy but more populous than the EU. NAFTA was born on 1 January 1989 when a bilateral agreement between the United States and Canada came into force, aimed at reducing their mutual barriers to trade. Because the agreement did not include the removal of all those barriers, it actually amounted to a

Table 1.2   *Regional integration associations*

Latin America	Latin American Free Trade Association (founded 1960, seven members; now defunct)
	Central American Common Market (1960, five members)
	Andean Group (1969, five members)
	Latin American Integration Association (1980, 11 members)
	Southern Cone Common Market (Mercosur) (1991, four members)
Caribbean	Caribbean Community and Common Market (1973, 14 members)
North America	North American Free Trade Agreement (1994, three members)
Asia	Association of Southeast Asian Nations (1967, nine members)
	South Asian Association for Regional Cooperation (1985, seven members)
	Commonwealth of Independent States (1991, 12 members)
Pacific Rim	Asia Pacific Economic Cooperation (1989, 18 members)
Middle East	Arab League (1945, 21 members)
	Council of Arab Economic Unity (1957, 11 members)
	Arab Cooperation Council (1989, four members)
	Arab Maghreb Union (1989, five members)
Europe	European Union (1951, 15 members)
Africa	Central African Customs and Economic Union (1964, six members)
	Economic Community of West African States (1975, 16 members)
	Economic Community of Central African States (1983, 10 members)
	Southern African Development Community (1992, 11 members)

freer trade agreement. Controversially, Mexico was admitted to NAFTA with the signing of a treaty in 1992 that came into force on 1 January 1994.

The goals of NAFTA are to phase out all tariffs on textiles, clothing, cars, trucks, vehicle parts and telecommunications equipment over ten years; to phase out all barriers to agricultural trade over 15 years; to allow banks, securities firms and insurance companies total access to all three markets; to open up the North American advertising market; to allow lorry drivers to cross borders freely; and to loosen rules on the movement of corporate executives and some professionals. At the same time, national energy and transport industries are still heavily protected under NAFTA, there is nothing approaching the free movement of people, and all three member states can apply their own environmental standards. No institutions have been created beyond two commissions to arbitrate disagreements over environmental standards and working conditions; special judges can also be empanelled to resolve disagreements on issues such as fishing rights and trade laws.

For some, NAFTA's real significance lies less in the content of the agreement than in the symbolism of its passage, representing as it does a shift in US foreign policy and in the structure of a US economy gearing up for unparalleled competition from abroad. Certainly it is a much looser arrangement than the European Union, or even the European Economic Community in its early years. It is strictly intergovernmental, and although it will result in the reduction of trade restrictions, it involves little surrender of authority or sovereignty.

Whether NAFTA will ever become anything like the EU remains to be seen. Neofunctional logic suggests it might, but many obstacles will need to be removed: Mexico's limited democracy and centralist/corporatist ideas of government that run counter to traditions in the United States and Canada; huge disparities in wealth, education and per capita production; concern among Canadians about the cultural dominance of the United States; significant gaps in mutual knowledge and understanding among the citizens of the three countries; and myths, misconceptions and sheer ignorance about free trade.

While the signing of the 1989 US–Canadian treaty attracted little public attention or political debate, the inclusion of Mexico raised questions in the United States about jobs, illegal immigration, drug trafficking and environmental standards, but it raised even more fundamental questions for Mexico. First, NAFTA has meant greater competition for Mexican companies and an increased trade deficit for Mexico because imports from the United States have grown more quickly than exports from Mexico. At the same time it offers considerable economic possibilities: Mexican companies now have greater access to the enormous markets to the north, more foreign investment is flowing into Mexico, and more jobs are being created in Mexico as US and Canadian companies take advantage of cheaper Mexican labour.

Second, NAFTA poses a challenge to Mexico's traditional economic policy, which has been heavily interventionist, in contrast to the more free market approach taken by the United States and Canada. In 1960 Mexico was a founder member of the seven-nation Latin American Free Trade

Association (LAFTA, see below), but was unable to achieve the very modest LAFTA goals of reducing tariff and trade barriers on selected items. Membership of NAFTA immediately removed tariffs from two thirds of Mexican exports to the United States and from nearly one half of imports from the United States. By 2009 all US–Mexican trade should be tariff-free.

Third, the investment and trade offered by NAFTA may improve the quality of life for the average Mexican worker, but there are doubts about whether this will happen quickly enough to reduce illegal immigration to the United States in the short term. Finally, NAFTA is likely to mean substantial political and social changes for Mexico because of the links between economic liberalization and democratization. A free trade partnership with wealthy liberal democracies brings with it greater pressure for democratic reform. Spain, Portugal and Greece all joined the European Union within a few years of shaking off authoritarian regimes; membership of the EU brought all three countries economic benefits, which in turn underpinned their efforts at democratization.

Regional integration in Latin America

While the United States and Canada are relative newcomers to the idea of regional integration, several much older exercises have been under way south of the Rio Grande since the 1960s, with mixed results. A combination of overly ambitious objectives, persistent protectionism, authoritarian politics and bad timing has undermined most of the agreements reached so far, forcing the participating states regularly to change their objectives and methods. The result has been a complex and constantly changing web of bilateral and multilateral free trade agreements.

The first step was taken with the signing in 1960 of the Treaty of Montevideo, creating the Latin American Free Trade Association (LAFTA). Seven countries – Argentina, Brazil, Chile, Mexico, Paraguay, Peru and Uruguay – signalled their intention to create a free trade zone by 1972, but the process was quickly derailed by the difficulties inherent in negotiating the abolition of trade barriers, the ambitious timetable and the authoritarian nature of most of the governments involved. In 1969, Chile and Peru – frustrated by the lack of progress – joined Bolivia, Colombia and Ecuador in the creation of the Andean Group, a more dynamic attempt at economic integration involving reduced taxes, a common external tariff and investment in poorer industrializing areas.

In the same year LAFTA postponed the deadline for the free trade zone to 1980, but when even this proved too ambitious it focused instead on establishing a preferred tariff area based on bilateral rather than multilateral agreements. Domestic economic problems in most South American countries made it difficult to reach the necessary agreements, so a new Treaty of Montevideo was signed in 1980, replacing LAFTA with the Latin American Integration Association (LAIA). This emphasized the importance of regional preferences aimed at increasing exports, reducing imports and developing more favourable balances of trade as a prelude to regional integration. Although the replacement of authoritarian regimes by democratically elected governments augured well, the Latin American debt crisis of the 1980s discouraged those governments from opening up their markets.

The focus began to change in 1985–86 when Argentina and Brazil started to concentrate on the reduction of barriers to bilateral trade. Just as Franco-German cooperation provided the early engine for regional integration in Europe, the Argentina–Brazil nexus had a spillover economic effect on neighbouring states. In 1991 the effect expanded with the signing of the Treaty of Asunción between Argentina, Brazil, Paraguay and Uruguay, creating the Southern Cone Common Market, or Mercosur. This involves progressive tariff reduction, the adoption of sectoral agreements, a common external tariff, the agreement of free trade areas with neighbouring countries or subregional groups, and the ultimate creation of a common market.

A new dimension has been added to free trade in North and Latin America in recent years with US-led attempts to work towards a free trade zone covering the entire western hemisphere. The idea was raised in 1990 by President George Bush, who spoke of the possibility of a free trade area of the Americas (FTAA), stretching from Alaska to Cape Horn. It was taken up enthusiastically by President Bill Clinton, who played host to the leaders of 34 states at a 'summit of the Americas' in Miami in December 1994, the first meeting among leaders of American states for 27 years. They agreed a target date of 2005, with 'concrete progress' to have been made by 2000, and trade ministers have since held meetings to decide the agenda for negotiations. A second summit of the Americas was held in Santiago, Chile, in April 1998 formally to launch the negotiations. However, while trade within regional subgroupings such as NAFTA, Mercosur and the Central American Common Market has grown substantially in recent years, the FTAA has many obstacles to overcome.

Regional integration in Asia

Until 1997–98, dynamic economic growth underlined the potential for regional economic integration among the newly industrializing countries of southeast Asia. The most important initiatives have come out of the Association of Southeast Asian Nations (ASEAN), established in August

1967 to replace an earlier organization founded in 1961. Headquartered in Jakarta, Indonesia, ASEAN now has nine members: the founding states were Indonesia, Malaysia, the Philippines, Singapore and Thailand, which were joined in 1984 by Brunei, in 1995 by Vietnam and in 1997 by Laos and Burma. From an initial interest in security issues (protecting the region from big-power rivalry and providing a forum for the resolution of intraregional problems), ASEAN has moved steadily towards economic cooperation and trade, its members agreeing in 1992 to create an ASEAN Free Trade Area within 15 years.

ASEAN has a much looser institutional system than the EU. The major decision-making body is their equivalent of the European Council, the Meeting of the ASEAN Heads of Government, or the ASEAN Summit. The first such summit took place in 1976, but no plans were made to reconvene regularly until the fourth summit in 1992, when it was decided that the heads of government would meet formally every three years and informally at least once in between. While summits lay down the general direction of ASEAN activities, foreign ministers meet annually (inviting along other ministers as and when necessary) to develop overall policies, and economics ministers meet annually to work on the development of the free trade area. In recent years, sectoral ministers have also met more regularly to discuss energy, agricultural, tourism and transport issues. When necessary, joint ministerial meetings take place to promote cross-sectoral coordination. A standing committee headed by a secretary-general takes care of business between ministerial meetings, providing a very modest bureaucracy for ASEAN (ASEAN Homepage, 1998).

Further west, the most obvious candidate to head a regional economic grouping is India, with a population of about one billion. India has been reluctant to become involved in regional economic arrangements, however, thanks mainly to strained relations with most of its neighbours, especially Pakistan, with which it has had three wars since 1947. India's giant presence has also caused an unequal distribution of power in south Asia, and successive Indian governments have tended to prefer to deal bilaterally with other countries in the region. For their part, India's smaller neighbours fear that India would inevitably dominate a regional association, and use it to institutionalize its hegemony (Hardgrave and Kochanek, 1993, pp. 409–10).

Despite these concerns, greater regional cooperation began slowly to emerge in the early 1980s, leading to the creation of the South Asian Association for Regional Cooperation (SAARC) with seven members: India, Pakistan, Bangladesh, Nepal, Bhutan, Sri Lanka and the Maldives. Together they are home to more than 1.2 billion people, or one fifth of the world's population. Meeting in 1983, the foreign ministers of the seven countries agreed to promote 'collective self-reliance' in nine areas, includ-

ing agriculture, transport and telecommunications, and since 1985 the
leaders have met at annual summits rotating among the different countries,
with the host country assuming the chairmanship for that year.

The commerce ministers met for the first time in 1996, a move that was
seen as recognition of the need to address what Indian Prime Minister
Narasimha Rao called 'neoprotectionism' among SAARC members, notably India and Pakistan. The seven countries had earlier agreed to set up a
South Asian Preferential Trading Arrangement (SAPTA) with a view to
encouraging the removal of tariff and non-tariff barriers and working
towards the creation of a free-trade area (SAFTA) by 2005. At the moment
SAARC has no institutional arrangements, its goals are very modest in
comparison with those of the European Union, or even NAFTA, and much
work still needs to be done if India and Pakistan's long-standing mutual
distrust is to be overcome.

Meanwhile, broader economic integration has been taking place around
the Pacific rim under the aegis of APEC (Asia Pacific Economic Cooperation). APEC is not so much an institution as a forum for the discussion of
economic issues affecting 18 Asian, Pacific and American states, including
Japan, the United States and Canada. Although it has been promoted most
actively since 1989 by the United States and Australia, Japan and China are
widely seen as the leading contenders for leadership of APEC in the
twenty-first century. The medium-term goal is the creation of a free trade
zone among these countries by 2020. Progress so far has been slow, and
China appears to see Japan less as a partner than as a rival for leadership
in the region. At the same time, the Japanese role is welcomed by many of
its neighbours as offering a counterbalance to the economic weight of the
United States.

The 18 APEC members include some of the world's fastest-growing
economies, and APEC already accounts for about 58 per cent of global
GDP; the economic potential of APEC is enormous, and if the experiment
is successful it will almost certainly promote economic liberalization
throughout the region.

Regional integration in the Middle East

The Middle East has had less success with experiments in regional
integration than any other part of the world, which is ironic given the
Islamic belief in a worldwide community of Muslims transcending race,
language and national identity. Greater cooperation among the states of
the Middle East makes sense at many levels: several countries are too small
to sustain themselves once the oil runs out, the profits of the oil producers
could be used to invest in non-producers and help promote manufacturing

in the region, cooperation would allow better control of the already considerable flow of workers to the oil-rich states, and intraregional trade could help the Middle Eastern states to reduce their dependence on oil exports to the West and to develop regional transportation networks.

There have been a number of attempts at regional cooperation. The first began in 1945 with the creation of the Arab League to promote political, economic, social and military cooperation. The League is headquartered in Cairo, and currently has 21 members. A second step was taken in 1957 with the creation of the Council of Arab Economic Unity, whose goal is to promote economic integration. Headquartered in Amman, Jordan, it has 11 members. A limited experiment in integration – the United Arab Republic, bringing together Egypt and Syria – took just three years to collapse (1958–61). In 1965 the Arab Common Market was set up to promote economic cooperation and integration, but so far it has attracted only four members (Egypt, Iraq, Jordan and Yemen). Finally, the Arab Monetary Fund was established in 1977 to promote economic and monetary integration. Headquartered in the United Arab Emirates, it has 19 members.

Why has the success of these organizations been so limited? Part of the problem stems from internal dissension, notably differences of opinion on how to deal with Israel: Egypt was expelled from the Arab League for ten years when it signed the 1979 peace treaty with Israel. Further divisions were caused by disagreement over how to respond to Iraq's invasion of Kuwait in 1990. Cooperation has been further undermined by differences between states over the interpretation of Islam, the fact that less than 10 per cent of trade in the Middle East and North Africa is intraregional, the dominance of oil in national economies, protectionist national economic policies and severe cross-border restrictions on the movement of people. It will take a significant shift in attitudes and policies for the Middle East to create the right conditions for greater economic cooperation.

Economic Community of West African States (ECOWAS)

In May 1975 Nigeria became a founder member of – and the driving force behind – the Economic Community of West African States (ECOWAS). Headquartered in Abuja, Nigeria, it now has sixteen member states with a total population of more than 210 million. ECOWAS set out to achieve first a customs union and then a full common market along the lines of the European Union. By harmonizing their policies on agriculture, industry, transport and communications and paving the way for the free movement of people and labour, its members felt they could change the balance of power between themselves and the richer Western countries. To promote cooperation, a development fund was created through which the wealthier ECOWAS members could channel investment funds to the poorer members.

Organizationally, ECOWAS revolves around meetings of the heads of government, which took place annually until 1997, when it was decided to hold them twice a year. A council of ministers, consisting of two representatives from each of the member states, meets twice a year to oversee the running of ECOWAS, which is left to a small secretariat and five commissions dealing with issues such as trade, customs, industry and transport. A tribunal meets to interpret provisions laid down in the founding treaty of ECOWAS and to settle disputes between member states.

With its growing oil revenues in the late 1970s, Nigeria was initially an active member of ECOWAS and exerted a substantial regional influence through grants, loans and technical assistance to other member states. During the 1980s, however, when Nigeria began to tighten its belt and put domestic economic priorities above those of regional cooperation, the cracks in the ECOWAS structure began to show. Some of its members (notably Côte d'Ivoire, Ghana and Senegal) have achieved relative political and economic stability, but others (such as Burkina Faso, Liberia and Sierra Leone) have persistent instability. However, the main problem has been the unequal size of the member states. With 53 per cent of the population of ECOWAS, Nigeria is by far the largest, wealthiest and most powerful member, which has not only caused nervousness among the smaller members (such as Benin, Cape Verde, Gambia and Togo) and poorer members (Guinea, Guinea-Bissau, Mali, Mauritania and Niger), but has also led to resentment among Nigerians, who feel that their country has borne too much of the financial burden of ECOWAS.

Nigeria is a large and valuable market for the smaller states, but they have been unwilling to reciprocate by opening their markets to Nigeria and have long suspected Nigeria of working towards regional domination. Also, ECOWAS members often have conflicting economic and trade policies, have made little progress in stabilizing exchange rates among themselves and regularly fail to pay their membership fees. One of its few tangible achievements to date was its contribution to monitoring a cease-fire in war-torn Liberia in 1990–93, which prompted its members to agree a new treaty in 1993 in which they adopted the additional objective of working together on regional peacekeeping.

European integration has been driven largely by the efforts of its larger member states – notably France and Germany – and the future of NAFTA is closely tied to events and policies in the United States. In few places, however, are the fortunes of an experiment in regional integration so patently dependent upon one of the members as is the case with ECOWAS. If Nigeria were to become democratic and stable, and if its oil wealth were harnessed for the benefit of the national economy and the greater good of all its citizens, Nigeria could become a powerful and influential force for democratic change and economic development throughout West Africa. Until such time, the aspirations of ECOWAS will be more significant than its achievements.

Conclusions

The European Union is the most highly evolved example of regional integration in the world, but as this chapter reflects, it is far from the only example. Clusters of states on every continent have found that cooperation on a variety of issues is in their interests, so much so that several have decided to take that cooperation to another level, moving into the realms of integration. In other words, rather than simply working together on matters of mutual interest, they have surrendered powers to decision-making systems that function beyond the level of the state. Some of these systems are informal, consisting, for example, of regular meetings among ministers or national leaders and agreement to reach decisions jointly rather than individually. Others are more formal and have moved beyond the intergovernmental level to the institution of supranational organizations and bodies of common law.

As a result, regional integration is a concept with which we are all becoming more familiar. This is especially true in Europe, because the laws and decisions that govern the lives of Europeans are being made less at the local or national level, and increasingly as a result of negotiations and compromises among the EU member states. Developments in Brussels, Strasbourg and Luxembourg are becoming as important to understand as those in the national capitals. Not long ago an 'informed citizen' was someone who knew how their national system of government worked, how their national economy functioned and how their national society was structured. To be 'informed' now demands a much broader horizon, and familiarity with a new set of institutions, processes, and political, economic and social forces.

Yet Europeans are still some way from understanding how and why regional integration takes place, or even deciding whether or not it is a good idea. Western Europe has come a long way since 1945, and has survived political and economic crises to become an economic superpower that has enjoyed the longest period of peace in its history, domestic conflicts excepted. But to what extent can this be credited to the European Union? What would Europe look like today without the EU? Would it be richer or poorer, more or less peaceful? Is there anything that the rest of the world can learn from the European experience, and is there anything that Europeans can learn from the steps being taken towards regional integration in the Americas, Asia or Africa?

Opinions on the value of regional integration – and its long-term prospects – will remain divided as long as they are confused and obscured by questions and doubts about the conditions that encourage integration, the logic of the steps taken towards integration, and the end product. Comparing the European case with other examples of regional integration around the world can give us more insight into its advantages and disadvantages, but we are still some way from agreement on what drives the process, and from understanding what we have created. Most confusingly, the goals of regional integration are only very vaguely defined. How will Europe know when it has gone as far as it should? What exactly is the end goal? The following chapters will attempt to answer these questions by looking at the evolution, structure and effects of the European Union.

Chapter 2

The Idea of Europe

The evolving identity of Europe
Where is Europe?
Western Europe today
Conclusions

We live in a European world. It is a multicultural world, to be sure, but most if it has been colonized at some point by one European power or another, and the vast majority of people live in societies that are either based on the European cultural tradition or influenced on a daily basis by the norms and values of that tradition. The 'world culture' described by the American political scientist Lucien Pye (1966) is ultimately European in origin, even if it is most actively promoted and exported by the United States (which is itself primarily a product of European culture).

It is all the more ironic, then, that the idea of Europe is so hard to pin down. We talk easily and routinely about 'the West' and 'the Western tradition', and we know where Europe sits on a map, but we have difficulty in defining its physical and cultural boundaries and in being certain about what makes it distinctive. Europeans have much that unites them, but much more that divides them. They lack a common history, they speak many different languages, they have different social values, their views of their place in the world often differ, they have gone to war with each other with tragic regularity, they have often redefined their allegiance and their identity, and they have frequently redrawn their internal frontiers in response to changes in political affiliation.

However, since 1945 the differences have slowly been replaced by common interests, goals and values, prompted in part by a redefinition of Europe's place in the world. Helen Wallace (1992, p. 16) argues that in trying to improve the way they manage their own affairs, taking on more responsibility for each other and dealing with the uncertainties posed by changes in the Soviet Union and then in Russia, Europeans have become more introverted and their internal preoccupations have heavily shaped their attitudes towards the rest of the world. Outsiders have also had to review their understanding of Europe, which is now less a collection of freestanding sovereign states and more a potential superstate. North Americans and the Japanese see the EU as a new source of competition for economic power and political influence, while most eastern Europeans

31

298304

see it as a new force for positive economic and political change, and as a club that many of them would very much like to join.

Despite this redefinition of Europe, the idea of European unity that has taken root and expanded since 1945 is nothing new. In fact it is a very old idea that has simply been revived and, more importantly, adopted voluntarily by Europeans for the first time. Monarchs, popes, generals and dictators have dreamed about variations on the theme of unity since the Early Middle Ages, and intellectuals have been writing and talking about unity as a means of defending Europe against itself and outsiders since at least the fourteenth century. The key difference between the times in which they wrote and the contemporary age is that there is now much wider political and public support for the idea of integration than there ever has been before.

This chapter will attempt to draw a portrait of Europe. It begins with a discussion of the meaning of the terms 'Europe' and 'European', providing a brief history both of the idea of Europe and of the arguments in favour of integration and unity, and setting the scene for developments after 1945 (covered in Chapter 3). The second half of the chapter is a political, economic and social profile of Europe today, which compares and contrasts the character of the member states of the EU and their immediate neighbours.

The evolving identity of Europe

Defining 'Europe' and 'European' has always been fraught with problems, mostly because of disagreements about the outer limits of the region and the inner character of its inhabitants. Today those inhabitants are experiencing political and economic change that is encouraging them to think of themselves less as Germans or Greeks or Finns and more as 'Europeans', but this is a trend that begs several questions. What is Europe, and what exactly does being a European mean? Is there a coherent and distinctive European identity and a set of core European values with which the inhabitants of the region can identify? When and how did the idea of European unity emerge, and how has it evolved? Where does Europe begin and end?

Europe has never been united, and its history has been one of fragmentation, conflict and changing administrative boundaries. Large parts of Europe have been brought together at different times for different reasons – beginning with the Romans and moving through the Franks to the Habsburgs, Napoleon and Hitler – but while many have dreamed of unification, it has only been since the Second World War that Europeans have finally begun to embrace the notion that nationalism might be put aside in the interests of regional cooperation. For the first time in its history, almost the entire subcontinent is engaged in a voluntary exercise in integration that is encouraging its inhabitants to think and behave as Europeans rather than as members of smaller cultural groups that just happen to inhabit the same landmass.

The word Europe is thought to come from Greek mythology: Europa was a Phoenician princess who was seduced by Zeus disguised as a white bull, and was taken from her homeland in what is now Lebanon to Crete, where she later married the King of Crete. However the origin of the application of the term to a specific territory is unclear, as is the use of the term European to describe the inhabitants of that territory. The terms appear first to have taken on substance when Greeks began to settle on the Ionian Islands and came across the Persians. The expansion of the Persian empire led to war in the fifth century BC, when Greek authors such as Aristotle began to make a distinction between the languages, customs and values of Greeks, the inhabitants of Asia (as represented by the Persians) and the 'barbarians' of Europe, an area vaguely defined as being to the north. Maps drawn up by classical scholars subsequently showed the world divided into Asia, Europe and Africa, with the boundary between Europe and Asia marked by the River Don and the Sea of Azov (Delanty, 1995, pp. 18–19; den Boer, 1995).

The Romans – whose power was at its peak from approximately 200 BC to 400 AD – were the first to bring a substantial part of Europe under a common system of government. However the Roman Empire, which emerged with the rule of Augustus in 27 BC, was centred around the Mediterranean and took in North Africa and parts of the Middle East as well, and so was not exclusively European. Because the Romans were presiding over an empire, there was no prevailing sense that everyone living under Roman rule was part of a region with a common identity. Furthermore the inhabitants of Europe were (and still are in some places) known as Franks or Romans by the inhabitants of the Middle East and North Africa. The situation was further confused after the end of Roman hegemony in the last part of the fourth century AD, when Rome was invaded by the northern 'barbarians' and Europe broke up into a series of feuding kingdoms. The invasions separated western Europe culturally from its classical past, and the dark ages that followed witnessed substantial movements of people as different tribes – notably the Huns, the Vikings and the Magyars – invaded other parts of Europe.

The birth of Europe is often dated to the Early Middle Ages (500–1050), when a common civilization evolved that was based on Christianity, with Rome as the spiritual capital and Latin as the language of education. The beginnings of a sense of a European identity can be dated to the emergence of a rift between the western and eastern branches of Christianity, the expansion of Frankish power from the area of what are now Belgium and the Netherlands, and the development of a stronger territorial identity in the face of external threats, notably from the Middle East. The retreat of Europeans in the face of Asian expansionism reached its peak in the seventh and eighth centuries with the advance of Arab forces across North Africa. Crossing the Strait of Gibraltar in 711, they conquered most of Spain and southern France, and their advance ended only in 732 with their defeat by Charles Martel at Poitiers.

The term European was used by contemporary chroniclers to describe the forces under the command of Martel (Hay, 1957, p. 25), but it did not become widely used until the year 800, when Charlemagne was crowned Holy Roman Emperor by the Pope and was described in poems as the king and father of Europe. The Frankish Empire over which he presided covered most of what are now France, Switzerland, western Germany and the Benelux countries, and proponents of European union in the 1950s liked to point out that the territory of the six founders of the European Economic Community closely correlated with that over which Charlemagne had ruled. Although the Frankish Empire helped promote the spread of Christianity, it was quickly divided up among Charlemagne's sons after his death in 814, and while the Holy Roman Empire persisted until the middle of the fourteenth century, it was – as Voltaire later quipped – 'neither Holy, nor Roman, nor an Empire'.

Europe at that time was technologically backward in comparison with China, and the west was to remain peripheral to the development of civilization until well into the Middle Ages. Central authority declined and intra-European trade ended in the wake of further invasions from Scandinavia and central Europe, and feudalism became the norm as large landowners exercised growing authority over their subjects. By the beginning of the High Middle Ages in the mid-eleventh century, however, commerce had revived, agricultural production was growing, the population was beginning to increase, towns were becoming centres of intellectual and commercial life, a new class of merchants was emerging, monarchs and the aristocracy were imposing greater control over their territories and the threat of invasion from outside Europe had largely disappeared. In fact, through the crusades and the development of external trade, Europe – long the target of foreign invaders – was now the aggressor. As Christian armies came together from all over the region to take part in the crusades, Europe developed a tighter identity.

Safe from invasion, European politics and culture began to take root in the High Middle Ages, and by the fifteenth century it had become increasingly common for scholars to use the term 'Europe', which to outsiders became synonymous with 'Christendom'. Indeed the latter term was used more often than the former to describe the region. This was ironic given the turbulence that followed in the wake of famines, the Black Death and the Hundred Years' War (1337–1453), the emerging power of monarchs, and the questioning of the authority of the papacy that led to the Reformation and the growth of the modern state. Europe became divided among a variety of Protestant churches and the Roman Catholic church, and for much of the sixteenth and early seventeenth century was destabilized by religious warfare. Nonetheless Europeans began voyages of discovery to Africa, the Americas and Asia, there was an expansion of education based on the classical works of Greek and Latin authors, and a scientific revolution was sparked by the findings of Copernicus, Sir Isaac Newton and others – all these developments combined to give Europeans a new confidence and a new sense of their place in the world.

Delanty (1995, p. 42) argues that cultural diversity within Europe ensured that European unity was restricted to matters of foreign conquest and a focus on hostility beyond its borders. The earliest proponents of unity were motivated in part by their belief that a united Christian Europe was essential for the revival of the Holy Roman Empire and by concern about Europe's insecurity in the face of gains by the Turks in Asia Minor; most of the proposals for unity were based on the notion that the supremacy of the papacy should be revived (Heater, 1992, p. 6). A notable example was the suggestion made in 1306 by the French lawyer and diplomat Pierre Dubois (b. 1255). Noting that war was endemic in Europe despite the teachings of Christianity, Dubois suggested that the princes and cities of Europe should form a confederal 'Christian Republic', overseen by a permanent assembly of princes working to ensure peace through the application of Christian principles. In the event of a dispute, a panel of nine judges could be brought together to arbitrate, with the Pope acting as a court of final appeal (Heater, 1992, p. 10; Urwin, 1995, p. 2).

The Renaissance (roughly 1350–1550) saw the loyalty of individuals shifting from the Church to ideas based on individualism and republicanism, and the state system began to emerge, beginning in England and France. Under the circumstances, the idea of regional unity was far from the minds of all but a small minority of idealists. Among these were King George of Bohemia and his diplomatist Antoine Marini, who proposed a European confederation to respond to the threat posed by the Turks in the mid-fifteenth century. Their plan – which was remarkably similar to the structure eventually set up for the European Union – involved an assembly, which would meet regularly and move its seat every five years, a college of permanent members using a system of majoritarian decision making, a council of kings and princes, and a court to adjudicate disputes (de Rougemont, 1966, p. 71).

The church had become so divided by the end of the sixteenth century that the idea of a united Christian Europe was abandoned, and those who still favoured the idea of European unity saw it as based less on a common religion than on addressing the religious causes of conflict and the growing threat of Habsburg power. These were the motives behind the Grand Design proposed by the Duc de Sully (1560–1641) in France in the early seventeenth century. He proposed a redrawing of administrative lines throughout Europe so as to achieve an equilibrium of power, and the creation of a European Senate with 66 members serving three-year terms (Heater, 1992, pp. 30–5).

One of those influenced by de Sully's ideas was William Penn (1644–1718), who in the midst of yet another war between England and France published *An Essay Towards the Present Peace of Europe* (1693), in which he proposed the creation of a European diet or parliament that could be used for dispute resolution. He suggested that quarrels might be settled by a three-quarters majority vote, weighted according to the economic power of the various countries: Germany would have 12 votes, France 10, England 6 and so on (Heater, 1992, pp. 53–6; Salmon and Nicoll, 1997, pp. 3–6). In 1717 the Abbé de Saint-Pierre (1658–1743) published his three-volume *Project for Settling an Everlasting Peace in Europe*, in which he argued for free trade and a European Senate. (His ideas were later to inspire Schiller to write 'Ode to Joy' which – sung to Beethoven's Ninth Symphony – has become the European anthem; Heater, 1992, p. 85.)

The theme of peace through unity was subsequently explored by a number of prominent thinkers and philosophers. For example Jean-Jacques Rousseau wrote in favour of European federation; Jeremy Bentham, in *A Plan for An Universal and Perpetual Peace* (1789), wrote of his ideas for a European assembly and a common army; Immanual Kant's *Thoughts on Perpetual Peace* (1795) included suggestions for the achievement of world peace; and the Comte de Saint-Simon, in response to the Napoleonic wars, published a pamphlet in 1814 titled *The Reorganization of the European Community*, in which he argued the need for a federal Europe with common institutions, but within which national independence would be maintained and respected.

For political figures, the desire to overcome Europe's political divisions usually led them to the narrow view that conquest was the best response, but found themselves foiled by the sheer size of the task and the resistance of key actors to changes in the balance of power. The attempts by Charlemagne, Philip II of Spain and the Habsburgs to establish a European hegemony all failed, argues Urwin (1995, p. 2), because of the 'complex fragmented mosaic of the continent . . . [and] the inadequate technical resources of the would-be conquerors to establish and maintain effective control by force over large areas of territory against the wishes of the local populations'.

The first attempt to achieve unity by force in modern times was made by Napoleon, who brought together France, Belgium, the Netherlands and large parts of Italy under his direct rule. One of his objectives was the unification of Europe under French domination. He saw himself as the 'intermediary' between the old order and the new, and hoped for a European association with a common body of law, a common court of appeal, a single currency and a uniform system of weights and measures. In stark contrast to Napoleon's idealistic notion of unity, and despite rapid economic, social and technological change, nineteenth-century Europe was actually characterized by nationalism, which emerged during the French Revolution and led most notably to the unification of Italy in the 1860s and Germany in 1871. Nationalism led to rivalry among European states, both within Europe and further afield in the competition among those states for colonies.

The concept of a United States of Europe continued to be promoted by nineteenth-century intellectuals such as Victor Hugo, who in 1848 declared that the nations of Europe, 'without losing [their] distinctive qualities or . . . glorious individuality, will merge closely into a higher unity and will form the fraternity of Europe. . . . Two huge groups will be seen, the United States of America and the United States of Europe, holding out their hands to one another across the ocean.' However, political leaders did not embrace such ideas, and a combination of nationalism and competition for colonial possessions led to increased militarization and the outbreak in 1914 of the Great War, in which all the competing tensions within Europe finally boiled over. The result of the war was chaos in much of central Europe, and it is clear in retrospect that the 1919 Treaty of Versailles avoided as many questions and problems as it addressed.

Before, during and after the war, philosophers and political leaders continued to put their minds to the question of how to encourage Europeans to rise above nationalism and consider themselves part of a broader culture, thereby helping them to face up to – and remove – the causes of conflict and allowing Europe to defend itself against external threats. Such ideas had already been explored by Dubois, Penn, Saint-Simon and others, but they had all been writing in a vacuum of public interest. The horrors of the First World War now created an audience that was much more open to the idea of European integration, and discussions involved not just intellectuals but political leaders as well. The most enthusiastic proponents tended to be smaller states that were tired of being caught up in big power rivalry, and several made practical moves towards economic cooperation. For example, Belgium and Luxembourg created a limited economic union in 1922, and in 1930 joined several Scandinavian states in an agreement to limit tariffs.

Prominent among the intellectual contributors to the idea of European unity was Count Richard Coudenhove-Kalergi, who developed the idea of a Pan-European Union (Box 2.1). While he failed to generate a mass following, his ideas did attract the interest of a number of leading figures in the arts, such as Richard Strauss and Ortega y Gasset, and several current or future political leaders, including Georges Pompidou, Thomas Masaryk, Konrad Adenauer, Winston Churchill and – most significantly – two French prime ministers, Édouard Herriot and Aristide Briand (1862–1932). Immediately after the war, the prevailing view in France was that European cooperation was an impossible ideal and that the best hope for peace lay in French strength and German weakness (Bugge, 1995, p. 102). Herriot was one of those who disagreed, and in 1924 he called for the creation of a 'United States of Europe', to grow out of the postwar cooperation promoted by the League of Nations.

For his part, Briand called for a European confederation working within the League of Nations, and in May 1930 distributed a memorandum to governments outlining his ideas (Salmon and Nicoll, 1997, pp. 9–14). In it he wrote of the need for 'a permanent regime of solidarity based on international agreements for the rational organization of Europe'. He used such terms as 'common market' and 'European Union', and even listed specific policy needs, such as the development of trans-European transport networks, and anticipated what would later become the regional and social policies of the EU. Although he is often described in France as one of the founding fathers of European integration, attention was diverted from his memorandum by the gathering tensions that led to the Second World War.

All prospect of discussions of this kind leading to European unity was swept violently aside by the rise of Nazi Germany, which was intent on correcting the 'wrongs' of the Versailles Treaty and creating a German 'living space'. Hitler spoke of a 'European house', but only in terms of the importance of German rule over the continent in the face of the perceived threat from communists and 'inferior elements' within and outside Europe. Many of the nationalist tensions that had built up in Europe during the nineteenth century – and had failed to be resolved by the Great War – now boiled over once again into conflict. Hitler was able to expand his Reich to include Austria, Bohemia, Alsace-Lorraine and most of Poland, and to occupy much of the rest of continental Europe.

The ideological division of Europe after 1945 added to the pre-existing economic and social divisions, so that it became normal to think of the region as having multiple identities: the capitalist west, the socialist east, the industrial centre, the Mediterranean south and the Nordic north. However, the end of the cold war in 1990–91 also brought an end to the ideological and social divisions that had been represented by the Berlin

Box 2.1 Paneuropa

The period of peace after the First World War saw the publication of a flood of books and articles exploring variations on the theme of European union. The most influential of these were written by Count Richard Coudenhove-Kalergi (1894–1972), the son of an Austrian diplomat and his Japanese wife, and founder in 1922 of the Pan-European Union.

The problems facing Europe after the war convinced Coudenhove-Kalergi that the only workable guarantee of peace was political union, and he expounded his ideas in a book titled *Paneuropa*, published in 1923. He argued that while Europe's global supremacy was over, the internal decline of Europe could be avoided if its political system was modernized, with a new emphasis on large-scale cooperation. Changes in Europe could not happen in isolation from those in the rest of the world, however, and Coudenhove-Kalergi felt that the best hope of world peace lay in the creation of five 'global power fields': the Americas (excluding Canada), the USSR, Eastern Asia (China and Japan), Paneuropa (which would include Europe's colonies in Africa and southeast Asia) and Britain and its empire (including Canada, Australia, southern Africa, the Middle East and India). He excluded the USSR from Europe because it was too diverse and did not have the democratic traditions necessary for the development of Paneuropa. He was uncomfortable about excluding Britain, but did so because he felt it was so powerful as to be a political continent in its own right. It could serve as a mediator with the United States, however, and could become part of Paneuropa if it lost its empire.

Coudenhove-Kalergi argued that an arms race among European states would be destructive and keep Europe in a permanent state of crisis. Instead, he proposed a four-stage process for the achievement of European union: a conference of representatives from the 26 European states, the agreement of treaties for the settlement of European disputes, the development of a customs union, and the drafting of a federal European constitution. He also suggested that English should become the common second language for Europe, since he felt that it was becoming the dominant global language.

wall and the iron curtain, and as the differences between east and west began to decline it became more normal to think of the region as a whole.

Eastern Europe has yet to divest itself of the heritage of state socialism, and Germans still make a distinction between Germans from the east and those from the west. Furthermore, cultural and economic differences continue to influence perceptions of Europe: the Mediterranean states to the south have features that make them distinctive from the maritime states to the west or the Scandinavian states to the north. Compared with just a generation ago, however, the differences that separate Europeans have become much less distinct and much less obvious. Language differences still stand as a potent reminder of cultural divisions, but the increased mobility of Europeans and the growth in trade that has seen a greater variety of European products on the shelves of shops across the region have helped build a sense among Europeans that there is less to distinguish them from one another than they once thought.

Where is Europe?

Even as Europeans move along the path of economic, social and political integration, the definition of Europe remains ambiguous, for several reasons. First, few of the EU's member states are culturally homogeneous, and there is no such thing as a European race; as the historian H. A. L. Fisher once remarked, 'Europe is a continent of energetic mongrels'. The constant reordering of territorial lines over the centuries has created a situation in which every European state has national minorities, and several of those minorities – notably the Basques and the Irish – are divided by national frontiers. Many states have also seen major influxes of immigrants in the last forty years, including Algerians to France, Turks to Germany and Indians to Britain. Not only is there nothing like a dominant culture, but most Europeans shudder at the thought of their separate identities being in any way subordinated to some kind of homogenized Euroculture.

Second, the EU embraces at least 36 languages (Keegan and Kettle, 1993, p. 92), which are vigorously defended as symbols of separate national identities and act as a constant reminder of the differences between the European peoples – one of the factors that eased the development of the United States was the existence of a common language. Multilingualism also means that all official EU documents are translated into the 11 official languages of the member states, although an increasing volume of the work of EU institutions is carried out in English and French. Supported by its rapid spread as the language of global commerce and diplomacy, the dominance of English grows, and it may eventually become the language of Europe. This worries the French in particular and other Europeans to some extent, but it is probably irresistible and will at least give Europeans a way of talking to each other, and perhaps help reduce the cultural differences that divide them.

Third, the histories of European states overlapped for centuries as they colonized, went to war or formed alliances with each other. However, those overlaps served to emphasize their differences rather than give them a sense of shared past, and European integration grew in part out of the essentially reactive idea of putting an end to the conflicts that arose from those differences. Historical divisions were further emphasized by the colonial interests of some European states, which long encouraged them to develop competing sets of external priorities at the expense of cultivating closer ties with their neighbours – even today they continue to have different priorities, with Britain, France, Spain and Portugal having close ties with their former colonies, while Germany – for different reasons – has interests in eastern Europe.

Finally, and most fundamentally, the confusion over the definition of Europe arises out of uncertainty about its political and geographical boundaries. Every other continent is defined by its coastline, but while the western, northern and southern boundaries of Europe are marked by the Atlantic, the Arctic and the Mediterranean, respectively, it has no clear eastern boundary. Strictly speaking it is not even a continent (usually defined as a large, unbroken land mass), but is part of the Asian continent. However it has been seen as distinct from Asia for the last 2000 years or more, even if no-one can really agree on where Europe ends and Asia begins.

The eastern boundary of Europe is conventionally defined as running down the Ural Mountains, across the Caspian sea, and along the Caucasus Mountains, but these are merely geographical features that have been adopted as the meeting place of Europe and Asia in spite of political reality. The Urals, for example, were nominated as a boundary by an eighteenth-century Russian cartographer, Vasily Tatishchev, simply so that Russia could claim to be an Asian as well as a European power. If we continue to accept the Urals as a boundary, then six former Soviet republics – Belarus, Ukraine, Moldova and the three Baltic states – are part of Europe. The three Baltic republics have historically been bound to Europe, and have been moving into the western European orbit since the break-up of the USSR, but questions remain about the orientation of Belarus, Ukraine and Moldova.

The biggest problem with the Urals is that they do not mark the frontier between two states, but are deep in the heart of Russia. Russians have sometimes been defined – and have seen themselves – as European, but Russia west of the Urals was long known as Eurasia because of the distinctions imposed on the region by Europeans, and contemporary Russia sees its political and economic interests as being significantly different from those of Europe. The most obvious problem with defining Russia as European is that three quarters of its land area lies east of the Urals and more than forty ethnic minorities live within Russia, most of whom are unquestionably non-European.

In central Europe, changes in the balance of power long meant that the Poles, the Czechs and the Slovaks were caught in the crossfire of great-power competition, which is why this region was known as the 'lands between'. The Slavs in particular became divided between those who accepted Catholicism, Greek Orthodoxy or Islam, which resulted in cultural heterogeneity in spite of the greater linguistic homogeneity among Slavs than among the peoples of western Europe (Delanty, 1995, p. 54). The west looked on this area as a buffer zone against Russia, a perception that was helped by the failure of its people to form lasting states identified with dominant ethnic groups. During the cold war the distinctiveness of eastern Europe was emphasized by the ideological divisions between east and west, despite the historical ties that meant Poland was closer to western Europe than to Russia.

For their part, the Balkans occupy an ambiguous position between Europe and Asia, being a geographical part of the former but historically drawn towards the latter. They were long regarded as an extension of Asia Minor, and until relatively recently were still described by Europeans as the Near East (Hobsbawm, 1991, p. 17). The Balkans have long been regarded as a zone of transition between two 'civilizations', whether the term is applied to religions (the boundary between Islam, Catholicism and Eastern Orthodoxy) or to political communities (the boundary between the eastern and western Roman empires, between the Habsburg and Ottoman empires, and more recently between Slavic–Russian, western and eastern influences).

Historical maps of the region show that its affiliations have constantly changed: it has come under the Macedonians, the Romans, the eastern Roman empire, Slavic tribes, Christianity, the Kingdom of Hungary, the Venetians and – from the sixteenth century until 1918 – the Ottoman Turks. Except during the Tito regime (1945–80), the region has never come close to being united, and the allegiance of its inhabitants has always been torn in several directions. These changes created what Delanty (1995, pp. 51–2) describes as 'frontier societies in the intermediary lands' between great powers. The Slavs continue to have affiliations with Russia, which is part of the reason why NATO has been loathe to become too deeply involved in the conflicts in Bosnia and Kosovo.

Finally there is the question of Turkey, which has long been seen by Europeans as part of the Islamic sphere of influence and squarely as part of Asia Minor. However, Europe and Asia are conventionally seen as meeting at the Bosphorus, which means that about 4 per cent of Turkey lies in Europe. Should we not then consider Turkey to be a European state? Turkey has applied for EU membership, but the EU has so far refused to open negotiations, expressing concern about Turkey's poverty, its large population and its mixed record on human rights. However, questions about the south-eastern limits of Europe have not prevented the EU from engaging in membership negotiations with Cyprus, which is further from Brussels than most of Turkey and is divided into Greek and Turkish zones.

The cold war has not been over for very long, and most of us still find it difficult to disregard the political, economic and social distinctions that divided the countries on either side of the iron curtain; try as they might, most older Europeans still look on Hungary and Poland as being somehow different from Belgium and France. A further distinction has been added since the 1970s by the accelerating closeness among EU member states, which has divided Europe into countries that are members of the EU and those that are not. There is little question, however, that Europe is closer than it has ever been to being considered a region with common interests and a common identity.

Western Europe today

If its borders with Turkey and Russia are taken as its eastern limits, then Europe at the turn of the millennium comprises 38 countries: the 15 members of the EU, three other western European states (Switzerland, Norway and Iceland), 12 eastern European states, six former Soviet republics and two Mediterranean states (Malta and Cyprus). It is one of the wealthiest regions of the world: its 582 million people constitute about 10 per cent of the world's population and live on just 4 per cent of the world's land area, but they generate about 31 per cent of the world's economic wealth. Nearly all of that wealth is concentrated in western Europe: the 15 EU members, together with Switzerland, Norway and Iceland, generate more than $8 trillion in GNP, while in 1995 the 18 eastern European states and former Soviet republics had a combined GNP that was less than that of Spain (Table 2.1).

While there is a large measure of political, economic and social cohesion in western Europe, there are also significant differences and these have had an impact on the process of integration. The leaders of the member states do not always meet as equals: their powers are based on different political and administrative foundations, and they face different sets of economic and social criteria that sometimes oblige or encourage them to take conflicting positions at the negotiating table.

Political structure

Most European countries use variations on the theme of parliamentary government, with either a monarch or a president as figurehead; executive power is vested in an elected prime minister who is the leader of the largest political party (or coalition) in the national legislature. One of the legacies of monarchies in most European societies is the distinction between head

Table 2.1   *Europe – basic indicators*

	Area (000 sq. km)	Population (million)	GNP (billion $) (1997)	Per capita GNP ($)	Political system (1995)	Admin system (1995)
European Union:						
Germany	357	82.2	2252	27 400	Rep. PD	Federal
France	457	58.5	1451	24 800	Rep. P/P	Unitary
Britain	245	58.2	1095	18 800	CM. PD	Unitary
Italy	301	57.2	1088	19 000	Rep. PD	Unitary
Spain	505	39.7	532	13 400	CM. PD	Unitary
Netherlands	37	15.7	371	23 600	CM. PD	Unitary
Greece	132	10.5	86	8 200	Rep. PD	Unitary
Belgium	31	10.2	250	24 500	CM. PD	Unitary
Portugal	92	9.8	97	9 900	Rep. PD	Unitary
Sweden	450	8.8	210	23 900	CM. PD	Unitary
Austria	84	8.2	216	26 300	Rep. PD	Federal
Denmark	43	5.2	156	30 000	CM. PD	Unitary
Finland	337	5.1	105	20 600	Rep. PD	Unitary
Ireland	70	3.6	53	14 700	Rep. PD	Unitary
Luxembourg	2	0.4	17	42 500	CM. PD	Unitary
Sub-total	3143	373.3	7979	21 400		
Other Europe:						
Switzerland	41	7.3	286	39 200	Rep	Federal
Norway	324	4.4	136	30 900	CM. PD	Unitary
Cyprus*	9	0.7	8	11 400	Rep	Divided
Malta*	0.3	0.4	4	10 000	Rep. PD	Unitary
Iceland	103	0.3	7	23 330	Rep. PD	Unitary
Sub-total	477	13.1	441	33 670		

* States that have applied for EU membership.
Rep. = republic, PD = parliamentary democracy, Pres. = presidential,
CM = constitutional monarchy, Imp. = imperial, P/P = presidential/parliamentary

of state and head of government, which stands in contrast to the fusion of these two positions in the US system. Heads of state take several different forms:

● Eight European countries still have monarchies: Britain, Spain, Belgium, the Netherlands, Luxembourg, Denmark, Norway and Sweden. However, these are all constitutional monarchies, meaning that the monarchs have negligible political power and government is carried out in their name (they reign, but they do not rule). All are limited to

Table 2.1 *continued*

	Area (000 sq. km)	Population (million)	GNP (billion $) (1997)	Per capita GNP ($)	Political system (1995)	Admin system (1995)
Eastern Europe:						
Ukraine	604	51.4	84	1 630	Rep. P/P	Unitary
Poland*	313	38.6	108	2 800	Rep. P/P	Unitary
Romania*	238	22.6	33	1 460	Rep. PD	Unitary
Yugoslavia	102	10.4	21	2 020	Rep. PD	Unitary
Belarus	208	10.3	21	2 040	Rep. P/P	Unitary
Czech Rep*	79	10.2	40	3 900	Rep. PD	Unitary
Hungary*	93	10.0	42	4 200	Rep. PD	Unitary
Bulgaria*	111	8.4	11	1 310	Rep. PD	Unitary
Slovakia*	49	5.4	16	2 960	Rep. PD	Unitary
Croatia	56	4.5	15	3 330	Rep. PD	Unitary
Moldova	38	4.4	4	900	Rep. PD	Unitary
Bosnia H.	51	3.8	1	260	Rep. PD	Unitary
Lithuania*	65	3.7	7	1 890	Rep. PD	Unitary
Albania	29	3.4	2	590	Rep. PD	Unitary
Latvia*	64	2.5	6	2 400	Rep. PD	Unitary
Macedonia	25	2.2	2	900	Rep. PD	Unitary
Slovenia*	20	1.9	16	8 420	Rep. PD	Unitary
Estonia*	45	1.5	4	2 660	Rep. PD	Unitary
Sub-total	2190	195.2	433	2 220		
Europe total	5810	581.6	8853	15 220		
Other:						
United States	9372	272.0	7100	26 100	Rep. Pres.	Federal
Russia	17075	147.7	332	2 250	Rep. P/P	Federal
Japan	378	126.0	4963	39 400	Imp. PD	Unitary
Turkey*	781	63.5	379	6 100	Rep. PD	Unitary
World	148 429	5848.7	28182.8	–		

Sources: GNP figures from World Bank, *World Bank Atlas 1996* (Washington, DC: World Bank, 1997); population figures from UN Population Fund, *The State of the World* (Geneva: UN, 1997).

ceremonial roles, and are afforded little opportunity to advise or influence the elected heads of government.

- Most other European states have a figurehead president who has similar powers and a similar standing to that of a monarch, but instead of inheriting the job by an accident of birth, they are either appointed or elected to their position for a fixed term. In several countries – including Germany, Italy and Switzerland – the president is elected by the legislature; elsewhere he or she is elected directly by the people, but is not expected to be a political figure. The only slight exception is in

Finland, where the president has a central role in foreign policy and can become involved in domestic policy if the situation allows.

- Four countries have a mixed presidential/parliamentary system of government: France, Poland, Belarus and Ukraine. Executive power is vested in the president, who is directly elected by the people, but legislative power is vested in the legislature, overseen by a prime minister and a council of ministers. If the president's party dominates the legislature, the president has substantial powers over appointments, and the legislative programme – the prime minister and the council of ministers are appointed by the president, and the country is ruled by this triumvirate, the political agenda being set by the president. If the president's party is in a minority, however, the prime minister and council of ministers come from a different party, base their power on their support in the legislature and are much less beholden to the president.

Non-executive presidents and monarchs have the advantage of being able to act as symbols of national unity. They can provide stability and continuity, especially in the case of monarchs, who often outlast a succession of prime ministers – by 1998 Queen Elizabeth, for example, had worked with eleven prime ministers. In Italy various presidents have played a crucial role in helping offset the disruptive effects of the frequent collapse of governments, and holders of that office have been known to become involved in public debates; President Cossiaga, for example, came out in support of electoral reform in the wake of the financial scandals of the early 1990s and the subsequent collapse of credibility of Italian political parties.

The president of France (and in eastern Europe, the presidents of Poland, Belarus and Ukraine) has a significantly different position within his domestic political structure, which gives him a different status at meetings with other European leaders. As noted above, when a president's party dominates the legislature, that president has considerable powers over the legislative programme and is in a strong position when it comes to negotiating international agreements. However, in France, recent elections have resulted in presidents having to work with opposition party prime ministers. This was the case for President Chirac after the 1997 National Assembly elections – with the socialists winning the majority of votes, domestic affairs were taken over by Prime Minister Lionel Jospin and Chirac could do little more than immerse himself in foreign affairs. Even there he found himself disadvantaged in his discussions with other EU leaders because he could not rely on the backing of the National Assembly.

Executive power in most European states is vested in the prime minister (or the chancellor in Germany and Austria). In contrast to the fixed term imposed on legislators in the United States, prime ministers and legislators in Europe are elected for a maximum term – usually four or five years (three years in Sweden) – and the leader has the power to call elections any time within that term. The main power of prime ministers is vested in their virtual monopoly over appointments to senior government positions, and the fact that they can normally rely on parliamentary majorities that are strong enough to ensure the success of their legislative programmes. This is certainly true of prime ministers in states that regularly return majority governments, but much less true of those with coalition governments, such as Germany and Italy. While the former have substantial political powers, the latter must base their programmes on consensus and bipartisanship, and are driven by the need to achieve compromises that keep all the party groups within their coalition happy.

Almost all European legislatures are based on the parliamentary model, with a government consisting of a prime minister and cabinet that is answerable to – and usually part of – the elected legislative body. By definition, a legislature is where laws are introduced, discussed, amended if necessary, and either accepted or rejected. Most European parliaments have two chambers, a lower and more powerful chamber that is directly elected by the people, and an upper and usually less important chamber that may be elected directly or indirectly, or appointed. Italy, Spain and Belgium have upper chambers where most of the members are elected by the people and the rest are appointed, while Germany, the Netherlands and Austria have upper chambers whose members are elected or appointed by the state or local governments. Several smaller European states, including Denmark, Finland, Norway and Sweden, have only one chamber.

Europeans have a wide variety of political parties from which to choose at elections, with every part of the ideological spectrum represented. On the left, communists have seen their support declining significantly in recent years, and now receive far fewer votes than they did in the heyday of Eurocommunism in the 1970s. The strongest and most enduring of the left-wing ideologies is social democracy, which now forms the foundation of political parties in almost every EU member state. After steadily losing support from the 1960s to the 1980s, social democracy has strengthened its base in recent years as traditional socialist parties have shifted more towards the centre, one of the results being that in late 1998 only one major EU state – Spain – was still governed by a conservative party.

The ideological right is dominated by Christian democratic parties, which are active in most of the EU member states. More concerned than secular conservative parties about social issues, and more willing to support welfare as a means of avoiding social conflict, Christian democratic parties have been particularly influential in Germany, France and Italy, where they have adopted more liberal positions than British and Irish conservatives. One of the effects of the European Parliamentary elections (see Chapter 4) has been to encourage social democrats and conservatives to form trans-European blocs, and while they do not as yet run on a European platform, these two blocs have consistently been the biggest in the European Parliament.

A recent phenomenon in national European politics has been the rise of political parties representing more focused sectors of society: these include greens, subnational and regionalist parties, and nationalist parties of the far right. Greens have done particularly well in Germany, Belgium and some of the Scandinavian states, their views representing a backlash against unsustainable consumerism and economic development. Regional parties, while still small, have evolved in economically or culturally divided EU member states such as Belgium, Britain and Italy. The far right, building on xenophobia and opposition to immigration, has had its biggest impact in France and Italy.

Electoral systems are far from standardized in Europe. Although most countries offer their voters proportional representation (PR), several different forms of PR are practised. The most common is the straight party list system, whereby the country is divided into districts with multiple representatives, all parties field a list of candidates in each district, and the votes are shared out among the candidates according to the proportion of votes they receive. This system is practised in Spain, Portugal, the Benelux countries, and the five Nordic states. The most notable exception to the PR rule is Britain, which has a plurality or majority system (sometime known as first past the post), in which candidates from different parties compete against each other and the person who wins the most votes wins the seat, irrespective of whether or not they win a majority of votes. The advent of the Blair government in 1997 marked the beginning of discussions on the possibility of introducing PR, certainly for European elections and possibly for general elections.

The plurality system has two advantages: it usually results in one party winning a clear majority (and so contributes to governmental stability), and it assigns a single member of parliament to each electoral district, allowing constituents to develop political and psychological links with one representative. However the system tends to be unfair in that the proportion of seats won by competing parties is often very different from the proportion of votes cast; parties that have solid blocs of support around the country turn those into parliamentary seats, while parties whose support is strong but more thinly spread often come second, and win fewer seats. This was particularly obvious in the 1997 British elections, when Labour won 44.4 per cent of the votes, but nearly 64 per cent of the seats in the House of Commons, while the Conservatives won 31.4 per cent of the votes, but 25 per cent of the seats.

PR is more representative of voters' preferences, but voters are represented by a group of legislators rather than just one. More problematically, the system also results in more parties being able to win seats in the legislature, making it less likely that any one party will win a majority. The result is usually a coalition government, with two or more political parties reaching an agreement to govern together. This often means that they have to compromise their policy goals in order to maintain the coalition, and they may only have a small majority, thereby creating instability. The most extreme case of such instability is Italy, which has had nearly 60 governments since 1945, some of which have lasted only a matter of weeks before collapsing. In order to promote stability, Italy changed its electoral system in 1993 from one based exclusively on PR to one using a combination of PR and first past the post.

The result of this variety of political structures is that the power of the individual leaders of the member states is often based on different foundations, which may affect their ability to negotiate with their counterparts. For example, French presidents and British prime ministers that head a strong majority in their respective legislatures are able to adopt a relatively uncompromising position in intra-EU negotiations, while French presidents without a legislative majority, or Italian or Danish prime ministers who lead a finely balanced coalition government, may be in a weak negotiating position and more inclined to follow than to lead.

Administrative structure

All but three European states are unitary systems, meaning that all significant power is focused at the national government level. Local units of government exist, but have relatively few independent powers or rights, and must generally follow the lead set by the national government. In other words, government in western Europe tends to be highly centralized. The only exceptions are Germany, Austria and Switzerland, which are federations in which national government coexists with local units of government with their own independent powers and responsibilities, and powers are more decentralized.

Federations are generally rare, some of the key examples outside Europe being the United States, Canada, Australia, Russia, Mexico and Nigeria. Federalism usually works best in large countries where strong local government makes sense simply for reasons of convenience, or in countries that have significant social divisions and decentralization gives different groups more power over their own affairs. The United States is often taken as the model of federalism, an arrangement that was used as a means of bringing the original 13 colonies together under a joint system of government. It began with a brief confederation (1781–89) in which national government had very little power, and switched to a federation once a constitution had been agreed that outlined the relationship between national and local government.

Federalism in Switzerland is rooted in differences in language and religion, so that the populations of individual cantons speak French, German or Italian, and are either mostly Protestant or mostly Catholic (Gallagher *et al.*, 1992, p. 137). In contrast, federalism in Germany was imposed by the occupying powers after the Second World War as a means of decentralizing the German state, and several of the states created under the new system had no historical traditions. Federalism is sometimes proposed as a possible answer for the problems of culturally or historically divided societies such as Belgium, with its two language groups, or Britain, which is already experiencing federalizing tendencies as Scotland, Wales and Northern Ireland are developing their own regional assemblies.

The vast majority of European states have unitary administrative systems, although the literal meaning of 'unitary' is debatable; local government in Sweden and Denmark has more functions than do Swiss cantons, and the balance continues to change as administration in Switzerland becomes more centralized (ibid.). In practice, unitary administration means that a state has two or even three levels of government, with the national government being responsible for foreign and defence policy, managing the national economy, welfare policy, transport, environmental management, industrial development policy and other matters that are considered as best dealt with from a national perspective. Meanwhile a network of local units of government – which come under labels as varied as municipality, commune, county, parish, district, borough, province, department or region – are usually responsible for overseeing public services such as land use planning, policing, local transport, schooling, public housing, refuse collection, road maintenance and social services.

Federalism has become controversial in Europe in recent years, being regularly used by Eurosceptics as a red flag with which to warn against the loss of powers by EU member states. They often talk of the possibility of a federal government in Brussels, associating the term with such notions as 'big government' and 'loss of sovereignty'. The Thatcher and Major governments in Britain were particularly leery of the idea. In 1988 Margaret Thatcher made her views clear in one of her most oft-quoted statements: 'We have not successfully rolled back the frontiers of the state in Britain, only to see them re-imposed at a European level, with a European super-state exercising a new dominance from Brussels'. For John Major, federalism became a critical issue during the debate over the Maastricht treaty. The draft included the objective of achieving a federal Europe, but British opposition led to the removal of all references to the idea, and the treaty was eventually described as 'a new stage in the process of creating an ever closer union among the peoples of Europe'.

However it is questionable whether most Europeans really understand how federalism works, since so few of them have experienced it firsthand. It is also questionable whether a federal Europe – should it ever be created – would have the same characteristics as a federal Germany or Austria. There is no one fixed definition of a federal system; in some cases (such as Russia and India) national government is relatively strong, in others (such as Switzerland) it is relatively weak, and in almost all cases the balance of power between national and local government changes according to economic and political realities; this has certainly been the case in the United States, where there has long been a debate about which level has the advantage in that balance. The seeds of a federal European government have been planted, but whether they will eventually flower or instead grow into a much looser confederal arrangement remains to be seen.

Economic structure

All western European states are predominantly free-market capitalist systems, meaning that most economic activity is driven – and prices set – by supply and demand, and governments limit their intervention in the marketplace. This has been particularly true since the 1980s, when the Thatcher government privatized many state-owned industries and services, and several continental European states followed suit. The size of the public sector in most countries declined markedly, and free market enterprise and competition grew.

Western European states are also predominantly postindustrial, meaning that their economies have gone through a transition from agriculture to industry to heavy reliance on services, that is, economic activities that do not produce tangible commodities, for example the retail sector, food services, banking, insurance and other financial activities. Typically, services account for about 65–70 per cent of gross national product, industry for about 25–30 per cent and agriculture for the balance. The poorer states tend to have the largest agricultural sectors: while 21 per cent of the population of Greece works in agriculture and 13 per cent of the population of Ireland, only 2–3 per cent of the populations of Belgium, Germany, Luxembourg, Britain and Sweden are similarly engaged (see Table 2.2).

While the national economic systems of Europe are similar in principle, levels of national economic development are not, and the balance of power is tilted in favour of the big four western European states: Germany, France, Britain and Italy account for just over two thirds of the population of the European Union (and 44 per cent of the population of Europe), for

Table 2.2   *Population structure of the EU, 1994*

	Population density (people per sq. km)	Urban population (%)	Population employed in agriculture (%)	Population employed in industry (%)	Population employed in services (%)
Austria	96	56	6.9	35.4	57.7
Belgium	331	97	2.9	28.9	68.2
Britain	239	90	2.1	27.8	70.1
Denmark	121	85	5.1	26.5	68.4
Finland	15	63	8.6	26.3	65.1
France	106	73	5.2	26.9	67.9
Germany	228	87	3.3	37.0	59.7
Greece	79	65	20.8	23.6	55.6
Ireland	51	58	13.2	27.1	59.7
Italy	190	67	7.7	32.1	60.2
Luxembourg	155	89	3.2	27.0	69.8
Netherlands	372	89	4.0	23.3	72.7
Portugal	107	36	11.8	32.5	55.7
Spain	78	77	9.9	30.1	60.0
Sweden	19	83	3.4	25.0	71.6

Source: Eurostat.

nearly three quarters of the gross national product (GNP) of the EU (and 66 per cent of the GNP of Europe) and for most of Europe's industrial production and trade.

All of western Europe has experienced substantial economic growth since 1945, and prosperity has begun slowly to spread to eastern Europe in recent years, but the levels of growth and prosperity have always differed from one region to another (Box 2.2, p. 55). Broadly speaking there is something of an economic heartland in the centre of Europe, running from northern Italy across Switzerland to the Benelux countries and neighbouring parts of France and Germany, and continuing across the Channel from London to the English midlands. This is the area where most industry and energy production is focused, with the greatest concentration of population, the highest levels of GNP and the fewest people employed in agriculture.

More generally, Europe has pockets of both economic dynamism and underdevelopment. The highest degree of economic activity is found in the economic heartland, particularly in the Rhineland, around northern Italian cities and in and around Paris, Rotterdam and London. These have neighbouring zones of balanced economic development, with a combination of prosperous agriculture, moderate urban growth, light industry and services. Balanced against these areas are the depressed industrial regions of Europe, such as the Ruhr, the English midlands and south Wales.

Table 2.3 *Quality of life indicators for the EU*

	Life expectancy (years) (1990–95)	Infant mortality rate (per 1000 live births) (1990–95)	Population growth (%) (1990–95)	Calories available (as % of need) (1990–92)	Human Development Index ranking (1997)*
Austria	76.2	7	0.7	133	12
Belgium	76.4	6	0.3	149	13
Britain	76.2	7	0.3	130	15
Denmark	75.3	7	0.2	135	18
Finland	75.7	5	0.5	113	8
France	76.9	7	0.4	143	2
Germany	76.0	6	0.6	138	19
Greece	77.6	10	0.4	151	20
Ireland	75.3	7	0.3	157	17
Italy	77.5	8	0.1	139	21
Luxembourg	77.1	7	0.4	138	27
Netherlands	77.4	7	0.7	114	6
Portugal	74.6	10	−0.1	136	31
Spain	77.6	7	0.2	141	11
Sweden	78.2	5	0.5	111	10
Japan	79.5	4	0.3	125	7
Russia	67.6	21	−0.1	n/a	67
US	76.0	9	1.0	138	4

* The Human Development Index is calculated by the UN Development Programme, and ranks 175 countries on the basis of life expectancy, educational attainment and per capita income.
Source: UN Population Division, UNICEF, UN Development Programme.

Finally, the periphery of Europe tends to be the most underdeveloped, either because it has lacked adequate investment, because it is remote and sparsely populated or – in the case of most of eastern Europe – because it is less industrialized and still undergoing the transition from central planning, which was a feature of the Soviet hegemony during the cold war, to a more free market system.

The single market programme has to some extent exacerbated the problem by promoting cross-frontier competition, allowing industry and business to move to the areas of maximum efficiency and greatest profits, and promoting the movement of workers. At the same time, though, regional policies have helped provide more investment for poorer regions (see Chapter 5), and social policies have helped place workers on a more equal footing (see Chapter 6), at least in the European Union. The single market has also helped promote trans-European corporate mergers and joint ventures, improving economies of scale such that the biggest

European corporations are now able to compete more effectively with those from the United States and Japan.

Economic differences are reflected in population numbers. Western Europe is one of the most densely populated regions of the world: overall population density is about 100 people per square kilometre compared with 29/sq km in the United States, and 9/sq km in Russia. Within the EU, population density varies from 370/sq km in the Netherlands to 15–20/sq km in Sweden and Finland, the spread reflecting environmental factors and different levels of industrialization. The most densely populated parts of Europe are also among the wealthiest: northern Italy, western Germany, the Benelux countries, and southeastern and central England. The most sparsely populated include the poorest or the coldest: much of eastern Europe, central Spain, northwest Scotland, Iceland and Scandinavia.

Not surprisingly, the greatest population growth is taking place in and around the major centres of industry and services, and new residential and leisure areas. Capital cities have seen growth since the mid-nineteenth century, their attraction lying in their role as administrative, cultural, service and prestige centres, their central position in national transport networks, and their pools of skilled labour and large marketplaces (Minshull and Dawson, 1996, p. 209). Regions of postwar industrial redevelopment, such as the Rhine valley in Germany and the West Midlands in Britain, have also seen sustained population growth. Meanwhile rural and peripheral regions and declining industrial areas have undergone steady depopulation. These trends have made Europe one of the most urbanized parts of the world. While only 75 per cent of Americans live in towns or cities, the level of urbanization in European states is often well over 85 per cent, with Belgium coming highest at 97 per cent and Portugal lowest at 36 per cent.

The European Union has become the world's biggest trading power, and its exports and imports have grown rapidly since 1945, thanks in large part to the growth of intra-European trade. Worldwide exports from the EU consist mainly of manufactured goods, machinery, machine tools, motor vehicles, electronics, telecommunications equipment, aerospace products, chemicals, clothing, consumer durables and agricultural products, while major imports include oil, agricultural products and raw materials. While the EU member states still actively protect their sovereignty in many different areas, when it comes to economic issues it has become more realistic to think of them collectively – the near completion of the single market, the substantial easing of the movement of people and capital, the power of the European Commission to negotiate on behalf of the EU as a whole on trade issues and the steps taken towards conversion to a single currency have all taken Europe to the brink of full economic union (see Chapter 7).

Box 2.2 The quality of life in Europe

Assessed by almost any objective measure of the quality of life, Western Europeans are among the most privileged people in the world. The average European has access to an advanced system of education and health care, an extensive and generous welfare system, a vibrant consumer society and a sophisticated transport and communications system. An African infant is 21 times more likely to die at birth than a European infant, the average European can expect to live 24 years longer than the average African and 18 years longer than the average Indian, Europeans enjoy almost universal literacy, employed Europeans enjoy more paid holiday leave and leisure time than almost anyone else, and the provision of shelter and nutrition is more than adequate (see Table 2.3).

Much can be attributed to the philosophy adopted by most European governments after the Second World War that the state should provide a wide range of basic social services, creating a safety net through which even the poorest and the most underprivileged would not be allowed to slip. Hence every EU member state has some form of state education and national health care, and the provision of care for children and the aged has increased as the number of lone parent families and retirees has grown. Most European states even do well in comparison with the United States, which has the most technologically advanced health care in the world but lacks a national health service, and is one of the richest economies in the world but refuses to provide the average office worker with more than two weeks of paid leave per year.

Not all of Europe's welfare policies have succeeded, and it is one of the great ironies of life in modern industrialized democracies that considerable want continues to exist in the midst of plenty. Poverty has not gone away and in several places has worsened, creating considerable differences across Europe. For example, while the number of children living in poverty stands at 4–10 per cent in Sweden, Germany, and the Netherlands, it is as high as 16–18 per cent in Britain and Italy. However this is still much better than in the United States, where the figure is nearly 30 per cent (statistics quoted in Bradford, 1998, p. 265).

Conclusions

The idea of Europe – always a debatable proposition at the best of times – has undergone some dramatic changes over the past two generations. Not only have the eastern and southeastern borders of Europe maintained their historical tradition of change, but the nature of the internal relationship among the different administrative units that make up Europe has undergone a substantial redefinition. The concept of European unity has found a widespread audience for the first time. Where intellectuals and philosophers once argued in isolation that the surest path to peace in Europe was cooperation, or even integration, the horrors of two world wars fought largely on European soil finally ensured a wider airing of the idea, and prompted the first tangible changes needed to bring it about.

Europeans still have much that divides them, and those differences are immediately apparent to anyone who travels across the region. There are different languages, cultural traditions, legal, education and health care systems, social priorities, cuisines, modes of entertainment, patterns of etiquette, styles of dressing, ways of planning and building cities, ways of spending leisure time, attitudes towards the countryside, and even which side of the road to drive on. Europeans also have differences in the way they govern themselves, and in what they have been able to achieve with their economies and social welfare systems.

Increasingly, however, Europeans have more in common. The economic and social integration that has taken place under the auspices of the European Union and its precursors since the early 1950s has brought the needs and priorities of Europeans closer into alignment. It has also encouraged the rest of the world to see Europeans less as citizens of separate states and more as citizens of the same economic bloc, if not yet the same political bloc. Not only has there been integration from the Mediterranean to the Arctic Circle, but the 'lands between' – which spent the cold war as part of the Soviet bloc and part of the buffer created by the Soviet Union to protect its western frontier – are now becoming part of greater Europe for the first time in their history. The result has been a fundamental redefinition of the idea of Europe.

Chapter 3

The Evolution of the EU

The idea of 'Europe' has been with us for centuries, but the European Union has been a reality for barely fifty years. It was only after the Second World War that all the theories about the possible benefits of European integration were finally tested in practice. There were a number of false starts, but the birth of what is now the European Union took place at a press conference on 9 May 1950, at which French foreign minister Robert Schuman announced a plan he had agreed with French businessman Jean Monnet and West German chancellor Konrad Adenauer to bring the coal and steel industries of France and Germany under the administration of a single joint authority.

Other countries were invited to take part, but only Italy and the three Benelux countries expressed interest. Nevertheless, that modest experiment involving just six western European states would lead in stages to the European Union as we know it today. The original priorities were postwar economic construction, the need to prevent European nationalism leading once again to conflict, and the need for security in the face of the threats posed by the cold war. At the core of early ideas about integration was the traditional hostility between Germany and France, and the argument that if these two could cooperate they might provide the foundation for broader European cooperation.

Building on the European Coal and Steel Community, founded in 1952, its members created the European Economic Community in 1958, with a far broader remit, including the development of a common agricultural policy, agreement on a common external tariff for all goods coming into the Community, and the construction of a single market, within which there would be free movement of people, goods, money and services. Membership began to expand in 1973 with the accession of Britain, Ireland and Denmark, followed in the 1980s by Greece, Portugal and Spain.

Economic problems and disagreements about the actions needed to remove the internal barriers to trade threatened to undermine the development of the single market, but a new impetus was provided in 1987 with the passage of the Single European Act, which set a five-year deadline for agreement on all the remaining tasks. The single market is now almost complete, membership of the EU has grown to 15 countries and more than 370 million people, negotiations have opened with a view to extending membership eastward, and work is under way on the most ambitious – and most controversial – step in the short history of European integration: the implementation of a single currency. The achievements have been substantial, but many Europeans are still ambivalent about the benefits of integration and question the ultimate objectives of the European Union. And while membership has grown, doubts remain about the many items of unfinished business on the agenda of European integration.

This chapter provides a brief history of European integration since the Second World War, describing the key steps that have been taken during the evolution of the EU and their underlying motives. It moves from the Treaty of Paris to the Treaties of Rome, on to the construction of the single market and early attempts to bring about economic union and common social and foreign policies, and ends with the Single European Act, the treaties of Maastricht and Amsterdam, and the state of progress on the single currency.

Domestic developments

The European Union was born out of the ruins of the Second World War. Prior to the war, Europe had dominated global trade, banking and finance, its empires had stretched across the world and its military superiority had been unquestioned. However, Europeans had often gone to war with each other, and their conflicts undermined the prosperity that cooperation might have brought. Many had described the First World War as the war to end all wars, but it was to take yet another conflagration finally to convince Europeans that the nature of the relationship among European states needed to be changed if lasting peace was to be achieved.

The Second World War resulted in the death of more than 40 million people and caused widespread devastation. Cities lay in ruins, agricultural production was halved, food was rationed and communications were disrupted by the destruction of bridges, railways and harbours. While the physical damage caused by the First World War had been relatively restricted, every country involved in this latest conflict sustained heavy casualties and physical damage. The war also dealt a severe blow to European power and influence, clearing the way for the emergence of the United States and the Soviet Union as superpowers, and creating a nervous new balance in the distribution of political influence in the world.

Against this background a number of European leaders revived an idea that had often been mooted before but had never taken hold of the collective European imagination: that European states should set aside their differences and build bridges of cooperation aimed at removing the causes of war, and perhaps even leading to European economic and political union. While the argument took on new significance given the scale of the postwar reconstruction effort, Europeans had different opinions about its merits.

France was destabilized by the national trauma created by wartime collaboration and the structural weaknesses of the government of the Fourth Republic (created in 1946), and was to suffer further blows to its national pride with the defeat of French forces in Indochina in 1954 and the Suez crisis in 1956. Three times in less than a century it had gone to war with Germany, and three times had suffered substantial losses; there was no certainty that the defeat of Nazism meant the removal of the German threat.

Germany had become introverted, not only because of the scale of the destruction it had suffered in the war, but also because of shame over its role in starting and fighting the war. It found itself occupied by four victorious allied powers, whose disagreement over what to do with Germany led to its division into a socialist eastern sector and three capitalist western sectors. Few Germans were happy with this arrangement, but few felt they could do much about it. The conservative Christian Democratic government of Konrad Adenauer set about aligning West Germany with the Western alliance and rebuilding West German respectability. Economic integration with its neighbours, especially France, fitted well with these goals.

Austria was also divided into separate zones of occupation, but had been relatively undamaged by the war and was able to return to its constitution of 1920, and quickly to hold democratic elections. Although it declared itself neutral in 1955, its economic interests pulled it increasingly towards economic integration with its western neighbours (Schultz, 1992).

Italy, like Germany, emerged from the war both introverted and devastated. It was less successful than Germany in creating political stability and suffered regular changes of government. For the administration of pro-European prime minister Alcide de Gasperi, European integration offered a means of fostering peace and helping Italy to deal with its internal economic problems, notably unemployment and the underdevelopment of the south.

Britain's sense of national identity had been strengthened by its resistance to Nazi invasion. It was politically stable and wealthier and more powerful than France and Germany, but many of its major cities had been bombed, its exports had been cut by two thirds and its national wealth had fallen by 75 per cent. Voters looking for change elected a Labour government in 1945, which embarked on a popular programme of nationalization and welfare provision, and signalled the demise of Britain's imperial status by granting independence to India and Pakistan in 1947. However, cooperation with the rest of Europe was far from British minds, and few Britons even thought of themselves as European. Ireland, meanwhile, had remained neutral during the war but was economically tied to Britain, so its attitude towards European cooperation was highly influenced by Britain's stance.

Belgium, the Netherlands and Luxembourg had all been occupied by the Germans, and remained concerned after the war about their inability to protect themselves from larger and more powerful neighbours. Agreement was reached in 1944 among the three governments-in-exile to promote trilateral economic cooperation after the war, and the creation in 1948 of the Benelux customs union led to the abolition of internal customs and the agreement of a joint external tariff. While all three countries retained many protectionist measures, their governments went on to agree the Benelux Economic Union in 1958, emphasizing their integrationist credentials.

The five Nordic states (Denmark, Finland, Iceland, Norway and Sweden) began their postwar cooperation with the creation in 1946 of the Committee on Legislative Cooperation, which was charged with ensuring that new national laws were in line with one another and encouraging a common Nordic position at international conferences. In 1952 Denmark, Iceland, Norway and Sweden formed the Nordic Council, a consultative body to promote the abolition of passport controls, the free movement of workers and the development of joint ventures. The Council had its own governing institutions, and its development was helped by the fact that all its members had small populations, were relatively wealthy and homogeneous, had few major social problems and were governed by socialist or social democratic governments. Finland joined in 1956.

Spain and Portugal were exceptions to the prevailing rule of democratic stability in western Europe, and were both poor and politically marginalized. Spain languished from 1939 under the rule of Francisco Franco, who declared Spain neutral in 1943. Portugal had 25 revolutions and military coups between 1910 and 1928, the last of which launched Antonio Salazar on a term of office that would not end until 1968. Neither Franco nor Salazar were in favour of cooperating with neighbouring countries immediately after the war, and both states remained on the margins of the international community for many years. The same was true of Greece, which enjoyed economic growth after the war thanks to US financial and military assistance, but remained poor and experienced protracted domestic political tensions that led to military dictatorship in 1967–74.

Economic reconstruction and security

While west Europeans worried about domestic reconstruction, changes were taking place at the global level that demanded new thinking. In July 1944 representatives from the United States, Britain and 42 other countries met at Bretton Woods in New Hampshire to make plans for the postwar global economy. All those involved agreed to an Anglo-American proposal to promote free trade, non-discrimination and stable exchange rates. It was also agreed that Europe's economies had to be rebuilt and placed on a more stable footing.

Because wartime resistance had been allied with left-wing political ideas, there was a political shift to the left after the war, with socialist and social democratic parties winning power in several European countries. Many of the new governments launched programmes of social welfare and nationalization, emphasizing central economic planning. Fundamental to this approach were the theories of the British economist John Maynard Keynes, who argued for some government control over some aspects of the economy in order to control the cycle of booms and busts. Keynesianism became the basis of postwar economic reconstruction and west European governments increasingly intervened in their economies to control inflation and rebuild industry and agriculture. However, it soon became clear that substantial capital investment was needed if Europe was to rebuild itself. The readiest source of such capital was the United States, which saw European reconstruction as essential to its own economic and security interests, and made a substantial investment in the future of Europe through the Marshall Plan (Box 3.1).

As one of the two new postwar superpowers, the United States found itself playing the role of global policeman, its primary goal being to defend western Europe (and ultimately itself) from the Soviet threat. Its assumption that Europe had sufficient people, resources and wealth to recover, and that the Allies would continue to work together, proved to be wrong (Urwin, 1995, pp. 13–14). Furthermore, its European allies were divided over the extent to which they felt they could rely on the United States to defend Europe, and the doubters began to think in terms of greater European cooperation.

Box 3.1　The Marshall Plan, 1948–51

US policy on Europe after 1945 was to withdraw its military forces as quickly as possible. However, it soon became clear that Stalin had plans to expand the Soviet sphere of influence, and the US State Department began to realize that it had underestimated the extent of Europe's economic destruction; despite a boom in the late 1940s, sustained growth was not forthcoming. When an economically exhausted Britain ended its financial aid to Greece and Turkey in 1947, President Truman argued the need for the United States to fill the vacuum in order to curb communist influence in the region.

US policymakers also felt that European markets needed to be rebuilt and integrated into a multilateral system of world trade. Economic and political reconstruction would help forestall Soviet aggression and the rise of domestic communist parties (Hogan, 1987, pp. 26–7). Against this background, Secretary of State George Marshall argued that the United States should provide Europe with assistance to fight 'hunger, poverty, desperation and chaos'. The original April 1947 State Department proposal for the plan made clear that one of its ultimate goals was the creation of a western European federation (quoted in Gillingham, 1991, pp. 118–19).

The European Recovery Programme (otherwise known as the Marshall Plan) provided just over $12.5 billion in aid to Europe between 1948 and 1951 (Milward, 1984, p. 94), the disbursement of which was coordinated by the Organization for European Economic Cooperation (OEEC), a new body set up in April 1948 with headquarters in Paris. Governed by a Council of Ministers made up of one representative from each member state, the OEEC's goals included the reduction of tariffs and other barriers to trade, and consideration of the possibility of a free trade area or customs union among its members. Opposition from several European governments (notably Britain, France and Norway) ensured that the OEEC remained a forum for intergovernmental consultation rather than becoming a supranational body with powers of its own (Wexler, 1983, p. 209; Milward, 1984, pp. 209–10).

Although the effects of the Marshall Plan are still subject to debate, there is little question that it helped underpin economic and political recovery in Europe, and to bind more closely the economic and political interests of the United States and western Europe. It was a profitable investment for the United States, but it also had considerable influence on the idea of European integration – as western Europe's first venture in economic cooperation, it encouraged Europeans to work together and highlighted the mutual dependence among their economies (Urwin, 1995, pp. 20–2). It also helped liberalize inter-European trade, and helped ensure that economic integration would be focused on western Europe.

Most immediately, the western allies were undecided about what to do with Germany. In June 1948 they agreed to create a new West German state and a new currency for their three zones. The Soviets responded with a blockade around West Berlin, prompting a massive western airlift to supply the beleaguered city. The US Congress was resistant to direct US commitments or entanglements in Europe, but saw the need to counterbalance the Soviets and ensure the peaceful cooperation of West Germany. In 1949 the North Atlantic Treaty was signed, by which the United States agreed to help its European allies to 'restore and maintain the security of the North Atlantic area'. Canada too signed, along with Britain, France, Italy, the Benelux countries, Denmark, Iceland, Norway and Portugal. The pact was later given more substance with the creation of the North Atlantic Treaty Organization (NATO), headquartered in Paris until it was moved to Brussels in 1966. The United States was now committed to the security of western Europe.

The NATO members agreed that an attack on one of them would be considered an attack on all of them, but each agreed only to respond with 'such actions as it deems necessary'. The Europeans attempted to take their own defence a step further in 1952 and proposed the creation of a European Defence Community, but this was prevented by political opposition in Britain and France (see later in this chapter). Nonetheless Britain was anxious to encourage some kind of military cooperation, and invited France, West Germany, Italy and the Benelux states to become founding members of the Western European Union (WEU), which would oblige all members to give all possible military and other aid to any member that was attacked. However, the WEU went beyond purely defensive concerns, and the agreement signed by the seven founding members in Paris in October 1954 included the aim 'to promote the unity and to encourage the progressive integration of Europe'. Within days of the launch of the WEU in May 1955 and the coincidental admission of West Germany into NATO, the Soviet bloc created the Warsaw Pact. The lines of the cold war were now defined, and its implications were illustrated all too clearly by events in Hungary in 1956.

In October the government of Imre Nagy announced the end of one-party rule, the evacuation of Russian troops from Hungary and Hungary's withdrawal from the Warsaw Pact. Just as Britain and France were invading Egypt to retake the Suez Canal following its nationalization in July 1956 by Gamal Abdel Nasser, the Soviets responded to the Hungarian decision by sending in tanks. The United States wanted to criticize the Soviet use of force and boast to the emerging Third World about the moral superiority of the West, but obviously could not while British and French paratroopers were storming the Suez Canal. Britain and France were ostracized in the UN Security Council, British Prime Minister Anthony Eden resigned and the attempt to regain the Suez was quickly abandoned.

The consequences of France's problems in Indochina, the Suez crisis and the Hungarian uprising were profound: Britain and France began to reduce the size of their armed forces, finally recognizing that they were no longer world powers capable of independent action in the Middle East, or perhaps anywhere; both embarked on a concerted programme of decolonization; Britain looked increasingly to Europe for its economic and security interests; and it became obvious to Europeans that the United States was the dominant partner in the North Atlantic alliance, a fact that particularly concerned the French.

First steps towards integration (1945–50)

The priority for European leaders after the Second World War was to create conditions that would prevent Europeans from ever going to war with each other again. For many, the major threats to peace and security were nationalism and the nation-state, both of which had been discredited by the war. For many, Germany was the core problem – peace was impossible, they argued, unless Germany could be contained and its power diverted to constructive rather than destructive ends. It had to be allowed to rebuild its economic base and its political system in ways that would not threaten European security.

Meanwhile, the growing hostility between the two superpowers led Europeans to fear that they were becoming pawns in the struggle for supremacy. There was clearly a need to protect western Europe from the Soviet threat, but there was concern about the extent to which western Europe and the United States could find common ground, and the extent to which western Europe could rely on the US protective shield. Perhaps Europe would be better advised to take care of its own security. This, however, demanded a greater sense of unity and common purpose than Europe had ever been able to achieve.

The spotlight fell particularly on Britain, which had taken the lead in fighting Nazism and was still the dominant European power. Winston Churchill became the focus of Europeanist sentiment; his credentials were based on his charisma, his last-minute proposal for an Anglo-French Union in 1940, and suggestions he had made in 1942–43 for 'a United States of Europe' operating under 'a Council of Europe' with reduced trade barriers, free movement of people, a common military and a High Court to adjudicate disputes (quoted in Palmer, 1968, p. 111). He made the same suggestion in a speech at the University of Zurich in 1946, but it was clear that Churchill felt this new entity should be based around France and Germany and would not necessarily include Britain – before the war he had argued that Britain was 'with Europe but not of it. We are interested and associated, but not absorbed' (Zurcher, 1958, p. 6).

National pro-European groups decided to organize a conference aimed at publicizing the cause of regional unity. The Congress of Europe, held in The Hague in May 1948, was attended by delegates from 16 states and observers from the United States and Canada. Many ambitious ideas were discussed, but the most tangible outcome was the Council of Europe, founded with the signing in London in May 1949 of a statute by ten European states. The statute noted the need for 'closer unity between all the like-minded countries of Europe' and listed the Council's aims, including 'common action in economic, social, cultural, scientific, legal and administrative matters' but not defence.

The Council, which was headquartered in Strasbourg, had a governing Committee of Ministers, on which each state had one vote, and a 147-member Consultative Assembly made up of representatives nominated from national legislatures. Although membership of the Council expanded, it never became anything more than a loose intergovernmental organization. It made progress on human rights, cultural issues and even limited economic cooperation, but it was not the kind of organization that European federalists wanted.

Opening moves: from Paris to Rome (1950–8)

The OEEC and the Council of Europe encouraged Europeans to think and work together, but opposition by antifederalists in Britain, Scandinavia and elsewhere ensured that neither would promote significant regional integration. Among those who felt that a bolder initiative was needed were the French businessman Jean Monnet (1888–1979) and Robert Schuman (1880–1963), French foreign minister from 1948 to 1953. Both were enthusiastic Europeanists, both felt that practical steps needed to be taken that went beyond the noble statements of organizations such as the Council of Europe, and both felt that the logical starting point should be the resolution of the perennial problem of Franco-German relations.

By 1950 it was clear to many that West Germany had to be allowed to rebuild its industrial base if it was to play a useful role in the western alliance. One way of doing this without allowing Germany to become a threat to its neighbours was for it to rebuild under the auspices of a supranational organization, thereby tying Germany into the wider process of European reconstruction. Looking for a starting point that would be meaningful but not too ambitious, Monnet focused on the coal and steel industries, which offered strong potential for common European organization, for several reasons:

- Coal and steel were the building blocks of industry, and the steel industry had a tendency to create cartels. Cooperation would eliminate waste and duplication, break down cartels, make coal and steel production more efficient and competitive, and boost industrial development.
- Because the heavy industries of the Ruhr had been the traditional foundation of Germany's power and France and Germany had previously fought over coal reserves in Alsace-Lorraine, creating a supranational coal and steel industry would contain German power.
- Integrating coal and steel would ensure that Germany became reliant on trade with the rest of Europe, underpinning its economic reconstruction and helping the French lose their fear of German industrial domination (Monnet, 1978, p. 292).

Monnet felt that unless France acted immediately, the United States would become the focus of a new transatlantic alliance against the Soviet bloc, Britain would be pulled closer to the United States, Germany's economic and military growth could not be controlled and France would be led to its 'eclipse' (ibid., p. 294). As head of the French national planning commission, he could see for himself that effective economic planning was beyond the ability of individual states working alone. He also knew from personal experience that intergovernmental organizations had a tendency to be hamstrung by the governments of their member states, and to become bogged down in ministerial meetings. To avoid these problems he proposed a new institution independent of national governments; in other words it would be supranational rather than intergovernmental.

After discussions with Monnet and West German Chancellor Konrad Adenauer, Robert Schuman took these ideas a step further at a press conference on 9 May 1950, a date now widely seen as marking the birth of united Europe. In what later became known as the Schuman Declaration, he argued that Europe would not be united at once or according to a single plan, but step by step through concrete achievements. This would require the elimination of Franco-German hostility, and Schuman proposed that French and German coal and steel production be placed 'under a common High Authority, within the framework of an organization open to the participation of the other countries of Europe'. This would be 'a first step in the federation of Europe', and would make war between France and Germany 'not merely unthinkable, but materially impossible' (Schuman, quoted in Weigall and Stirk, 1992, pp. 58–9).

The proposal was revolutionary in the sense that France was offering to sacrifice a measure of national sovereignty in the interests of building a new supranational authority that might end an old rivalry and help build a new European peace (Gillingham, 1991, p. 231). Although membership of this new body was offered to all western European states, only four accepted: Italy, which wanted respectability and economic and political stability, and the Benelux countries, which were in favour because they were small and vulnerable, had twice been invaded by Germany, were heavily reliant on exports and felt that the only way they could gain a significant voice in world affairs and ensure their security was to become part of a bigger regional unit.

The other European governments had different reasons for not taking part: Spain and Portugal were dictatorships and had little interest in international cooperation; in Denmark and Norway the memories of German occupation were still too fresh; Austria, Sweden and Finland were keen on remaining neutral; Ireland was predominantly agricultural (and so had little to gain) and was tied economically to Britain; while Britain still had extensive interests outside Europe, exported very little of its steel to western Europe, and the new Labour government had just nationalized the coal and steel industries and did not like the supranational character of Schuman's proposal.

The lines of thinking now established, the governments of the Six opened negotiations and on 18 April 1951 signed the Treaty of Paris, creating the European Coal and Steel Community (ECSC). The new organization began work in August 1952 after ratification of the terms of the treaty by each of the member states. It was governed by a nominated nine-member High Authority (with Jean Monnet as its first president), and decisions were taken by a six-member Special Council of Ministers. A nominated 78-member Common Assembly helped Monnet allay the concerns of national governments regarding the surrender of powers, and disputes between states were to be settled by a seven-member Court of Justice.

The founding of the ECSC was a small step in itself, but remarkable in that it was the first time that any European government had given up significant powers to a supranational organization. It was allowed to reduce tariff barriers, abolish subsidies, fix prices and raise money by imposing levies on steel and coal production. It faced national opposition to its work, but its job was made easier by the fact that much of the groundwork had already been laid by the Benelux customs union. The ECSC showed that integration was feasible, and its very existence served to encourage the Six to work together. Although the ECSC failed to achieve many of its goals (notably the creation of a single market for coal and steel), it had ultimately been created to prove a point about the feasibility of integration, which it did.

While the ECSC was at least a limited success, two much larger, more ambitious and arguably premature experiments in integration failed dismally. The first of these was the European Defence Community (EDC), the object of which was to promote western European cooperation on defence and bind West Germany into a European defence system. A draft treaty was signed by the six ECSC members in 1952 but it failed to be ratified, mainly because the French were nervous about the idea of German rearmament so soon after the war and did not want to give up control over their armed forces. Furthermore Britain – still the strongest European military power – was not included, and Europe could not have a workable common defence force without a common foreign policy (Urwin, 1995, p. 63).

The European Political Community, meanwhile, was intended as the first step towards a European federation. A draft plan, completed in 1953, based the proposed community on a European Executive Council, a Council of Ministers, a Court of Justice and a popularly elected Parliament. With the collapse of the EDC, however, all hope of a political community died, at least temporarily. The failure of these two initiatives was a sobering blow to the integrationists and sent shockwaves through the ECSC. Monnet resigned the presidency of the High Authority in 1955, disillusioned by the political resistance to its work and impatient to further the process of integration (Monnet, 1978, pp. 398–404).

While the ECSC made modest but solid achievements in its first four years, there were limits to its abilities and Europeanists felt that something more needed to be done to give momentum to the cause of integration. While the six ECSC members agreed that coal and steel had been a useful testing ground, it was becoming increasingly difficult to develop these two sectors in isolation. A meeting of the ECSC foreign ministers at Messina in Italy in June 1955 resulted in a resolution that the time had come to 'relaunch' the European idea. They agreed to a Benelux proposal 'to work for the establishment of a united Europe by the development of common institutions, the progressive fusion of national economies, the creation of a common market, and the progressive harmonization of their social policies' (Messina Resolution, in Weigall and Stirk, 1992, p. 94).

A committee was set up under the chairmanship of Belgian Foreign Minister Paul-Henri Spaak to look into the options. Its report led to a new round of negotiations and the signing in March 1957 of the two Treaties of Rome, one creating the European Economic Community (EEC) and the other the European Atomic Energy Community (Euratom), both of which came into force in January 1958. The EEC had a very similar administrative structure to the ECSC, with a nine-member quasi-executive

Commission, a Council of Ministers with powers over decision making and a seven-member Court of Justice. A new 142-member Parliamentary Assembly was created to cover the EEC, ECSC and Euratom.

The EEC Treaty committed the Six to the creation of a common market and the harmonization of their economic policies. Action would be taken in areas where there was agreement, and disagreements could be set aside for future discussion. The creation of the common market was to be completed within 12 years by gradually removing all restrictions on internal trade, setting a common external tariff, reducing barriers to the free movement of people, services and capital among the member states, developing common agricultural and transport policies and creating a European Social Fund and a European Investment Bank. The Euratom Treaty, meanwhile, was aimed at creating a common market for atomic energy, but Euratom remained a very junior actor in the process of integration and focused primarily on research.

Integration takes root (1958–70)

By January 1958 the six founding members of the European Communities had signed three treaties, created a small network of joint institutions – some of which were more supranational in character than others – and set a number of ambitious goals aimed at integrating many of their economic activities. Problems were encountered along the way, but there were also many achievements:

- The Treaty of Rome set a deadline of 12 years for the staged removal of all barriers to a common market (Article 8). Although the deadline was not met, internal tariffs fell quickly enough to allow the Six to agree a common external tariff in July 1968, and to declare an industrial customs union.
- Bureaucratic bloat and replication were always a possibility, but although critics of European integration regularly pointed accusing fingers at the European Commission, its staff numbers remained low, and decision making was streamlined in April 1965 with the Treaty Establishing a Single Council and a Single Commission of the European Communities (the Merger Treaty). The decision-making process was given both authority and direction by the formalization in 1975 of regular summits of EC leaders coming together as the European Council. The EEC was also made more publicly accountable and more democratic with the introduction in 1979 of direct elections to the European Parliament.

- Integration brought the removal of the quota restrictions that the member states had used to protect their domestic industries from competition from imported products. Intra-EEC trade between 1958 and 1965 grew three times faster than that with third countries (Urwin, 1995, p. 130), the GNP of the Six grew at an average annual rate of 5.7 per cent, per capita income and consumption grew at 4.5 per cent and the contribution of agriculture to GNP was halved (Ionescu, 1975, pp. 150–4).
- The free movement of goods across borders would be restricted as long as EEC members had non-tariff barriers such as different standards and regulations on health, safety and consumer protection. Standards were harmonized during the 1960s and 1970s, although it was not until the passage of the Single European Act that a concerted effort was made to bring all EEC members into line.
- Another priority was to lift restrictions on the free movement of workers. While some limits remained well into the 1990s, steady progress was made towards easing them during the 1960s and 1970s.
- One of the goals of the Treaty of Rome was agreement on a Common Agricultural Policy (CAP), and this was eventually achieved in 1968. CAP was aimed at creating a single market for agricultural products and assuring EEC farmers of guaranteed prices for their produce. CAP initially encouraged both production and productivity, but it became the biggest single item in the EEC budget and provoked heated controversy (see Chapter 7).
- The Six worked increasingly close together on international trade negotiations and their joint influence was far greater than it would have been if they had negotiated individually. The EEC acted as one, for example, in the Kennedy Round of negotiations under the General Agreement on Tariffs and Trade (GATT) in the mid-1960s, and in reaching preferential trade agreements with 18 former African colonies under the 1963 Yaoundé Convention.

First rounds of enlargement (1973–86)

Britain was the most obvious absentee from the early attempts to integrate Europe. It continued to view itself after the war as a world power, but that notion ended with the Suez crisis, which shook the foundations of Britain's special relationship with the United States, and also made it clear that most of the key decisions on global political and economic issues were being driven (and often taken) by the United States and the USSR. Britain was not opposed to European cooperation, but was nervous about the closeness of the ties proposed by Monnet and Schuman. In 1957 Britain decided to pursue the idea of a wider but looser free trade area based on the OEEC states, but preparations for the EEC had gone too far, and then in 1960 the OEEC evolved into the Organization for Economic Cooperation and Development (OECD).

Hence Britain became a founding member of the European Free Trade Association (EFTA), a looser intergovernmental body whose goal was free trade rather than economic and political integration. It was founded in January 1960 with the signing of the Stockholm Convention by Austria, Britain, Denmark, Norway, Portugal, Sweden and Switzerland. Membership of EFTA was voluntary – in contrast to the contractual arrangements set up for the EEC by the Treaty of Rome – and involved no institutions beyond a Council of Ministers that met two or three times a year and a group of permanent representatives serviced by a small secretariat in Geneva.

EFTA helped cut tariffs, but achieved relatively little in the long term, mainly because several of its members did more trade with the EEC than with their EFTA partners. It soon became clear to Britain that political influence in Europe lay not with EFTA but with the EEC, that Britain risked political isolation if it stayed out of the EEC, and that the EEC was actually working – the member states had made impressive economic and political progress and British industry wanted access to the rich EEC market (Pinder, 1991, pp. 46–7). In August 1961, barely 15 months after the creation of EFTA, Britain applied for EEC membership, as did Ireland and Denmark. They were joined in 1962 by Norway.

Denmark's motive for applying for EEC membership was agricultural: it was producing three times as much food as it needed, and much of that was being exported to Britain. Furthermore, the EEC represented a big new market for Denmark's agricultural surpluses and would provide a boost for Danish industrial development. Ireland for its part saw membership of the EEC as way of furthering its industrial plans and reducing its reliance on agriculture, as well as loosening its ties with Britain. Norway followed the British lead because of the importance of the EEC market. With four of its members apparently trying to defect, EFTA ceased to have much purpose, so Sweden, Austria and Switzerland all applied for associate membership of the EEC; they were followed in 1962 by Portugal, Spain and Malta.

Negotiations between Britain and the EEC opened in early 1962, and appeared to be on the verge of a successful conclusion when they fell foul of Charles de Gaulle's Franco-German policy. De Gaulle had plans for an EEC built around a Franco-German axis, saw Britain as a rival to French influence in the Community, was upset that he had not been given equal status at the wartime summits of the allied powers and resented Britain's lack of enthusiasm for the early integrationist moves of the 1950s. He also felt that British membership would give the United States too much influence in Europe.

Monnet, however, was keen on British membership, and even tried to bring Adenauer to his point of view by suggesting that Adenauer refuse to sign a proposed Franco-German friendship treaty unless de Gaulle accepted Britain's application. But Adenauer shared de Gaulle's anglophobia, and agreed that development of the Franco-German axis was the key. In the space of just ten days in January 1963 de Gaulle signed the Franco-German treaty and vetoed the British application. He further upset Britain and some of his own EEC partners by reaching the veto decision unilaterally and making the announcement at a press conference in Paris. Since Britain's application was part of a joint package with Denmark and Ireland, their applications were rejected as well.

Britain reapplied in 1967, but its application was again vetoed by de Gaulle. Following de Gaulle's resignation in 1969 Britain applied for a third time, and this time its application was accepted, along with those of Denmark, Ireland and Norway. Following membership negotiations in 1970–71, Britain, Denmark and Ireland finally joined the EEC in January 1973. Norway would have joined as well but a public referendum in September 1972 narrowly went against membership. The Six had now become the Nine.

An additional round of enlargements took place in the 1980s and pushed the borders of the EEC further south and west. Greece had made its first overtures to the EEC in the late 1950s, but had been turned down on the ground that its economy was too underdeveloped. It was given associate membership in 1961 as a prelude to full accession, which might have come sooner had it not been for the Greek military coup of April 1967. With the return to civilian government in 1974, Greece almost immediately applied for full membership, arguing that EEC membership would help underpin its attempts to rebuild democracy. The Community agreed, negotiations opened in 1976 and Greece joined in 1981.

Spain and Portugal had both requested negotiations for associate membership in 1962, but both were dictatorships. Spain was given a preferential trade agreement in 1970 and Portugal in 1973, but it was only with the overthrow of the Caetano regime in Portugal in 1973 and the death of Franco in Spain in 1975 that EEC membership for the two states was taken seriously. Despite the relative poverty of Spain and Portugal, problems over fishing rights and concern about Spanish and Portuguese workers moving north in search of work, the EEC felt that membership would encourage democracy in the Iberian peninsula and help link the two countries more closely to NATO and western Europe. Negotiations opened in 1978–79 and both states joined in 1986, bringing the EEC membership to 12.

Map 2   *Growth of the EU*

KEY

= Founder Members of ECSC, 1952

= First Enlargement 1973

= Second Enlargement 1981–6

= Third Enlargement 1995

= East Germany 1990

The doubling of membership had several political and economic consequences: it increased the influence of the EEC (which was by now the biggest economic bloc in the world), it complicated the Community's decision-making processes, it reduced the overall influence of France and Germany, and – by bringing in the poorer Mediterranean states – it altered the internal economic balance of the EEC. Rather than enlarging any further, it was now time to deepen the relationship among the Twelve. Applications were made by Turkey (1987), Austria (1989), Cyprus and Malta (1990), and although East Germany in a sense entered through the back door with the reunification of Germany in 1990, there was to be no further enlargement until 1995.

Economic union and the single market (1979–92)

By 1986 the EEC had become known simply as the European Community (EC). Its member states had a combined population of 322 million and accounted for just over one fifth of all world trade. The EC had its own administrative structure and an independent body of law, and its citizens had direct (but limited) representation through the European Parliament, which also gave them a psychological and political stake in the evolution of the Community.

However, progress towards integration remained uneven. The creation of a common market was one of the key goals of the Treaty of Rome, but there was still a long way to go; the customs union was in place, but barriers remained to the free movement of people and capital, including different national technical, health, and quality standards, and varying levels of indirect taxation, such as VAT.

Back in the 1970s the term 'Eurosclerosis' had begun to gain currency to describe the economic stagnation, double-digit inflation and high unemployment that were afflicting Europe. European businesses were not competing well on the global market, scientists and industrialists were failing to collaborate, and the remaining barriers to internal trade stood in the way of a true single market. There could be no single market without monetary union and complete financial integration, and it would be a relatively short hop in neofunctionalist terms from monetary union to the creation of a single currency, a controversial idea because it would mean a certain loss of national sovereignty. Monetary union was also fundamental to the idea of real economic union and would represent a significant move towards political union. These issues had now begun to concern EC leaders, who were soon to take the three most important steps in the process of integration since the treaties of Paris and Rome: the launch of the European Monetary System, and agreement of the Single European Act and the Treaty on European Union.

The EEC treaty had mentioned the need to 'coordinate' economic policies, but had given the Community no specific powers to ensure this, so in practice coordination had been minimal. New momentum had come in 1969 with a change of leadership in France and West Germany: Georges Pompidou had been less averse than de Gaulle to strengthening EC ties and Willy Brandt had been in favour of monetary union (Pinder, 1991, pp. 120–1). Turbulence in the international monetary system in the late 1960s had given the idea new urgency and significance, but the EEC leaders had disagreed about whether economic union or monetary union should come first (Urwin, 1995, p. 155).

The principle of economic and monetary union (EMU) had beem agreed at a 1969 summit of EEC leaders in the Hague, who had agreed to control fluctuations in the value of their currencies and to make more effort to coordinate national economic policies, with their finance ministers meeting at least three times a year. In August 1971, however, the Nixon administration had taken the United States off the gold standard, and signalled the end of the Bretton Woods system by imposing domestic wage and price controls and placing a surcharge on imports. This had led to international monetary turbulence, which had been exacerbated in 1973 by the Arab–Israeli war and the OPEC oil crisis. Because only West Germany, the Benelux countries and Denmark had been able to keep their currencies reasonably stable, the goal of achieving EMU by 1980 had been quietly abandoned.

A new initiative – the European Monetary System (EMS) – was launched in 1979, again based on the goal of stabilizing exchange rates. It used an Exchange Rate Mechanism (ERM) founded on a European Currency Unit (ecu), and had the goal of creating a zone of monetary stability, with governments taking action to keep their currencies as stable as possible relative to the ecu, a unit of account whose value was calculated on the basis of a basket of national currencies, weighted according to their relative strength. The hope had been that the ecu would become the normal means of settling international debts between EC members, psychologically preparing them for the idea of a single European currency. Member states opting in to the EMS agreed to take whatever action they could, such as adjusting interest rates, to keep their currencies within an agreed band (commonly +2.25 per cent) relative to the ecu.

The EMS did help stabilize exchange rates and complemented the tendency among Western economies at the time to focus on controlling inflation (Kaufmann and Overturf, 1991, p. 186). So in 1989, Commission President Jacques Delors decided to take EMU a step further with the elaboration of a three-stage plan aimed at economic and monetary policy coordination, with the goal of bringing all 12 currencies into the ERM by July 1990, instituting a European central bank by 1994, fixing exchange rates and introducing a single currency. His hopes were dashed, however, by massive speculation on the world's money markets, which sent shockwaves through the ERM: Britain and Italy pulled out, Spain, Portugal and Ireland devalued their currencies, and by 1992–93 the ERM appeared to have collapsed. Ironically the crisis deterred speculation and reinforced currency stability, and EMU was back on track by 1994, but there was doubt about how soon Stage Three of the Delors plan could be reached.

Meanwhile there was concern that progress towards the single market was being handicapped by inflation and unemployment, and by the temptation of member states to protect their home industries with non-tariff barriers such as subsidies (Pinder, 1991, p. 65). Competition from the United States and Japan was also growing. In response, a decision was reached at the 1983 European Council meeting in Stuttgart to revive the original goal outlined in the Treaty of Rome of creating a single market. In June 1985 the Commission published the Cockfield report, listing the specific actions that would need to be taken in order to remove all remaining non-tariff barriers and create a true single market.

The Single European Act (SEA) was signed in Luxembourg in February 1986, and – after ratification by national legislatures – came into force in July 1987. It had several goals (Box 3.2), the most important of which was to complete all preparations for the single market by midnight on 31 December 1992. This involved the removal of all remaining physical barriers (such as customs and passport controls at internal borders), fiscal barriers (mainly in the form of different levels of indirect taxation) and technical barriers (such as conflicting standards, laws and qualifications). This would create 'an area without internal frontiers in which the free movement of goods, persons, services and capital is assured'. In practical terms it meant that the Commission and the Council of Ministers had to agree 282 new pieces of legislation by 1990, which then had to be applied at the national level. In the event the deadline came and went with only 92 per cent of proposals adopted by the Council of Ministers, and only 79 per cent adopted and transposed into national law (*Eurecom*, 4:11, December 1992). Nonetheless the single market went into force in January 1993 with the understanding that the backlog of legislation would be cleared as soon as possible.

Social and regional integration since 1974

For a long time social policy was a poor relation to economic and political integration. Although the EEC Treaty provided for the development of an

Box 3.2 The 1986 Single European Act

The passage of the Single European Act was widely acclaimed as the most important and successful step in the process of European integration since the Treaty of Rome. It had many important consequences:

- It created the single biggest market and trading unit in the world. Many internal passport and customs controls were eased or lifted, banks could do business throughout the Community, companies could do business and sell their products throughout the Community, there was little to prevent EC residents living, working, opening bank accounts and drawing their pensions anywhere in the EC, protectionism became illegal, and monopolies on everything from electricity supply to telecommunications were broken down.
- It gave the EC responsibility over new policy areas that had not been covered in the Treaty of Rome, such as the environment, research and development, and regional policy.
- It gave new powers to the Court of Justice, and created a Court of First Instance to hear certain kinds of case and ease the workload of the Court of Justice.
- It gave legal status to meetings of heads of government under the European Council, and gave new powers to the Council of Ministers and the European Parliament.
- It gave legal status to European Political Cooperation (EPC – foreign policy coordination) so that member states could work towards a European foreign policy and work more closely on defence and security issues.
- It made economic and monetary union an EC objective and promoted 'cohesion', or the reduction of the gap between rich and poor parts of the EC, thereby avoiding a 'two-speed Europe'.

EEC social policy, this was left in the hands of the member states and was very narrowly defined, emphasizing improved working conditions and standards of living for workers, equal pay for equal work among men and women, social security for migrant workers, and increased geographical and occupational mobility for workers. As the economic links among EEC member states tightened, however, so their differing levels of wealth and opportunity became more obvious. Even in the mid-1960s, per capita GDP in the EEC's ten richest regions was nearly four times greater than in its ten poorest regions. With the accession of Britain, Ireland and Greece the gap grew to the point where the richest regions were five times richer than the poorest (George, 1990, pp. 143–4). Social and regional policy has since focused on promoting cohesion by helping the poorer parts of Europe, revitalizing regions affected by serious industrial decline, addressing long-term unemployment, providing youth job training and helping the development of rural areas.

Economic assistance is given by the Commission in the form of grants from what are collectively known as structural funds. The oldest of these is the Guarantee section of the Common Agricultural Policy, which provides funds for rural areas. The European Social Fund (ESF) was established in 1974 with an initial focus on employment and retraining, and since 1983 has concentrated more on youth unemployment and job creation. Cohesion is also promoted by the European Regional Development Fund (ERDF), set up in 1975 in response to the regional disparities that arrived with the accession of Britain and Ireland to the Community. The Commission considered that these disparities were an obstacle to the 'balanced expansion' of economic activity and to EMU (Commission, 1973), and that something needed to be done. France and West Germany became interested in regional policy as a means of helping Britain integrate with its new partners, and the Heath government promoted the creation of a regional fund as a way of making EEC membership more palatable to Britons concerned about the potential costs of membership. It was made clear that ERDF funds would not replace national spending on the development of poorer regions, but would at most provide matching funds and could be spent only on projects that would create new jobs in industry or services, or improve infrastructure. The identification of priority regions was left up to the member states.

The SEA made cohesion a central part of economic integration, the assumption being that although the single market would create new jobs, this would not be enough. A boost for social policy came in 1989 with the Charter of Fundamental Social Rights for Workers (the Social Charter), which promoted the free movement of workers, fair pay, better living and working conditions, freedom of association, and protection of children and adolescents. The Maastricht treaty introduced the Cohesion Fund, which compensates the poorest EU member states for the costs of tightening environmental controls, and provides assistance for transport projects. The structural funds accounted for 18 per cent of EC expenditure in 1984 but by 1998 represented more than one third of EU spending.

Despite the increased focus on cohesion, regional disparities remain; the gap between the highest and lowest income levels in the EU is twice that in the United States, and neither the EU nor the member states have so far been able to deal effectively with unemployment, which was in the range of 6–22 per cent in most EU states in mid-1998, compared with just over 5 per cent in the United States and 3 per cent in Japan. The Amsterdam treaty not only incorporated the Social Charter into the Treaty of Rome, but also made the promotion of high employment an EU objective.

From Community to Union

The controversial idea of political integration was long left on the back burner because it was felt there was little hope of political union without economic union. False starts had been made with the European Political Community and an attempt in 1961 to draw up a political charter that would spell out the terms of political union (the Fouchet Plan, see Urwin, 1995, pp. 104–7). A later initiative came out of the 1970 Davignon report, which argued in favour of foreign policy coordination, quarterly meetings among the six foreign ministers, liaison among EC ambassadors in foreign capitals and common EC instructions on certain matters for those ambassadors.

Foreign policies were also coordinated under a process known as European Political Cooperation (EPC), which achieved some early successes, for example the 1970 joint EC policy declaration on the Middle East and the signature of the Yaoundé Conventions on aid to poorer countries. In 1975 the Final Act of the Conference on Security and Cooperation in Europe (held in Helsinki) was signed by Italian Prime Minister Aldo Moro 'in the name of the European Community'. EPC was eventually given legal status with the SEA. It worked well in some areas, but was more reactive than proactive and a truly European foreign policy has yet to emerge. This became clear during the 1990–91 Gulf crisis when the EC as a whole issued demands to the Iraqi regime, and imposed an embargo on Iraqi oil imports, but few individual member states wished to be actively involved in the allied response to the 1991 Iraq invasion of Kuwait. It became clear once again in 1998 when Britain supported US threats of military action against Iraq, but found little agreement among its EU partners.

Determined to reassert French leadership in the EC, President François Mitterrand had focused on the theme of political union at the Fontaineblue European Council in 1984, with the result that a decision had been taken in Milan in June 1985 to convene an intergovernmental conference (IGC) on political union. The outcome was the Treaty on European Union, agreed at the Maastricht European Council summit in December 1991 and signed by the EC foreign and economics ministers in February 1992 (Box 3.3). The draft treaty had included the goal of federal union, but Britain had balked at this so the wording was changed to 'an ever closer union among the peoples of Europe, in which decisions are taken as closely as possible to the citizen'.

The Maastricht treaty had to be ratified by the 12 member states before it could come into force and it received a major setback when it was rejected by Danish voters in a referendum in June 1992. Following agreement that Denmark could opt out of the single currency, common defence arrangements, European citizenship and cooperation on justice

Box 3.3 The 1992 Treaty on European Union

Better known as the Maastricht treaty after the town in the Netherlands where it was agreed, the Treaty on European Union has several elements:

- The creation of the European Union, a new label meant to symbolize the next stage in the process of European integration, and based on three 'pillars': a reformed and strengthened European Community; and two areas in which there was to be more formal intergovernmental cooperation: a Common Foreign and Security Policy (CFSP), and home affairs and justice. However, final responsibility for the CFSP remains with the individual governments rather than being handed over to the EU. Although the European Community still exists, one of the effects of Maastricht was that the label 'European Union' became more popular.
- A timetable for the creation of a single European currency by January 1999. Here Maastricht was simply confirming the essence of the plan outlined by Jacques Delors in 1989.
- Extension of EU responsibility to new areas such as consumer protection, public health policy, transport, education and (except in Britain) social policy.
- Greater intergovernmental cooperation on immigration and asylum, the creation of a European police intelligence agency (Europol) to combat organized crime and drug trafficking, the creation of a new Committee of the Regions, and increased regional funds for poorer EU states.
- New rights for European citizens and the creation of an ambiguous European Union 'citizenship', meaning, for example, the right of citizens to live wherever they like in the EU, and to stand or vote in local and European elections.
- Greater powers for the European Parliament, including a 'codecision procedure' under which certain kinds of legislation are subject to a third reading in the European Parliament before they can be adopted by the Council of Ministers.

and home affairs, a second referendum was held in May 1993 and the treaty was accepted by the Danes. With its passage in November 1993, the European Community became one of three 'pillars' that made up the new European Union.

Further enlargement

Any European state wishing to apply for membership of the EU must meet at least five basic requirements: as well as being European and democratic, applicants must follow free-market economic policies, accept the terms of the treaties and accept the *acquis communitaire* (the body of laws and policies already adopted by the EU – see Box 4.2, p. 108). Deciding whether applicants meet these criteria has proved difficult, not least because of the problem of defining 'Europe', as discussed in Chapter 2.

Throughout the 1980s, discussions about enlargement focused on other western European states, if only because they would have to make the fewest adjustments. In order further to prepare the prospective members, negotiations began in 1990 on the creation of a European Economic Area (EEA), under which the terms of the SEA would be extended to the seven EFTA members, in return for which they would accept the rules of the single market. The EEA came into force in January 1994, but had already begun to lose relevance because Austria, Sweden, Norway and Finland had applied for EC membership. Negotiations with these four applicants were completed in early 1994, each held a national referendum, and all but Norway (where the vote once again went against membership) joined the EU in January 1995. This left just Norway, Switzerland, Iceland and tiny Liechtenstein in EFTA.

Switzerland, which had considered applying for EC membership in 1992, rejected the EEA and now finds itself completely surrounded by the EU. Demands for Switzerland to open its highways to EU trucks and intra-EU trade will undoubtedly increase the pressure for EU membership, although its neutrality and unique system of government remain obstacles (Saint-Ouen, 1988). Iceland, with a population of just 300 000, relies largely on the exportation of fish and does more than half its trade with the EU; it too will find the logic of joining the EU increasingly difficult to resist. With a population of just 30 000, Liechtenstein is little more than an enclave of Switzerland and is likely to follow the Swiss lead.

Looking further east, Turkey has been anxious to join for some time and applied for membership in 1987. While its eligibility has been confirmed and it has been in a customs union with the EU since 1996, Turkey is populous (64 million people), poor and predominantly Islamic. In addition to the troubling economic and social questions thus raised, Turkey's human rights record is poor and its application has been opposed by Greece. It was angered by the decision of the European Council in December 1997 not to include it in the next round of enlargement negotiations, particularly as the EU said yes to Cyprus, which has been divided since 1975 into Turkish and Greek zones.

Among the likely prospects for medium-term accession are eastern European states that turned to free market policies after the collapse of the Soviet bloc in 1991. Negotiations opened in the spring of 1998 with Hungary, Poland, the Czech Republic, Slovenia, Estonia and Cyprus. Looking still further east, accession by the other Baltic states (Latvia and Lithuania) and three former Soviet republics (Ukraine, Belarus and

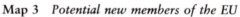

Map 3   *Potential new members of the EU*

Moldova) cannot be discounted, but will depend on the resolution of questions about their relationship with Russia and how quickly they make the transition to free market policies. Latvia, Lithuania, Slovakia, Bulgaria and Romania have all applied – the first three have reasonably strong credentials but the last two are unlikely to be seriously considered until after 2006 (see Box 8.3, p. 224).

The single currency and beyond

In June 1997 the EU leaders signed the Treaty of Amsterdam (Box 3.4), a new set of revisions to the founding treaties of the EU. The treaty fell far short of its original goal of political union to accompany the economic and monetary union promoted by the SEA and Maastricht, and the 15 leaders were unable to agree changes to the structure of EU institutions in preparation for a further expansion in membership. However, they were able to agree on instituting a single European currency in January 1999, enlarging the EU to the east, further developing policies on asylum, immigration, unemployment, social policy, health protection, consumer protection, the environment and foreign policy, and making modest reforms to EU institutions. Amsterdam also provided an opportunity to assess the progress made since the signing of the Treaty of Paris.

First, it is almost universally agreed that the single market has been a great success. Not all of the nearly 1340 separate pieces of legislation aimed at removing the final barriers to trade have been implemented, but the EU has become one of the two biggest markets in the world and intra-EU trade and competition has grown rapidly.

Second, the EU still has no joint foreign or defence policy, although it has made progress in some areas. It has become a major actor on the world stage in terms of aid to eastern Europe, has signed preferential trade agreements with 71 African, Caribbean and Pacific countries, and is helping to build a Mediterranean free trade area (to be completed by 2010 and encompassing nearly 700 million people). However, the 15 member states still pursue their own interests and take different positions on foreign policy problems. Organizational changes coming out of Amsterdam include agreement that foreign policy should be the responsibility of one commissioner rather than several, and the possibility of limited majority voting in the Council of Ministers on issues that have so far required unanimous agreement.

Third, there is no common policy on immigration, visas and asylum, but progress on the removal of border controls continues. In 1985 France, Germany and the Benelux states signed the Schengen Agreement, under which all border controls were to be removed. All EU member states

Box 3.4 The 1997 Treaty of Amsterdam

The most recent changes to the treaties that form the basis of European integration were the result of an intergovernmental conference (IGC) held between March 1996 and June 1997 to plan future developments, notably the inevitable eastward expansion of the EU. The result was a new treaty that was signed at the Amsterdam European Council in June 1997. Less notable and less controversial than either the SEA or the Maastricht treaty, the Amsterdam treaty includes the following elements:

- Matters relating to asylum, visas, immigration and external border controls were made subject to EU rules and procedures (with opt-outs for Britain, Denmark and Ireland), the Schengen Agreement was incorporated into the EU framework, and cooperation between national police forces (and the work of Europol) was strengthened.
- Policies on employment, sustainable development, human health protection and consumer protection were made formal objectives of the EU, and 'subsidiarity' was given a new definition (see Chapter 7).
- The treaty made a number of small changes to the structure of the EU institutions in anticipation of enlarged membership. It was also decided that at least one year before the membership of the EU grows to 20, a new IGC will be convened to carry out a comprehensive review of the treaties and the functioning of the institutions.
- In order to promote coherent, effective and visible foreign policy, a policy planning unit was established, decision-making procedures were simplified in order to reduce the risk of deadlock, cooperation with the WEU was emphasized, and provision was made for a single commissioner to be the EU representative on external relations.
- Several changes were made to institutional practices, including downgrading the cooperation procedure and changing the codecision procedure to place the European Parliament and the Council of Ministers on a more equal footing, increasing the number of policy areas that are subject to qualified majority voting, and giving additional powers to the Court of Auditors and the Committee of the Regions.

except Britain and Ireland have since joined, along with two non-members: Iceland and Norway. The terms of the agreement allow the signatories to implement controls at any time and not all have introduced truly passport-free travel (see Chapter 7), but it marked a substantial step towards the final removal of border controls.

Finally – and most critically of all – progress continues on the most ambitious project ever undertaken by the EU, the creation of a single European currency. A decision was taken in 1995 to call this currency the euro, and the timetable agreed under Maastricht required participating states to fix their exchange rates in January 1999. The euro would then be officially launched, and after a three-year gestation period, euro notes and coins would begin circulating in January 2002 and replace completely national currencies the following July.

At a special EU summit in May 1998 it was decided that all but Greece met the conditions necessary to join the single currency (see Chapter 7), but public and political opinion in the member states was divided on which should or would fix their exchange rates in January 1999. While inflation rates were low in member states in 1998, their unemployment rates were not, and the rate of industrial growth was slowing in several. There was also considerable public resistance to the idea of the single currency in Germany, and the Blair government in Britain decided not to consider joining until at least after the next general election, perhaps as late as 2002. However, while there may eventually be a multispeed approach to monetary union – as there has been to almost every element of European integration – the ambitious timetable set for the euro has forced European citizens and their leaders to think about the implications of a single currency (see Chapter 7).

Conclusions

Europe has come a long way in the past fifty years or so. Just after the Second World War, most European states were physically devastated, the suspicions and hostilities that had led to two world wars in the space of a generation still lingered, and western Europe found itself being pulled into a military and economic vacuum as power and influence moved outwards to the United States and the Soviet Union. Since then, new ties of cooperation have been built that have combined the interests of western European states and have helped give the region new confidence and influence.

Beginning with the limited experiment of integrating their coal and steel industries and building on an economic foundation and security shield underwritten by the United States, six European states expanded their economic ties and quickly moved on to agreement on a common agricultural policy, a customs union and the beginnings of a common market. The accession of new members in the 1970s and 1980s greatly increased the size of the Community's population and market. The global economic instability that followed the end of the Bretton Woods system and the energy crises of the 1970s, served to emphasize the need for western European countries to cooperate if they were to have more control over their own future rather than simply to respond to external events.

After several years of relative lethargy the European experiment was given new impetus by completion of the single market, and then by the more controversial notion of replacing the individual national currencies with a single European currency. The effects of integration have been felt in a growing number of policy areas, including agriculture, competition, transport, the environment, energy, telecommunications, research and development, working conditions, culture, consumer affairs, education and employment. At the core of all this has been a set of five major institutions, supported by a growing body of specialized agencies. The next chapter focuses on the structures and powers of those institutions, which are steadily taking on the characteristics of a new level of government to which the member states and their citizens are subject.

Chapter 4

The Institutions of the EU

The European Commission
The Council of Ministers
The European Parliament
The European Court of Justice
The European Council
Conclusions

As the European Union has grown, so has the body of laws and policies that drive its activities, and so have the powers and reach of the institutions that make, decide and implement those laws and policies. Unfortunately, changes made to the treaties have created an institutional structure that is both complex and confusing, where powers and roles have evolved slowly and unsteadily, often in opportunistic response to short-term needs without much sense of what the governments of the member states want them eventually to become. The Amsterdam treaty was to have included major innovations, but ended up doing little more than light tinkering, so more changes are anticipated as membership of the EU enlarges over the next few years.

To confuse matters further, the EU institutions (Figure 4.1, p. 94) cannot easily be compared with the conventional institutions of government at the national level. Comparisons can be made, but they must always be tempered: the College of Commissioners is not quite a cabinet, the European Parliament is not quite a legislature, the Commission is more than a bureaucracy, and so on. Furthermore, the institutions do not amount to a 'government' in the conventional sense of the word, because the member states still hold most of the decision-making powers and are still responsible for implementing EU policies. However, the institutions are becoming more powerful and significant, and their evolution is having the effect of slowly building a confederal Europe.

In brief, the five major institutions work as follows. The European Commission is responsible for developing proposals for laws and policies, upon which the final decisions are taken by the Council of Ministers in a complex interaction with the European Parliament. Once decisions are made, the European Commission is responsible for overseeing the implementation of laws and policies by the member states. The Court of Justice works to build a common body of law for the EU, and to make judgements on the correlation between EU law, national laws and the EU treaties. The European Council brings the leaders of the member states together regularly to guide the overall direction of the European Union.

As with any summary of administrative systems, this brief outline says nothing about the many subtle (and not so subtle) pressures that are brought to bear on European decision making, nor does it convey the many informal aspects of EU government: the different degrees of influence exerted by different member states; the political and economic pressures that drive the decisions of the member states; the key role played by interest groups, corporations, members of staff in the Commission and specialized working groups within the Council of Ministers; and all the muddling through and incremental change that often characterizes policy making in the EU, as in the member states.

This chapter looks at the structure and influence of each of the major EU institutions, explains how they fit into the policy process, and how they relate to each other and to the member states. It paints a picture of a system that is complex and occasionally clumsy, and is still in the process of construction. It shows how the EU institutions are caught in a web of competing national interests, and how the conflicting forces of intergovernmentalism and supranationalism are pulling each of them in different directions.

The European Commission

The process by which laws and policies are made in the EU begins with the European Commission, which is the executive–bureaucratic arm of the EU. It is responsible for developing proposals for new laws and policies, overseeing the implementation of law, 'guarding' the treaties and promoting the interests of the EU as a whole. It is the most supranational of the EU institutions, and has long been at the heart of the process of European integration. It has not only encouraged member states to harmonize their laws, regulations and standards in the interests of removing the barriers to trade, but has also been the source of some of the defining policy initiatives of the last forty years, notably the completion of the single market.

Despite its importance, the Commission is regularly the target of disdain and criticism. Eurosceptics grumble about waste and meddling by Eurocrats, and complain that the leaders of the Commission are not elected and that its staff have little public accountability. For some, 'Brussels' has become a codeword for some vague and threatening notion of government by bureaucracy, or 'creeping federalism'. But this is unfair. The Commission has much less power then its detractors often suggest, it is not a decision-making body, and its powers are being reduced as those of other

EU institutions grow. It is also very small given the size of its task; it has just over 20 000 staff, making it much smaller than many national government ministries.

Structure

The Commission is headquartered in Brussels, but its staff work in numerous buildings around that city, in regional cities throughout the EU and in national capitals around the world. It has four main elements: the College of Commissioners, the president of the Commission, directorates-general, and the Secretariat General.

The College of Commissioners

The European Commission is led by a group of 20 commissioners, who serve five-year terms and jointly function as something like a European cabinet, taking collective responsibility for their decisions. Each has a portfolio for which he or she is responsible (see Table 4.1, p. 90), and one is appointed president. The 20 posts are distributed among the EU member states, the five biggest countries (Germany, Britain, France, Italy and Spain) having two each, and the rest one each. This will be changed after the next enlargement, when all member states will have no more than one post each.

Commissioners are appointed by their national governments, but they are not national representatives and must swear an oath of office that they renounce all defence of national interests. There are no formal rules on appointments, but appointees usually must be acceptable to the other commissioners, to other governments, to the major political parties at home, and to the European Parliament (for details of the process, see Cini, 1996, pp. 107–11). Commissioners tend to be people who already have a national political reputation at home, albeit sometimes a modest one. They may be well-respected members of an opposition party, or someone the governing party would like to remove from the national political scene for some reason. As the powers of the Commission have increased, and the EU has become a more significant political force, postings to the Commission have become more desirable and more important, and commissioners are becoming both younger and more technocratic.

At the beginning of each term, the 20 commissioners are each given portfolios, the distribution of which is the prerogative of the president, has great political significance and is seen as an acid test of the ability of the president to lead (de Bassompierre, 1988, p. 8). Despite regular claims of collegiality among commissioners, the College has its own internal

Table 4.1 *The European Commissioners, January 1999*

Name	Country	Key portfolios
Jacques Santer	Luxembourg	President
Sir Leon Brittan	Britain	Trade policy, external relations (North America, Southeast Asia, OECD, World Trade Organization)
Hans van den Broek	Netherlands	External relations (Eastern Europe and former USSR), Common Foreign and Security Policy
Manuel Marin	Spain	External relations (Southern Mediterranean, Middle East, Latin America)
Jao de deus Pinheiro	Portugal	External relations (ACP states)
Yves-Thibault de Silguy	France	Economic and financial affairs
Martin Bangemann	Germany	Industrial affairs, information and telecommunications
Karel van Miert	Belgium	Competition
Padraig Flynn	Ireland	Employment and social affairs
Franz Fischler	Austria	Agriculture
Neil Kinnock	Britain	Transport
Erkii Liikanen	Finland	Budget, personnel and administration
Ritt Bjerregaard	Denmark	Environment, nuclear safety
Edith Cresson	France	Science, education, research and development, human resources
Emma Bonino	Italy	Consumer policy, fisheries
Mario Monti	Italy	Internal market, financial services, tax
Monika Wulf-Mathies	Germany	Regional policy, relations with the Committee of the Regions, Cohesion Fund
Christos Papoutsis	Greece	Energy
Marcelino Oreja	Spain	Relations with the European Parliament, culture, official publications
Anita Gradin	Sweden	Justice, home affairs, immigration and financial control

hierarchy of positions: the key posts are those concerned with the budget, agriculture and external relations. Once in office, each commissioner is supported by a personal staff of about half a dozen assistants and advisors, called a *cabinet*, which is headed by a *chef* and provides advice, information and the basic services that help commissioners do their jobs.

The president

The dominant figure in the Commission hierarchy is the president, the person who comes closest to being able to claim to be the leader of the EU, although this is a debatable proposition given the way that power is divided and dissipated within the system. The president is technically no more than a first among equals and can be outvoted by other commissioners, but – like prime ministers in parliamentary systems – the president's trump card is the power of appointment; the ability to distribute portfolios is a potent tool for patronage and political manipulation. The president also oversees meetings of the College, represents the Commission in dealings with other EU institutions and national governments, and is responsible for ensuring that the Commission gives impetus to the process of European integration.

The assertiveness of Commission President Jacques Delors in 1985–94 heralded the emergence of a more presidential style in the governance of the EU (Wallace, 1991). Delors personalized his position to an unprecedented degree, often issuing reports and papers with little or no prior consultation with his peers, and taking responsibility for economic policy issues that were really the job of the relevant commissioner. He also had firm ideas about a strong, federal Europe asserting itself internationally (Dinan, 1994, p. 203), and used this vision to push the EU in many new directions. He was succeeded in January 1995 by Jacques Santer, former prime minister of Luxembourg, who faced the task of guiding the EU towards economic and monetary union, preparing for further enlargement and developing a common foreign and security policy.

There are no formal rules on how the president should be chosen. It has become normal practice for the leaders of the member states to make the choice collectively at the European Council held in the June before the term of the incumbent ends, settling on someone acceptable to them all, to the Commission itself and to the European Parliament. Appointed for renewable five-year terms, the president is usually someone with a strong political reputation, a strong character and proven leadership abilities. The incumbents to date have proved very different in style and ability; Walter Hallstein (1958–67), Roy Jenkins (1977–80) and Jacques Delors (1985–94) are remembered as the most active, and the remainder as relatively passive (Table 4.2).

Table 4.2 *Presidents of the European Commission*

1958–67	Walter Hallstein (West Germany)
1968–69	Jean Rey (Belgium)
1970–72	Franco Maria Malfatti (Italy)
1972	Sicco Mansholt (Netherlands)
1973–76	Francois–Xavier Ortoli (France)
1977–80	Roy Jenkins (Britain)
1981–84	Gaston Thorn (Luxembourg)
1985–94	Jacques Delors (France)
1995–	Jacques Santer (Luxembourg)

Directorates-general

Below the College, the European Commission is divided into 24 directorates-general (DGs), which are the functional equivalent of national government ministries. Every DG is responsible for a particular area (Table 4.3), has its own director-general and is tied to a particular commissioner. Just as there is an informal pecking order among commissioners, so some DGs are more important (and larger and better funded) than others, the ranking being a reflection of the extent to which the EU is active in different policy areas. Hence those dealing with external affairs (DGI-IB), industry (DGIII) and agriculture (DGVI) are larger and more powerful, while those dealing with fisheries (XIV), energy (XVII) and education (XXII) are smaller and less influential.

The Commission employs temporary staff, and national experts are seconded for fixed terms according to need, but the bulk of DG employees are full-time and acquire their jobs through a competitive and rigorous recruitment process. The Commission is required to ensure there is balanced nationality representation at all levels, but nearly one in four Eurocrats is Belgian, mainly because the secretarial and support staff are locally recruited. Although those who will eventually become directors-general theoretically work their way up the ranks of the Commission, appointments at the higher levels are often based less on merit than on nationality and political affiliation.

About two thirds of Commission staff are engaged in drafting new laws and policies or overseeing implementation, about 20 per cent are involved in research, and the rest are involved in translation and interpretation – although the Commission works mainly in English and French, all documents must be translated into the 11 official EU languages. The majority of Commission staff work in offices in and around Brussels, and the remainder in Luxembourg, other parts of the EU or the Commission's overseas offices.

Table 4.3 *Directorates-general of the European Commission*

DG I	External relations: commercial policy and relations with North America, Far East, Australia, New Zealand
DG IA	External relations: Europe and newly independent states, Common Foreign and Security Policy, external missions
DG IB	External relations: southern Mediterranean, Middle and Near East, Latin America, South and Southeast Asia, North–South cooperation
DG II	Economic and financial affairs
DG III	Industry
DG IV	Competition
DG V	Employment, Industrial relations and social affairs
DG VI	Agriculture
DG VII	Transport
DG VIII	Development
DG IX	Personnel and administration
DG X	Information, communication and culture
DG XI	Environment, nuclear safety and civil protection
DG XII	Science, research and development
DG XIII	Telecommunications, information market and exploitation of research
DG XIV	Fisheries
DG XV	Internal market and financial services
DG XVI	Regional policy and cohesion
DG XVII	Energy
DG XVIII	*Disbanded*
DG XIX	Budgets
DG XX	*Disbanded*
DG XXI	Customs and indirect taxation
DG XXII	Education, training and youth
DG XXIII	Enterprise policy, distributive trades, tourism and cooperatives
DG XXIV	Consumer policy and consumer health protection

The Secretariat General

Administration is overseen by a secretary general, supported by a staff of about 350. The secretary general chairs the weekly meetings of the *chefs de cabinet*, sits in on meetings of the Commissioners, directs Commission relations with Parliament and generally makes sure that the work of the Commission runs smoothly.

Figure 4.1   *The European policy process*

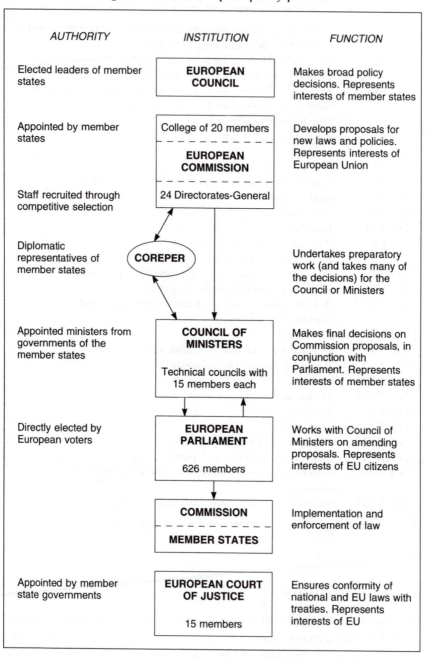

AUTHORITY	INSTITUTION	FUNCTION
Elected leaders of member states	**EUROPEAN COUNCIL**	Makes broad policy decisions. Represents interests of member states
Appointed by member states	College of 20 members — — — — — — — — **EUROPEAN COMMISSION** — — — — — — — —	Develops proposals for new laws and policies. Represents interests of European Union
Staff recruited through competitive selection	24 Directorates-General	
Diplomatic representatives of member states	COREPER	Undertakes preparatory work (and takes many of the decisions) for the Council or Ministers
Appointed ministers from governments of the member states	**COUNCIL OF MINISTERS** Technical councils with 15 members each	Makes final decisions on Commission proposals, in conjunction with Parliament. Represents interests of member states
Directly elected by European voters	**EUROPEAN PARLIAMENT** 626 members	Works with Council of Ministers on amending proposals. Represents interests of EU citizens
	COMMISSION — — — — — — — — **MEMBER STATES**	Implementation and enforcement of law
Appointed by member state governments	**EUROPEAN COURT OF JUSTICE** 15 members	Ensures conformity of national and EU laws with treaties. Represents interests of EU

How the Commission works

While the Commission is neither a full-blown 'government' nor a 'bureaucracy' in the true sense of either term, it has elements of both, because its key task is to ensure that EU policies accord with the treaties (for details, see Edwards and Spence, 1997). It does this in five ways.

Powers of initiation

The Commission is legally obliged to ensure that the principles of the treaties are turned into practical laws and policies, and in this respect it is sometimes described as the 'guardian' of the treaties. It has the sole power to initiate new legislation, and can also draw up proposals for entirely new policy areas – as it did with the Single European Act and the Delors package for Economic and Monetary Union – and pass them on to Parliament and the Council of Ministers for discussion and adoption.

Proposals can come from a commissioner or a staff member of one of the DGs, may come as a result of a ruling by the Court of Justice, or may flow out of one of the treaties. Member state governments, interest groups and even private corporations can exert direct or indirect pressure on the Commission. The last two decades have also seen more policy suggestions coming from the European Council.

Typically, a piece of EU legislation begins life as a draft written by middle-ranking Eurocrats in one of the DGs. It is then passed up the ranks of the DG and other interested DGs, being amended or revised along the way. The draft eventually reaches the College of Commissioners, which normally meets every Wednesday to go through the different proposals. By majority vote the College can accept a draft law, reject it, send it back down the line for redrafting or postpone making a decision. Once passed by the College, it is sent to the European Parliament for an opinion and the Council of Ministers for a decision. This process can take anything from months to years, and Commission staff are involved at every stage.

Powers of implementation

Once a law or policy is accepted, the Commission is responsible for ensuring that it is implemented by the member states. While it has no power to do this directly and has to rely heavily on the national bureaucracies, it does have the power to collect information from member states, to take to the Court of Justice any member state, corporation or individual that does not conform to the spirit of the treaties or follow subsequent EU law, and to impose sanctions or fines if a law is not implemented. The Commission has its own monitoring teams, but they do not have the personnel to police every member state so it usually has to rely on reports from member states, or whistle-blowing by member states, individuals, corporations or interests groups. The Commission adds to the pressure by publicizing the progress on implementation in the hope of embarrassing the laggards into action. Until 1993 compliance was based on goodwill and agreement to 'play the game', but Maastricht gave the Commission new powers to take non-compliant states to the Court of Justice, which is authorized to impose fines.

With regard to non-implementation, Italy, Greece, Belgium and Germany are the worst offenders – Italy has been taken to court more often than any other member state. Ironically, Britain and Denmark – two of the most lukewarm members of the EU – have among the best records on compliance, a reflection of the seriousness with which both countries have traditionally taken their international treaty obligations. Most cases of non-compliance are due not so much to deliberate avoidance by a member state as to differences over interpretation or differences in the efficiency of national bureaucracies; for example, the latter accounts for many of the infringements by Italy, where the national bureaucracy is notorious for delay, inefficiency and corruption.

Acting as the conscience of the EU

The Commission is expected to rise above national interests and to represent and promote the general interest of the EU, however that is defined. The Commission is also expected to smooth the flow of decision making by mediating disagreements between or among member states and other EU institutions.

Management of EU finances

The Commission makes sure that all EU revenues are collected, plays a key role in drafting and guiding the annual budget through the Council of Ministers and Parliament, and administers EU expenditure, especially under the Common Agricultural Policy and the structural funds.

External relations

The Commission acts as the EU's main external representative in dealings with international organizations such as the United Nations and the World Trade Organization. It is also a key point of contact between the EU and the rest of the world; more than 140 governments have opened diplomatic missions in Brussels accredited to the EU, while the EU has opened more than 120 offices in other parts of the world, staffed by Commission employees. The Commission also oversees the process by which applications for full or associate membership are considered; it looks into all the implications and reports back to the Council. If the Council decides to open negotiations with an applicant, the Commission oversees the process.

The Council of Ministers

The Council of Ministers is the decision-making branch of the EU, the primary champion of national interests and arguably the most powerful of the EU institutions. Once the Commission has proposed a new law or policy, it is discussed and amended by the European Parliament and the Council of Ministers, but cannot become law without the approval of the Council. The Council consists of national government ministers and its make-up changes according to the topic under discussion; hence employment ministers will meet to deal with employment issues, transport ministers to discuss new proposals for transport policy and law, and so on. Overall direction is provided by the presidency of the Council, which is held for six-month terms by each EU member state in turn.

Despite its powers, the Council is less well known and understood than the Commission and the Parliament. Most Europeans tend to associate the actions of the EU with the Commission, forgetting that the Council of Ministers must approve all new laws. In many ways its powers make the Council more like the legislature of the EU than the European Parliament, although the new powers given to Parliament in recent years have made the two bodies into 'colegislatures'.

Structure

The Council of Ministers – officially titled the Council of the European Union – is based in the Justus Lipsius Building in Brussels, across the road from the Berlaymont, the former headquarters of the Commission. It has four main elements: the councils of ministers themselves, the permanent representatives, the presidency and the secretariat general.

The Councils

Nearly two dozen so-called technical councils come under the general heading of the Council of Ministers. The most important is the General Affairs Council (GAC), which brings together the EU foreign ministers to deal broadly with internal and external relations, and to discuss politically sensitive policies and proposals for new laws. Ecofin brings together economics and finance ministers, the Agriculture Council brings together agriculture ministers, and below them are councils dealing with issues such as the environment, research, fisheries and education. With the launch of the single currency, a new euro-11 council was formed in 1998, comprising the finance ministers of the eleven participating member states.

Each council normally consists of the relevant national government ministers, together with the relevant European commissioner, whose presence ensures that the councils do not lose sight of broader EU interests. How often each council meets depends on the importance of its area of responsibility. The GAC, Ecofin and the Agriculture Council tend to meet monthly because of the sheer volume of the work with which they have to deal, but the councils dealing with other issues may meet only twice or four times a year. Most meetings last no more than one or two days, and are held in Brussels.

Permanent representatives

Between meetings of ministers, national interests in the Council are protected and promoted by national delegations of about 30–40 professional diplomats, each headed by a Permanent Representative. The representatives meet every week in the powerful Committee of Permanent Representatives (COREPER), act as a link between Brussels and the member states, and ensure that the views of the governments of the member states are represented and that the capitals are kept in touch with developments in Brussels.

As a body, COREPER acts as a clearinghouse for proposals and a melting pot of ideas, where national positions are outlined and debated, and compromises are often agreed that result in most of the key decisions on proposals being taken before they even reach the ministers. COREPER sets up specialist working groups to study the law or policy under discussion, and to try to reach common positions. It plays a key role in organizing Council meetings by preparing the agendas, deciding which proposals go to which council, deciding which of those proposals can be automatically approved and which need discussion, and overseeing the committees and working parties set up to sift through the proposals.

The presidency

The presidency of the Council of Ministers (and of the European Council) is held not by a person but by a country, which in effect means the prime minister – or president in the case of France – and the foreign minister. Successive member states hold the presidency for spells of six months each, beginning in January and July each year. Six months is usually long enough to make an impression on the direction of the EU, but is also short enough to ensure that each member state regularly takes a turn at the helm.

As the breadth and depth of European integration have grown, so have the value, influence and power of the presidency. The state holding the presidency has several responsibilities:

- It sets the agenda for European Council meetings, and for the EU as a whole.
- It arranges and chairs meetings of the Council of Ministers and COREPER, and oversees Council relations with other EU institutions.
- It mediates and bargains, and is responsible for promoting cooperation among member states: the success of a presidency is measured by the extent to which the incumbent is able to encourage compromise and agreement among the EU members, as well as by what is delayed, opposed or promoted (Brewin and McAllister, 1991).
- It oversees EU foreign policy for six months, acts as the main voice of the EU on the global stage, coordinates member state positions at international conferences and negotiations in which the EU is involved, and (along with the president of the Commission) represents the EU at meetings with the president of the United States and at the annual meetings of the G7 group of industrialized countries.
- It hosts summits of the European Council.

Holding the presidency allows a member state to convene meetings and launch initiatives on issues of national interest, to try to bring those issues to the top of the EU agenda, and to earn prestige and credibility, assuming it does a good job. It allows the leaders of smaller states to negotiate directly with other world leaders and also helps the process of European integration by making the EU more real to the citizens of the country holding the presidency: it helps them to feel more involved and to see that they have a stake in the development of the EU.

The Secretariat General

This is the bureaucracy of the Council and consists of about 2400 Brussels-based staff, most of whom are translators and service staff. The office is headed by a secretary general, appointed for a five-year term. The secretariat supports the presidency and the Council by preparing draft agendas, keeping records and generally providing the work of the Council with some continuity. It does this by working closely with the permanent representatives, and by briefing every Council meeting on the status of each of the items on the agenda.

How the Council works

Once the European Commission has proposed a new law, it is sent to Parliament and the Council of Ministers for debate and possible adoption. The more complex proposals usually go first to one or more specialist working parties within the Council, which look over the proposal in detail, identify points of agreement or disagreement, and respond to suggestions for amendments made by Parliament (for more details see Hayes-Renshaw and Wallace, 1997). The proposal then goes to COREPER, which considers the political implications and tries to clear as many of the remaining problems as it can, ensuring that the meeting of ministers is as quick and as painless as possible. The proposal then moves on to the relevant Council, which has three voting options:

- *Simple majority.* Formerly, this was needed mainly when the Council was dealing with a procedural issue or working under treaty articles, but the SEA and Maastricht broadened the number of issues and areas in which a majority vote could be used, notably matters related to the single market.
- *Unanimity.* This was formerly needed for new laws that would launch an entirely new policy area or substantially change an existing policy, but its use is now heavily restricted. The Amsterdam treaty introduced a 'constructive abstention' procedure whereby a member state is not obliged to apply a particular decision, but recognizes that the EU is committed.
- *Qualified majority.* This is needed for almost every other kind of decision where ministers have failed to reach a consensus. Instead of each minister having one vote, each is given several votes roughly in proportion to the population of his/her member state (see Table 4.4). To be successful, a proposal must win 62 out of a possible 87 votes, but it can also be defeated by a blocking minority of 26 votes. Political pressure has been growing for a redistribution of the votes, notably by larger member states concerned about erosion of their relative voting power. The next enlargement of the EU will certainly see a recalculation.

Because the Council of Ministers is a meeting place for national interests, the key to understanding how it works is provided by terms such as compromise, bargaining and diplomacy. The ministers are leading political figures at home, so they are motivated by national political interests. They are also ideologically driven, and their authority depends to some extent on the stability of the governing party or coalition at home. All these factors combine to pull ministers in many different directions, and to deny the Council the kind of permanence and regularity enjoyed by the Commission.

Table 4.4 *Qualified majority voting in the Council of Ministers*

Member state	Number of votes	Number of citizens per vote (millions)
Germany	10	8.09
Britain	10	5.82
France	10	5.77
Italy	10	5.71
Spain	8	4.89
Netherlands	5	3.04
Greece	5	2.06
Belgium	5	2.02
Portugal	5	1.97
Sweden	4	2.18
Austria	4	1.98
Denmark	3	1.73
Finland	3	1.68
Ireland	3	1.17
Luxembourg	2	0.12
Total	87	4.24*
Qualified majority	62	
Blocking minority	26	

* Average.

The European Parliament

The European Parliament (EP) is the only directly elected institution in the EU system but has relatively few powers over how law and policy is made. It has many of the trappings of a conventional legislature but lacks three critical powers: it cannot introduce laws, enact laws or raise revenues. It can suggest that the Commission propose a new law or policy, it can amend laws as they go through the Commission and the Council of Ministers, it can delay and even reject proposals, and it has equal powers with the Council over the EU budget, but the Commission still holds the power of initiation and the Council the power of decision-making. In short the EP is a junior member in the EU decision-making system.

Most of the EP's handicaps can be traced to the unwillingness of the member states to give up their power over decision-making in the Council of Ministers, and to the emphasis placed in the Treaty of Rome on

Parliament's 'advisory' and 'supervisory' powers. Parliament also has a credibility problem: few EU citizens know what it does, or have the same kind of psychological ties to the EP as they have to their national legislatures.

Despite its handicaps the EP has managed to use arguments about democratic accountability to win added responsibilities and to be taken more seriously. It has become less a body that merely reacts to Commission proposals and Council votes, and has increasingly launched its own initiatives and forced the other institutions to pay more attention to its opinions. The EP has won a greater right to amend laws and check the activities of the other institutions, it has been a valuable source of ideas and new policy proposals, and it has acted as the conscience of the EU and the guardian of its democratic ideals (Lodge, 1993). Since the introduction of direct elections in 1979, the EP has been able to claim that it is the only democratically elected institution in an EU system that is often undemocratic and secretive. This gives it a critical role in building bridges between EU citizens and EU institutions.

Structure

The European Parliament is the only directly elected international assembly in the world. It consists of a single chamber, and its 626 members (MEPs) are directly elected by universal suffrage for fixed, renewable five-year terms. The seats are divided between the member states roughly on the basis of population, so Germany has 99 while Luxembourg has just six. This formula means that the larger countries are underrepresented and the smaller countries overrepresented. (Hence Germany has 1 seat per 830 000 citizens, while Luxembourg has 1 seat per 66 000 citizens.)

The parliamentary functions are divided among three cities: the administrative headquarters are in Luxembourg, parliamentary committees meet in a forum in Brussels for about two weeks every month (except August), and the parliamentary chamber is situated in Strasbourg, where MEPs meet in plenary session for about 3–4 days each month (except August). Since committees are where most of the real bargaining and revising take place, and since 'additional' plenaries can be held in Brussels, the Strasbourg plenaries are relatively poorly attended and MEPs tend to spend most of their time in Brussels.

The president

The president of the EP presides over debates during plenary sessions, passes proposals to committees and represents the EP in relations with other institutions. The president must be an MEP and is elected by other MEPs for two-and-a-half year renewable terms (half the life of a parliamentary term). The president would probably be a member of the majority party bloc if there was one, but since no one party has ever had a majority, he or she is chosen as a result of interparty bargaining. To help with the task of dealing with the numerous party groups in Parliament, the president has 14 vice-presidents. These 15 officials make up the Bureau of the EP, which functions much like a governing council.

Committees

Like most national legislatures the EP has standing and *ad hoc* committees, which meet in Brussels to consider legislation relevant to their area. The committees have their own hierarchy, which reflects the varying levels of parliamentary influence over different policy areas: among the most powerful are those dealing with the environment and the budget. Seats on committees are distributed on the basis of a balance of party groups, the seniority of MEPs and national interests. For example, there are more Irish and Danish MEPs on the agriculture committee than on committees dealing with foreign and defence matters.

European elections

The European Parliament is elected for fixed five-year terms and all its members stand for reelection at the same time. Every country uses multimember districts and variations on the theme of proportional representation (PR), either treating their entire territory as a single electoral district or dividing it into 3–5 'Euro constituencies'. Seats are then divided among parties according to their share of the votes. France, for example, has 87 seats, so if French Party A wins 50 per cent of the votes, it will be given 50 per cent of the French seats (44), if Party B wins 40 per cent of the votes, it will be given 40 per cent of the seats (35) and so on. For many years, the UK (except for Northern Ireland) used the same first-past-the-post, single-member district system as it uses for domestic elections, finally adopting PR for the 1999 EP elections.

PR has the advantage of reflecting more accurately the proportion of votes given to different parties, but it also results in the election of many small parties, spreading the distribution of seats so thinly that no one party has enough seats to form a majority. While that encourages legislators from different parties to work together and reach compromises, it also makes it more difficult to get anything done. Also, PR leads to voters being represented by a group of MEPs from different parties and constituents may never get to know or develop ties with a particular MEP.

Table 4.5   *Distribution of seats in the European Parliament, 1998*

	PES	EPP	UPE	ELDR	GUE	V	ERA	EDN	Ind	Total
Austria	6	7	–	1	–	1	–	–	6	21
Belgium	6	7	–	6	–	2	1	–	3	25
Denmark	4	3	–	5	–	–	–	4	–	16
Finland	4	4	–	5	2	1	–	–	–	16
France	16	12	16	1	7	–	12	12	11	87
Germany	40	47	–	–	–	12	–	–	–	99
Greece	11	9	2	–	3	–	–	–	–	25
Ireland	1	4	7	1	–	2	–	–	–	15
Italy	18	14	27	6	5	4	2	–	11	87
Luxembourg	2	2	–	1	–	1	–	–	–	6
Netherlands	7	9	1	10	–	2	–	2	–	31
Portugal	10	9	3	–	3	–	–	–	–	25
Spain	22	30	–	2	9	–	1	–	–	64
Sweden	7	5	–	3	3	4	–	–	–	22
UK	63	19	–	2	–	–	2	–	1	87
EU	217	181	56	43	32	29	18	18	32	626

Notes:
PES = Party of European Socialists
EPP = European People's Party
UPE = Union for Europe
ELDR = European Liberal Democrat and Reform Party
GUE = Confederal Group of the European United Left
V = Greens, ERA = European Radical Alliance
EDN = Europe of the Nations
Ind = Independent/non-attached.
All elections held 9–12 June 1994 except Sweden (17 September 1995), Austria
(13 October 1996), and Finland (20 October 1996).

Voters must be 18 years of age and a citizen of one of the EU member states. Some member states restrict voting to their own citizens, but there is a trend towards abolishing national distinctions and allowing EU citizens to vote – and even to run for parliament – wherever they live, regardless of their citizenship. The Maastricht treaty included the goal of extending this to all member states.

The turnout for European elections is lower than that for national elections in the member states, and the average has fallen steadily from more than 67 per cent in 1979 to just under 59 per cent in 1994. Among the explanations for this are that European elections are a novelty, few European voters know what the EP does or what issues are at stake, there is no change of government at stake, party groups in the EP are still learning how to coordinate their election campaigns across all the member states, the media and national governments still tend to play down the significance of European elections, and Eurosceptic voters may be disinclined to take part. In addition, European elections are still treated by most voters as a poll on their national governments rather than an opportunity to influence EU policies, about which many voters are still confused. As European integration deepens, as more voters understand what is at stake in European elections and, as the powers of the EP grow, the turnout may improve.

How Parliament works

Although it cannot introduce legislation, Parliament's powers to influence and amend EU law have grown. As well as the advisory and supervisory powers set out in the treaties, the EP can exert a number of essentially negative powers: the Commission tries to anticipate the EP's position when drawing up proposals, Parliament can delay or kill a proposal by sitting on it, and it also has the power to dismiss the Commission (for details see Westlake, 1994, Chapter 3). Unfortunately the concern of member states with preserving their power over decision making in the Council of Ministers has created a complex legislative process.

Powers over legislation

The legislative powers of the EP were once very modest, but changes to the treaties have resulted in those powers growing significantly in recent years. The Treaty of Rome provided the EP with a 'consultation procedure', whereby it was allowed to offer its non-binding opinion to the Council of Ministers before the latter adopted a new law in selected areas, such as aspects of transport policy, citizenship issues, the EC budget and amendments to the treaties. The Council could then ask the Commission to amend the draft, but the Commission was under no obligation to comply.

The SEA introduced a 'cooperation procedure', whereby the EP gained the right to a second reading for certain laws being considered by the Council of Ministers, notably those relating to aspects of economic and monetary policy. Subsequently, Maastricht introduced a 'codecision procedure', under which Parliament was given the right to a third reading on selected laws, notably those relating to the single market and the environment, and hence shared powers with the Council in these areas. Maastricht also extended Parliament's power over foreign policy issues by obliging the presidency of the European Council to consult with the EP on the development of a common foreign and security policy. Finally, under

Box 4.1 The party system in the European Parliament

MEPs do not sit in national blocs, but instead come together in cross-national ideological groups with roughly similar goals and values. European elections bring as many as 50–60 different parties to the EP, many of which consist of as few as one or two members; since there is little they can achieve alone, it is in their interests to build alliances with other parties. Some of these have been marriages of convenience, but over time the groups have achieved greater consistency and focus. A minimum of 26 MEPs is needed to form a group if they all come from one member state, 21 if they come from two member states, 16 if they come from three and 13 if they come from four or more.

No one party group has ever had enough seats to form a majority, so multipartisanship has been the order of the day. Moving from left to right on the ideological spectrum, the major party groups in 1998 were as follows:

- European United Left (GUE): mainly Spanish, French and Italian communists.
- Party of European Socialists (PES): consistently the largest group in the EP, with shades of opinion ranging from ex-communists on the left to more moderate social democrats towards the centre. It has members from every EU country, with the British Labour Party forming the single biggest national bloc.
- Liberal Democrat and Reform Group (ELDR): contains members from every EU member state except Germany, Greece, and Portugal, but is difficult to pinpoint in ideological terms. The political persuasions of most of its members lie in or around the centre.
- Union for Europe (UPE): consisting mainly of French, Irish and Italian conservatives, the UPE is a centre-right group that has been reluctant so far to link up with its most natural ally, the European People's Party.
- European People's Party (EPP): the major group on the right and consistently the second largest bloc in Parliament. Right of centre, it contains MEPs from every EU member state, the delegations from Germany, Italy and Spain being the largest.

the 'assent procedure', the EP has equal power with the Council over decisions on the admittance of new EU members, on giving other countries associate status and on the EU's international agreements – decisions on all these must have the support of a parliamentary majority.

Amsterdam significantly increased the powers of Parliament by abolishing the cooperation procedure on everything except issues related to economic and monetary union, and increasing the number of areas to which the codecision procedure applies from 15 to 38; these now include public health, the movement of workers, vocational training, the structural funds, transport policy, education and customs cooperation.

Powers over the budget

Parliament has joint powers with the Council of Ministers to fix the EU budget, so that the two institutions constitute the 'budgetary authority' of the EU. It meets biannually with the Council to adopt a draft and discuss amendments. It can ask for changes to the budget, ask for new appropriations for areas not covered (but cannot make decisions on how to raise money) and even (with a two-thirds majority) reject the budget.

Powers over other institutions

Parliament has several direct powers over other EU institutions, including the right to debate the Commission's annual programme, to take the Commission or the Council to the Court of Justice over alleged infringements of the treaties, and to approve the appointment of the president and all the commissioners. The most potentially disruptive of Parliament's powers is its ability – with a two-thirds majority – to force the resignation of the entire College of Commissioners through a vote of censure. This is mainly a deterrent power and has never been used, although it came very close in January 1999 following a controversy over the misuse of EU funds.

The European Court of Justice

The Court of Justice has been one of the most important champions of European integration but has pursued this cause largely out of the public eye. While media and political attention has focused on the Commission and the Council of Ministers, the Court has quietly gone about its business, working far away from the political fray in its Luxembourg headquarters.

Its job is to rule on interpretations of the treaties and EU laws, and to ensure that national and European laws and international agreements being considered by the EU meet the terms and the spirit of the treaties. It can rule on the 'constitutionality' of all EU law, gives rulings to national courts in cases where there are questions about the meaning of EU law, and rules in disputes involving EU institutions, member states, individuals and corporations. The Court's role has been vital to the development of the EU: without a body of law capable of uniform interpretation and application, the EU would have no authority and its decisions and policies would be arbitrary and largely meaningless.

The Court made its most fundamental contribution to European integration in 1963 and 1964 when it declared that the Treaty of Rome was not just a treaty, but a constitutional instrument that imposed direct

Box 4.2 European Union law

The most important difference between the EU and any other "international organization" is that it has built a body of law that is binding on all member states, supersedes national laws when these conflict and is backed up by rulings from the Court of Justice. The creation of this body of law has involved the voluntary surrender of powers by the member states in a broad range of policy areas, and the development of a new level of administrative authority to which the member states are subject.

Collectively, all the principles, policies, laws, practices and goals agreed and developed within the EU are known as the *acquis communitaire.* This includes case-law that has resulted from decisions taken by the Court of Justice, but the foundation of the EU legal order is provided by the six major treaties: the Treaty of Paris, the two treaties of Rome, the Single European Act, Maastricht, and Amsterdam. These set out the basic goals and principles of European integration, and describe – and place limits on – the powers of EU institutions and of the member states in their relationship with the EU. They have also spawned thousands of individual laws, which come in five main forms.

Regulations are the most powerful and play a central role in developing a uniform body of European law. Usually fairly narrow in intent, they are often designed to amend or adjust an existing law, are binding on all member states, are directly applicable in the sense that they do not need to be turned into national law, and take immediate effect in all member states on a specified date. The EU adopts about 250–300 new regulations each year.

Directives are binding on member states in terms of goals, but it is up to the states to decide how best to achieve those goals. For example Directive 88/609 on emissions from large combustion plants set targets for the reduction of pollutants implicated in acid rain, but left it up to each member state to decide how to go about meeting those targets. Directives usually include a date by which national procedures must be established, and member states must tell the Commission what action they are taking. The EU adopts about 50–80 directives each year.

Decisions are also binding, but are usually fairly specific in their intent and are aimed at one or more member states, at institutions or even at individuals. Some involve changes in the powers of EU institutions, some are directed towards internal administrative matters (such as staff appointments and promotions) and others are issued when the Commission has to adjudicate disputes between member states or corporations. The EU adopts about 160–190 decisions each year.

Finally, *recommendations and opinions* are not binding so it is debatable whether they can be termed law. They are sometimes used to test reactions to a new EU policy, but they are mainly used to encourage or provide adherence to classification of regulations, directives and decisions and common obligations on member states and took precedence over national law. It established important additional precedents through decisions such as *Costa* v. *ENEL* (1964), which confirmed the primacy of EU law, and the Cassis de Dijon case of 1979, which greatly smoothed the path to the single market by establishing the principle of mutual recognition: a product made and sold legally in one member state cannot be barred from another (see Chapter 7). More recent Court rulings have helped increase the powers of Parliament, strengthened individual rights, promoted the free movement of workers, reduced gender discrimination, and helped the Commission break down the barriers to competition (for examples of this see Van Hamme, 1991).

Structure

The Court of Justice is based in the Centre Européen, a cluster of EU buildings situated on a plateau above the city of Luxembourg. The Palais de Justice building was opened in 1973, extended in 1988 and 1992, and now makes up part of a modest complex that includes the EP Secretariat and the headquarters of the Court of Auditors and the European Investment Bank. The Court has four main elements: the judges, the president, the advocates general and the Court of First Instance.

The judges

The Court of Justice has 15 judges, each appointed for a six-year renewable term of office. The terms are staggered and about half come up for renewal every three years. In theory the judges are appointed by common accord among the member state governments. There is no official national quota, but because each member state has the right to make one appointment, all 15 are effectively national appointees. The persistence of the quota emphasizes once again the role of national interests in EU decision making.

Apart from being acceptable to all member states, judges must be scrupulously independent, must avoid promoting the national interests of their home states, and must also be legally competent. Some European judges have come to the Court with experience as government ministers, some have held an elected office and others have had careers as lawyers or academics, but they are not allowed to hold administrative or political office while they are on the Court. They can resign their positions but can only be forcibly removed by their fellow judges and the advocates general (not by member states or other EU institutions) – and then only when there is unanimous agreement that they are no longer doing their job adequately (Lasok, 1984, pp. 7–8).

To speed up its work, the Court is divided into chambers of 3–5 judges, which are allowed to make the final decision on cases unless a member state or an institution asks for a hearing before the full Court. To assist further with the workload, all judges and advocates general have their own teams of assistants and legal secretaries, known as *cabinets* (chambers). These are roughly equivalent to the *cabinets* of the European commissioners and are responsible for helping with research and keeping records. Unlike all the other EU institutions, where English is becoming the working language, the Court works mainly in French, although a case can be heard in any one of 12 languages (the 11 official languages and Irish) at the request of the plaintiff or defendant.

The president

The judges elect the president from among their own ranks by majority vote for a three-year renewable term. The president presides over Court meetings, is responsible for distributing cases among the judges and setting the dates for hearings, and has considerable influence over the political direction of the Court.

The advocates general

Copied from the French legal model, the nine advocates general are advisors who look at each case as it comes in, study the arguments and deliver a preliminary opinion before the judges on what action should be taken and which EU law applies. The judges are not obliged to agree with the opinion or even to refer to it, but it gives them a point of reference from which to reach a decision. Although in theory advocates general are appointed by common accord, one is appointed by each of the five largest member states and the rest by the smaller states. One advocate general is appointed as first advocate general on a one-year rotation.

The Court of First Instance

The Court of Justice has become much busier over the years: in the 1960s it heard about 50 cases a year and made about 15–20 judgements, but today it hears more than 400 cases a year, and makes about 300 judgements. As the volume of work grew during the 1970s and 1980s, it was taking the Court up to two years to reach a decision on more complex cases. To clear the logjam, agreement was reached in 1989 to create a subsidiary Court of First Instance. One judge is appointed to the court from each of the member states, to a total of 15, and the court follows the same basic procedures as the Court of Justice, although it has no advocates general and does not have its own staff. Its job is to provide the first ruling on less complicated cases – if cases are lost at this level the parties concerned may appeal to the Court of Justice.

How the Court works

The European Commission is often described as the guardian of the treaties, but it is the Court of Justice that is charged with ensuring that the principles of the treaties are observed when EU law is being interpreted and applied. The Court is the supreme legal body of the EU and the final court of appeal on all EU laws, and as such has played a vital role in determining the character of the EU and extending the reach of EU law. It has been particularly involved in cases and judgements relating to the internal market, and the Cassis de Dijon decision (see Chapter 7) has been credited by some as facilitating the SEA and restoring the progress of the EU (Colchester and Buchan, 1990).

The overall purpose of the Court is to build a body of common EU law that is equally, fairly and consistently applied throughout the member states. It does this by interpreting EU treaties and laws, and in some cases by ensuring their application. EU law takes precedence over the national laws of member states when the two come into conflict, but only in areas where the EU is active and the member states have given up powers to the EU. Hence the Court has no power over criminal law or family law, and most of its decisions have involved the kinds of economic issue in which the EU has been most actively involved. It has had much less to do with policy areas where the EU has been less active, such as education and health.

Court proceedings usually begin with a written application, describing the dispute and the grounds upon which the application is based. The president assigns the case to a chamber, and the defendant is given one month to lodge a statement of defence, the plaintiff a month to reply, and the defendant a further month to reply to the plaintiff. The case is then argued by the parties at a public hearing before a chamber of three or five judges, or – for the most important cases – the full Court. The judges wear gowns of deep crimson; the lawyers appearing before them wear whatever is deemed appropriate in their national court. Once the hearing is over the judges retire to the Deliberation Room, with its sweeping views over the city of Luxembourg. Having reached a conclusion they return to Court to deliver their judgement.

The whole process can take a year for preliminary rulings, but most other cases take as long as two years. Court decisions are supposed to be unanimous but usually involve a simple majority. All decisions are made in secret and it is never made public who, if anyone, dissented. The Court has no direct power to enforce its judgements, so implementation is left mainly to national courts or the governments of the member states, with the Commission keeping a close watch. Maastricht gave the Court of Justice new power by allowing it to impose fines, but the question of how the fines were to be collected was left open and the implications of this new power are unclear.

The work of the Court falls under two main headings:

Preliminary rulings

These are the most important part of the Court's work and account for about 60 per cent of the cases it considers. Under this process a national court can ask for a ruling from the European Court on the interpretation or validity of an EU law that arises in a national court case. The question of validity is particularly important, because chaos would reign if national courts could declare EU laws invalid (Brown and Kennedy, 1994, pp. 173–6). Members of EU institutions can also ask for preliminary rulings, but most are made on behalf of a national court and are binding on the court for the case in question.

An example of a preliminary ruling with profound implications for individual rights took place in 1989. A British citizen named Ian Cowan was mugged outside a subway station in Paris during his holiday in France. Under French law he would have been able to claim state compensation for damages, but the French courts held that he was not entitled to damages because he was neither a French national nor a resident. Cowan argued that this amounted to discrimination, so the Court of Justice was asked for a ruling. In *Cowan* v. *Le Tresor Public* (case 186/87) the Court declared that since Cowan was a tourist and was receiving a service, he could invoke Article 7 of the EEC Treaty, which prohibits discrimination on the grounds of nationality among nationals of member states.

Direct actions

These are cases where an individual, company, member state or EU institution brings proceedings before the Court of Justice rather than a national court, usually with an EU institution or a member state as the defendant. Direct actions take several forms.

Actions for failure to fulfil an obligation   When a member state has failed to meet its obligations under EU law a case can be brought by the Commission or a member state. For example, the Commission has regularly taken member states to court for not fulfilling their obligations under the SEA. Private companies can also bring actions if they think a member state is discriminating against their products.

Actions for annulment These are aimed at ensuring that EU laws (even non-binding opinions and recommendations) conform to the treaties, and are brought in an attempt to annul those that do not. The defendant is almost always the Commission or the Council because proceedings are usually brought against an act they have adopted (Lasok, 1984, p. 323).

Actions for failure to act These relate to the failure of an EU institution to act in accordance with the terms of the treaties and can be instituted by other institutions, member states or individuals if they are directly and personally involved. The European Parliament brought one such action against the Council of Ministers in 1983 (case 13/83), charging that the Council had failed to agree a common transport policy, as required by the Treaty of Rome. The Court ruled that while there was an obligation, no timetable had been agreed so it was up to the member states to decide how to proceed.

Actions for damages These are cases where damages are claimed by third parties against EU institutions or their employees. For example a claim could be made that an institution was acting illegally, or that someone's business was being harmed by a piece of EU law.

Actions by staff These are cases involving litigation against EU institutions by their staff, and are the only cases where a private individual can go directly to Court. For example someone working for the European Parliament might ask the Court for a ruling on the application of a staff regulation, an instance of gender discrimination or a decision to hold a civil service exam on a day that was a religious holiday in their home country.

The European Council

The European Council is the newest and arguably the most powerful of the EU's five major institutions, although it is really more of a process or a forum than an institution. Simply defined, it is a collective term for the heads of government of EU member states, their foreign ministers, and the president and vice-presidents of the Commission. This small group periodically convenes for short summit meetings and provides strategic policy direction for the EU. The Council is something like a steering committee or a board of directors for the EU; it sketches out the broad picture and leaves it to the other institutions to fill in the details.

The Council was created in 1974 in response to a growing feeling among European leaders that the EEC needed stronger leadership to clear

Box 4.3 Specialized EU institutions

As the work of the EU has grown, so too has the number of specialized agencies that deal with specific aspects of its work. They include the following.

- Committee of the Regions (CoR) (Brussels). Set up under the terms of Maastricht, the CoR provides a forum in which representatives of local units of government can meet and express their views on matters relating to regional and local issues. Most of its 222 members are elected local government officials.
- Court of Auditors (Luxembourg). Founded in 1977, this is the EU's financial watchdog. Its 15 auditors and 400 staff carry out annual audits of the accounts of the EU institutions to ensure that funds have been raised and spent in a lawful and acceptable manner.
- Economic and Social Committee (ESC) (Brussels). This is an advisory body that gives employers, workers and other sectional interests a forum in which they can meet, talk and give advice to the Commission and the Council of Ministers. It has 222 members, drawn from a variety of backgrounds, mainly in industry, agriculture and the professions.
- European Central Bank (ECB) (Frankfurt). Created in 1998 to replace the European Monetary Institute (EMI) (set up in 1994), the job of the Bank is to ensure monetary stability by setting interest rates in relation to the euro (see Box 7.3).
- European Environment Agency (EEA) (Copenhagen). Established in 1993, the EEA collects information from the member states and neighbouring non-EU states in order to help develop environmental protection policies, and to measure the results of existing policies. The EEA also publishes three-yearly reports on the state of the European environment.
- European Investment Bank (EIB) (Luxembourg). The EIB is an autonomous institution set up in 1958 to encourage 'balanced and steady development' by granting loans and giving guarantees. Its projects are designed to help poorer regions and to support the modernization and improve the competitiveness of industry, and they must be of common interest to several member states or the EU as a whole. Its largest project was the Channel Tunnel. It is managed by a board of governors consisting of the finance ministers of the member states.
- European Agency for the Evaluation of Medicinal Products (EMEA) (London). This was set up in 1995 to harmonize (but not replace) the work of national drug regulatory bodies, to help reduce the costs that drug companies incur by having to win separate approval from each member state, and to eliminate the protectionist tendencies of states that are unwilling to approve new drugs that might compete with those being produced by domestic drug companies.
- European Police Office (Europol) (The Hague). Fully operational since 1998, this is charged with promoting police cooperation within the EU through a system of information exchange targeted at combatting terrorism, drug trafficking and other serious forms of international crime.

blockages in decision making and give it a clearer sense of direction. Nothing was said in the treaties of Paris or Rome about a European Council, however, and its existence was only given legal recognition with passage of the SEA. Maastricht elaborated on its role, but without much clarity: it states that the Council should 'provide the Union with the necessary impetus for its development and shall define the general political guidelines thereof'.

The Council has been an important force for integration and has launched major new initiatives (for example the European Monetary System in 1978, the Maastricht treaty in 1991 and the IGC that led to the Amsterdam treaty), issued major declarations on international crises, reached key decisions on institutional changes (such as the 1974 decision to introduce direct elections to the European Parliament) and given new momentum to EU foreign policy. It has been argued that without these regular summits the Community would not have survived the Eurosclerosis of the 1970s, launched the single market programme in the 1980s or adjusted to changes in the international environment in the 1990s (Dinan, 1994, p. 230). However, the Council has also had its failures, including its inability to speed up agricultural and budgetary reform, or to agree a common EU response to the Iraqi and Balkan crises.

How the Council works

The first meeting of the European Council was held in Dublin in March 1975 under the lumbering title 'the Heads of Government Meeting as the Council of the Community and in Political Cooperation'. It met more or less triannually throughout the 1970s and 1980s, but a decision was taken at the December 1985 summit to hold just two regular summits each year, in June and December, with emergency summits as needed.

Meetings are hosted by the country holding the presidency of the EU, and take place either in the capital of that country or in a regional city or town, such as Milan, Cardiff or Strasbourg. In December 1991 it took place in Maastricht in the Netherlands, where the Treaty on European Union was agreed. Organization is left largely to the presidency, which in effect means the prime minister and foreign minister of the country holding the presidency. Some heads of government take a hands-on approach to determining the agenda, while others are more low-key. The goal of each summit is to agree a set of Conclusions of the Presidency. An advance draft of this is usually awaiting the leaders at the start of the summit, and provides the focus for the discussions.

Summits usually run for a period of two days, beginning with informal discussions over breakfast and moving on to the nuts and bolts of the agenda at plenary sessions in the morning and afternoon. Formal dinners in the evening were once routinely followed by a 'fireside chat' among the heads of government and the president of the Commission, but it has become more common for another plenary session to be held instead. Overnight, officials from the presidency and the secretariat of the Council of Ministers work on the draft conclusions, which are discussed at a second plenary on the morning of the second day, and if necessary at a third in the afternoon. The summit normally ends with the publication of the conclusions.

During summit plenaries the leaders of the member states sit around a table with their respective foreign ministers and two officials from the Commission, including the president. In order to keep the meeting intimate and manageable, few others are allowed into the meeting chamber: no more than one adviser per country, plus interpreters, two officials from the country holding the presidency, one from the Council of Ministers secretariat and three from the Commission – about 60 people in all.

European Council decisions are usually taken on the basis of unanimity, or at least consensus, but the occasional lack of unanimity may force a formal vote, and sometimes member states wish to attach conditions or reservations to the conclusions. As well as the formal plenary sessions, summits usually involve a number of meetings (for example between foreign ministers) and regular bilateral meetings between prime ministers over breakfast or coffee.

The summits are always major media events and are surrounded by extensive security. As well as the substantive political discussions that take place, enormous symbolism is attached to the outcomes of the summits, which are assessed according to the extent to which they represent breakthroughs, or show EU leaders to be bogged down in disagreement. Failure and success reflect not only on the presidency, but on the whole process of European integration. The headline-making nature of the summits is sufficient to concentrate the minds of the participants and encourage them to reach agreement. The opportunity is also provided for a 'family picture' to be taken of the 15 leaders and the president of the Commission.

Preparation is the key to the success of European summits (for details see de Bassompierre, 1988, pp. 80–7). Officially the Council has no set agenda, but there has to be some direction, so it is usual for senior officials from the country holding the presidency to work with the Council of Ministers to identify agenda items. Preparation begins as soon as a member state takes over the presidency in January or July. At their monthly meetings the foreign ministers try to resolve potential disagreements, and as the date for the summit approaches the prime minister and foreign minister of the state holding the presidency become increasingly involved. The more agreements they can broker in advance, the less likely it is that the summit will end in failure (Johnston, 1994, pp. 27–31).

About ten days before the summit the foreign ministers meet to finalize the agenda and iron out any remaining problems and disputes. The items on the agenda depend on circumstances; national delegations normally have issues they want to raise, there must be some continuity with previous summits, and leaders often have to deal with an emerging problem or an emergency that needs a decision. Some issues (especially economic issues) are routinely discussed at every summit. The Commission may also promote issues it would like to see discussed, and an active presidency might use the summit to bring items of national or regional interest to the attention of the heads of government. Calls are occasionally made for the launch of a major policy initiative, such as the decision taken at the 1989 Strasbourg summit to call an IGC on economic and monetary union. Some summits are routine and result in general agreement among leaders; others involve deep differences of opinion, with some member states perhaps refusing to agree a common set of conclusions.

The exact role of the European Council has always been kept deliberately ambiguous by its members. An attempt to define its role occurred at the Stuttgart European Council in 1983 with the agreement of the 'Solemn Declaration on European Union'; combining this with earlier declarations produced the following list of goals:

- To exchange views and reach a consensus.
- To give political impetus to the development of the EU.
- To begin cooperation in new policy areas.
- To provide general political guidelines for the EU and the development of a common foreign policy.
- To guarantee policy consistency.
- To reach common positions on foreign policy issues.

More specifically, the European Council makes the key decisions on the overall direction of political integration and EMU, internal economic issues, foreign policy issues, budget disputes, treaty revisions, new membership applications and institutional reforms (such as enlargement of the European Parliament). The summits achieve all this through a combination of brain-storming, intensive bilateral and multilateral discussions, and bargaining. The mechanics of decision making depend on the quality of organization and preparation, the leadership skills of the presidency and the ideological and personal agendas of the individual leaders. The interpersonal dynamics among the participants is also important: the Franco-German axis has always been politically significant, and has been given added influence by the good personal relations that usually exist between the leaders of the two states. Leaders who have been in office a long time or have a solid base of political support at home are in a very different negotiating position from those who do not. Some leaders are respected and have strong credibility, others do not.

Because the European Council has more power over decision making than any other EU institution, it has tended to take power away from the other institutions. It can, in effect, set the agenda for the Commission, override decisions reached by the Council of Ministers and largely ignore the Parliament altogether. Any hope that the Commission might once have had that it could develop an independent sphere of action and power has largely disappeared with the rise of the European Council. Certainty about the present and future role of the Council is clouded by its ambiguities, and opinion remains divided over whether it is an integrative or a disintegrative body (Johnston, 1994, pp. 41–8).

Conclusions

Over the last few decades, the European Union has developed a substantial body of governing institutions to make broad policy decisions, develop and adopt laws, oversee the implementation of laws and policies by the member states, ensure that those laws and policies meet the terms of the major treaties, and oversee activities in a variety of specialized areas, from environmental management to drug regulation and police cooperation.

The governing institutions amount to a confederal government of Europe in all but name. They fit the standard definition of confederalism: a general system of government coexisting with local units of government, each with shared and independent powers, but with the balance in favour of the local units (the member states). Despite concern about the construction of a federal Europe, the EU institutions still lack many of the powers of conventional federal governments; for example there is no European army or air force, no elected European president, no European foreign and defence policy, and no single postal system. Furthermore, the bulk of decision making still rests with the Council of Ministers, which is an intergovernmental body made up of national ministers rather than a supranational organization. Finally, the European Union is still ultimately a voluntary arrangement, and lacks the power to force its member states to implement European law and policy.

Nonetheless, while debates continue about the finer points of the decisions reached by the EU institutions, the national governments of the member states have surrendered powers to these institutions. If Europe is not yet federal, it is federalizing. Particularly since the passage of the Single European Act, the activities of the Commission, the Council of

Ministers, Parliament and the Court of Justice have become increasingly important to Europeans, and government in Europe is not just what happens in national capitals and regional cities, but also what happens in Brussels, Luxembourg and Strasbourg.

The relationship among the five major institutions, and between them and the governments of the member states, is constantly changing as the balance of power is adjusted and fine-tuned. Out of a combination of internal convenience and external pressure is emerging a new layer of government that is winning more powers as the member states cautiously transfer sovereignty from the local and national levels to the regional level. In the two chapters that follow we shall see what this has meant for the member states and the citizens of Europe.

Chapter 5

The EU and the Member States

The changing powers of the member states
Addressing regional differences
Improving environmental quality
An emerging European civil society
The changing character of the EU
Conclusions

The history of the European Union has been dominated by efforts to remove or reduce economic barriers among its member states. National leaders have focused most of their attention on such matters as trade, tariffs, competition, finance and labour mobility. However neofunctionalist logic suggests that the economies of Europe cannot be fully integrated unless the member states also address disparities in wealth, income and unemployment, different standards and regulations, different approaches to administration, and different positions on issues as varied as consumer safety, environmental protection, transport and relations with countries outside the EU. As the member states have addressed these needs, so the relationships among them have changed, and they have found themselves subject to complex integrative pressures.

Those pressure have been both formal and informal. William Wallace defines formal integration as the deliberate actions taken by authoritative policy makers to create and adjust rules, to establish and work through common institutions, to regulate, encourage or inhibit social and economic flows, and to pursue common policies. He defines informal integration as consisting of patterns of interaction that develop without the intervention of deliberate government decisions, following the dynamic of markets, technology, communications and social exchange, or the influence of mass movements. Wallace also makes a distinction between proactive and responsive integration, the former having deliberate and explicit political aims, while the latter involves a reaction to economic and social change (Wallace, 1990, pp. 54–5).

If all EU member states had the same political, economic and social structures, the same levels of wealth and productivity, and the same sets of standards and regulations, integration would be a relatively simple matter and would lean heavily towards the formal and the proactive. However the disparities within and among EU member states have posed complex challenges and have made it difficult for national leaders always to be able to anticipate or understand the needs or motives of integration. Concerned with avoiding the emergence of a 'two-speed' or even a 'multispeed' Europe, they have often had to react to problems revealed by the attempt to achieve the original goal of a common market, and have often allowed integration to be driven by informal pressures. For example, while they have expended considerable effort on the 'harmonization' of standards, laws and regulations, the complexities of integration have compelled them in some areas simply to agree to proceed through 'mutual recognition' (if something is good enough for one state, it is good enough for them all).

The list of the effects of integration on the EU member states is lengthy and complex. In order to illustrate these effects, this chapter looks first at some of the constitutional and legal issues raised by integration, and at what integration has meant for the relationship among the member states. In order to illustrate the changes, it then focuses on two policy areas that illustrate some of the pressures behind integration: regional policy and environmental policy. In the case of the former, member states have responded to the economic disparities in Europe by shifting resources and funds from wealthier to poorer regions. In the case of the latter, they have responded to the threats posed to the single market by differences in environmental quality and standards, and have developed a substantial body of common policy and law.

The changing powers of the member states

Human society is in a constant state of flux, and western Europe is no exception. Political, economic and social relationships among Europeans have undergone continuous change, generated in large part by changes in communications and economic activity. While subsistence economies revolved around the village and the tribal community, trade led to the development of roads and towns, and the expansion of political authority in the Middle Ages. As European society shifted from an agricultural to an industrial base in the eighteenth and nineteenth centuries, a combination of technological change and improvements in communications once again redefined political and social relationships.

Western Europe emerged from the Second World War with its place in the world substantially changed. While it had held the balance of global political, military and economic power until the 1930s, it now found itself squeezed militarily between the two superpowers and saw the focus of economic power shifting to new centres, notably the United States and

Japan. As discussed in Chapter 3, the need to save Europe from itself combined with the need to build economic and military security in the troubled postwar world to encourage western European elites to call for a new sense of community within the region, and for cooperation rather than competition.

As late as the 1960s and 1970s, western European states still approached each other as sovereign states with strong and independent national identities. They had considerable freedom over the making of law, and travellers were reminded of the differences between countries when they crossed national borders. Controls and limits were placed on the movement of people, money, goods and services, and citizens of one state who travelled to another felt very much that they were 'going abroad'. The nation-state was dominant, the focus of mass public loyalty and the source of primary political and administrative authority. Italians were clearly Italians, the Dutch were clearly Dutch, and Swedes were clearly Swedes – at least this is what Europeans were encouraged to think.

The situation today is quite different, and the relationship between the EU and its member states has undergone changes so fundamental as to be described by terms such as 'transformation' and 'metamorphosis' (Weiler, 1991, p. 2406). There has been a transfer of authority from the member states to the European Union, and an agreement to share or pool the exercise of power over selected policy areas. The member states have remained the essential building blocks in this process, but they have moved far beyond the simple cooperation normally associated with conventional international organizations to create a new layer of institutions underwritten by a common body of laws. Whether the member states have actually *surrendered* sovereignty, however, and thereby created a superstate with its own sovereign powers, is a debatable and contentious point.

Much of the debate revolves around our understanding of the concept of sovereignty, and where it resides. The term is usually understood to mean the ability of an individual or a collective body of some kind to exercise control over the territory in which he/she or its members reside. In most democracies it is claimed that sovereignty rests with the people, and that elected officials simply represent the interests of the people in the exercise of sovereignty. Since national governments have negotiated the major European treaties, and since the interests of the member states are still represented by the Council of Ministers, the argument might be made that there has in fact been no transfer of sovereignty. Instead there has been a transfer of the right to exercise sovereignty in selected areas from national governments to the EU institutions. In other words, sovereignty still rests with the people, but new kinds of institutions have been created with new rights over the exercise of that sovereignty, over the development of policy and over the administration of the needs of the people.

Put another way, developments since the Treaty of Rome led to the member states of the European Community/Union surrendering control over selected policy areas (wittingly or unwittingly, formally or informally), and they now reach most decisions in these areas through negotiation with other member states. Debates on the effects and the meaning of the treaties have combined with day-to-day discussions within the Commission and the Council of Ministers to encourage national leaders to work towards multinational compromises, and towards a European consensus. As this has happened, it has become increasingly difficult for leaders to define and pursue 'national interests', because these interests have been subsumed under European interests. Spillover of many different kinds has led to the development of complex networks of cooperation at almost every level: trade, transport, communications, labour relations, policing, agriculture, research and development, financial services, the environment and so on. The result, argues Wallace (1996, p. 452), has been that governments have had to decide 'which issues they choose to define as key to the preservation of sovereignty, autonomy, or national idiosyncrasy, conscious of the political costs of defining too many issues in the symbolic terminology of high politics'.

The question of the transfer of powers – or at least of the most appropriate level at which to make decisions – has been at the heart of a growing debate about subsidiarity, the principle that decisions should be taken at the lowest level possible for effective action. It was first raised in the European context in 1975 when the European Commission – in its response to the Tindemans report (see Chapter 6) – argued that the Community should be given responsibility only for those matters which the member states were no longer capable of dealing with efficiently. There was little further discussion until the mid-1980s, when member states opposed to increasing the power of the Commission began quoting the principle. It was finally brought into the mainstream of discussions about the EU by Article 3b of Maastricht: 'In areas which do not fall within its exclusive competence, the Community shall take action, in accordance with the principle of subsidiarity, only if and in so far as the objectives of the proposed action cannot be sufficiently achieved by the Member States and can therefore, by reason of the scale or effects of the proposed action, be better achieved by the Community.'

There are at least three problems with the concept of subsidiarity. First, it cannot be used to reduce EU powers in areas that have already been defined as being within its 'exclusive competence'. Second, there are no absolutes in the debate about whether or not an action can be better achieved by the member states acting alone or the EU acting as a whole. Third, subsidiarity is aimed at limiting the powers of the EU through a political–judicial discussion about 'competence' rather than through a clarification of the relative powers of European citizens, member states and EU institutions.

European integration has been accompanied by growth in the body of European law and a reduction in the ability of national governments independently to make policy and law, according to national interests and priorities. Simultaneously, national legislatures have become weaker and more marginalized in a process that has been described (pejoratively) as 'creeping federalism'. National legislatures once had almost complete authority to make laws as their members saw fit, within the limitations created by constitutions, public opinion, the powers of other government institutions and the international community. They now find themselves focusing increasingly on those policy areas in which the EU is not yet very active, and reacting to the requirements of EU law and the pressures of regional integration.

When trying to grasp the relative powers of the EU and the member states, it is important to remember two key points. First, the EU is a voluntary arrangement and there is nothing in theory to prevent a member state from leaving at any time. If a region of a nation-state were to declare its independence without first reaching some kind of agreement with the central government, it would be regarded as secession, and would probably lead to war; this is what happened, for example, with the attempted secession by the Confederacy from the United States in 1861, Biafra from Nigeria in 1967 and Chechnya from Russia in 1994–95. In contrast, membership of the EU is reversible, and several anti-European movements within the member states have called for their country to leave the EU, but while this is legally permissible it is practically unlikely, because the economic ties among the member states would make it more costly to leave than to stay in.

Second, the old 'Community method' by which all the member states were obliged to proceed at the same pace and adopt and implement the same laws and policies, has been replaced in recent years by a Europe *à la carte*, or a Europe of 'variable geometry'. This is Euro-speak for an arrangement that allows different member states to adopt different elements of European policy: for example Britain was allowed to opt out of the Social Charter (see Chapter 6), only eleven member states have so far chosen to go ahead with the single currency, not all member states have opted for the removal of border controls, as envisaged in the Schengen Agreement, and traditionally neutral states such as Ireland and Finland have decided not to participate in the proposed common European defence policy.

Under the circumstances it is debatable where the member states have given up the most power. In the realm of 'high politics' (a concept rarely defined, but usually taken to mean the universal, the persistent, or the most pressing concerns of government), they now have much less freedom of movement than before on many economic matters, such as trade, taxes, financial services, company law and banking (see Chapter 7). The adoption of a single currency will ensure that there are few elements of economic policy that are not primarily driven by Europe rather than by the member states – at least among those member states that decide to join.

In contrast the EU still has some way to go before it can claim a common foreign policy, and the member states still have considerable individual freedom in their relationships outside Europe and in the way they define and express their defence interests (see Chapter 8). The EU is slowly becoming a more distinctive actor on the world stage, most notably with regard to development aid to poorer countries, but non-European governments must still approach each of the member states as individual actors on issues such as security threats in the Middle East, nuclear testing, relations with former colonies and so on.

In the realm of 'low politics' (matters that are both more sectional and further down the agendas of most governments) there are still distinctions between issues that come under EU jurisdiction, are shared by the EU and the member states, and are the preserve of member states, but these distinctions have become less clear with time. There is little question that agricultural policy is almost entirely determined at the European level, the loosening of internal border controls has been accompanied by a tightening of external controls that has seen more pan-European cooperation, and the setting of environmental quality standards is now driven largely by EU law. Decisions on social matters such as education, employment and residence are increasingly being made at the European level as personal mobility moves up the policy agenda. Member states still make most of their own decisions on internal transport, but are working together on the development of trans-European highways and railways, and on the administration of airline systems and air transport. They still have national policies on investment in poorer rural areas and urban regeneration, but these are increasingly influenced by European regional policy.

Not only has there been a transfer of powers from the member states to the EU, but the member states now have a very different legal relationship with one another. Where national frontiers in the 1960s were potent reminders of the independence of the states, and of the political, cultural, economic and social barriers that divided Europeans, they have become increasingly porous. Particularly among the Schengen states, national frontiers have become almost invisible, and the differences among member states are determined less by lines on a map and questions of law and jurisdiction, and more by differences in language or culture. The number of policy areas in which the governments of member states can exercise real independence has declined, and the legal ties that bind their states have tightened.

There have also been important psychological changes in the relationship among the member states. There are still many reminders of the differences among Europeans – most notably language – but those differences have become less obvious as the mobility of Europeans has increased (see Chapter 6). Nationalism remains an issue, most notably among minorities and those most actively opposed to European integration, but increased individual mobility has allowed Europeans not just to visit other states on holiday, but to live in – and even 'emigrate' to – other states. Europeans are undergoing a process of transition in which they are transferring their loyalty from individual states to a more broadly defined European identity, and are thinking of themselves less as Germans or Belgians or Swedes and more as Europeans.

Critics of integration have long argued that one of the greatest dangers posed by integration has been the homogenization of Europe as the differences that give member states their character are being whittled away in the move towards Europe-wide standards and regulations. They argue that power is shifting away from national governments mandated by the people towards a European supergovernment that lacks such a mandate. However, while much still needs to be done to strengthen the ties between the EU and its citizens (see Chapter 6), it is unlikely that economic integration will lead to cultural integration. If anything it is most likely to lead to a reassertion of cultural differences as Europeans grow to understand and appreciate the variety of the regions in which they live (Box 5.1).

Indeed it is often argued that Europe of the regions may come to rival or even replace Europe of the states. European regions have become more important in the wake of changes within member states, and in the wake of EU policy on regional development (see below). In the interest of correcting economic imbalances, and prompted by growing demands for greater decentralization, European states began to regionalize their administrative systems in the 1960s, and as a result regions have emerged as important actors in politics and policy (Keating and Hooghe, 1996). Regions have come to see the EU as an important source of investment and of support for minority cultures, and in some cases this has given more confidence to nationalist movements (such as those in Scotland and Catalonia,) as they feel less dependent on the support of the state governments. The logical conclusion is that forces of this kind will lead to Europe integrating and decentralizing at the same time, with the member states as we know them today squeezed in the middle.

Box 5.1 The rise of regionalism

Ironically, as the nation-states of western Europe have been busy cooperating on the construction of the European Union, so national minorities within these states have become more visible, more vocal and more demanding of greater independence. In other words, as western European states have integrated at the macro level there has been a growing demand for self-determination at the micro level by cultural regions (Kellas, 1991).

We have been conditioned to look at western Europe as a region divided into three dozen nation-states, but it is more realistic in social terms to see it as a region divided into more than 100 nationalities, including Dutch and English in the maritime north, Portuguese and Cantabrians on the Atlantic coast, Alsatians and Franconians in the northwest, Bavarians, Swiss and Styrians in the Alpine regions, Castilians, Andalusians and Ligurians in the west-central Mediterranean, Serbs and Croats in the Balkans, Czechs, Slovaks and Ruthenians in the east, Poles and Lithuanians in the northern plains, and Lapps, Finns and Karelians in the northern Baltic (Fernández-Armesto, 1997).

In some cases, such nations have been fully integrated into the larger states of which they are part (the Cornish in England, Galicians in Spain and Lombards in Italy). In others, integration has never been complete, secessionist movements have long been active and calls for self-determination threatens a redrawing of the boundaries of member states. For example the Scots and the Welsh are establishing regional assemblies, and public opinion in Scotland is increasingly in favour of complete independence from England. There are similar demands for independence or devolution from Bretons and Corsicans in France, Basques in the Spanish–French borderland, Catalans in Spain and Walloons in Belgium.

The status of national minorities has traditionally been a domestic matter for individual national governments, but European integration has helped redefine the relationship of the parts to the whole. As the member states lose their distinctive political identity, so the cultural identity of minorities is strengthened and the pressure for 'disintegration' grows. It is possible that greater self-determination will lessen the demand among nationalists for complete independence, and that we will simply see a reassertion of cultural differences within the member states. It is also possible, however, that self-determination will lead to independence for minorities within the European Union, and a redrawing of administrative lines along cultural lines.

Addressing regional differences

The European Union is far from homogeneous – not only are there economic and social disparities within most of its member states, but there are disparities between one state and another. This becomes clear, for example, when comparing economic wealth, the standard measure of which is gross domestic product (GDP, or the total value of all goods and services produced by a country) adjusted to take account of the purchasing power of different currencies (purchasing power standard, or PPS). If the average of the EU as a whole is expressed as 100, the differences in per capita GDP in 1995 ranged from 135 in Luxembourg, to about 103–10 in Belgium, Denmark, Germany, France and Italy, to a low of 48 in Greece. Differences among regions within the member states were even greater, ranging from 195 in Hamburg and 172 in Brussels to 50 in the Azores and 43 in Ipeiros, Greece. About one quarter of Europe's more than 200 regions have a per capita GDP that is less than 75 per cent of the EU average (Eurostat, April 1998). The disparities are further highlighted by unemployment rates, which in mid-1998 ranged from as low as 4.5 per cent (the Netherlands) to as high as 19.6 per cent (Spain).

Generally speaking, the wealthiest parts of the EU are in the north-central area, particularly in and around the 'golden triangle' (or the 'hot banana') between London, Dortmund, Paris and Milan. The poorest parts are on the southern, western and eastern peripheries: Greece, southern Italy, Spain, Portugal, Ireland, Northern Ireland, western Scotland and eastern Germany. In the mid-1960s the gap in per capita GDP between the ten richest regions and the ten poorest was 4:1. By 1970 it had fallen to 3:1, but recession and Greek membership pushed it up to 5:1 by the early 1980s (Eurostat figures, various years). The EU's marginal areas are relatively poor for different reasons; some are depressed agricultural areas with little industry and high unemployment, some are declining industrial areas with outdated plants, some (notably islands) are geographically isolated from the prosperity and opportunity offered by bigger markets, and most suffer relatively low levels of education and health care and have underdeveloped infrastructure, especially roads and utilities.

Individual EU member states have tried to deal with their own internal problems in different ways. Britain, for example, has designated special Development Areas and provided industry with incentives to invest in those areas or to relocate their factories there. Italy created a Fund for the South to help provide infrastructure and encourage investment in the Mezzogiorno – everywhere south of Rome, including parts of Italy so riddled with corruption and so heavily controlled by organized crime that they are effectively independent subgovernments. Likewise the major industrialized states have tackled the problem of urban decline in different ways.

Box 5.2 European regional policy

The EU's regional policy has the following goals (Allen, 1996a, p. 225):

- Help for Objective 1 regions, defined as regions where per capita GDP is less than 75 per cent of the EU average. The biggest recipients are Spain, Portugal, Greece, Italy and Germany (for investment in the former East Germany), while Denmark and the Benelux countries receive the least. Objective 1 projects are funded mainly out of the ERDF and the Cohesion Fund, and now account for about 60 per cent of all structural fund spending.

- Help for Objective 2 areas, defined as those suffering high unemployment and job losses, and industrial decline; these are mainly in the older industrial regions of Germany, Britain, France, and Spain. Funded mainly out of the ERDF.

- Objectives 3 and 4 are programmes aimed at reducing long-term unemployment and creating jobs for young people. They are funded mainly out of the European Social Fund, and Britain, France, Germany, Spain and Italy are the biggest recipients. Objective 5 focuses on assistance to agricultural and rural areas, and is funded mainly out of the EAGGF, while Objective 6 was added after the 1995 enlargement to deal with the problems of the thinly populated parts of Northern Europe.

- There are also a host of specialized programmes with specific objectives, some of which overlap with social policy and all of which have provided a field day for the authors of clever acronyms. These include RECHAR (converting coalmining areas), REGIS (help for overseas regions of the EU), INTERREG (helping border regions prepare for completion of the single market) and PRISMA (aid for infrastructure and business services in poorer regions).

While it has always been made clear by national leaders that EU regional policy will not replace national policies, but will simply provide an additional economic impact (known as the principle of 'additionality'), Armstrong (1993) suggests that there are several arguments in favour of a joint EU approach: it ensures that spending is concentrated in the areas of greatest need, it ensures coordination of the spending of the different member states, and it encourages the member states to work together on one of the most critical barriers to integration. At the same time a common regional policy means that the member states have a vested interest in the welfare of their EU partners, helps member states deal with some of the potentially damaging effects of integration (such as loss of jobs and greater economic competition), and introduces an important psychological element: citizens of poorer regions in receipt of EU development spending are made more aware of the benefits of EU membership, while citizens of the wealthier states that are net contributors have a vested interest in ensuring that such spending is effective.

It would be unrealistic to hope that there will ever be completely equal conditions throughout the EU – economic inequalities are a fact of life, and cultural differences will always ensure that different communities take different approaches to common problems. The EU has recognized this, and has agreed that its regional policy should be aimed at promoting 'cohesion', defined as 'reducing disparities between the various regions' in the interests of promoting 'economic and social progress'. In order to do this, the EU has increased efforts to help bring the poorer member states closer to the level of their wealthier partners. While free marketeers have always hoped that the single market would have a 'trickle-down' effect by directing more investment towards the poorer parts of Europe, the EU has taken a more proactive approach by setting up several 'structural funds', or baskets of money aimed at spending in the interests of cohesion. There are now four of these:

- The Guidance section of the European Agricultural Guidance and Guarantee Fund (EAGGF), which is part of the Common Agricultural Policy and is aimed at the reform of farm structures and rural areas.
- The European Social Fund (ESF), which is designed to promote employment and worker mobility, combat long-term unemployment and help workers adapt to technological change.
- The European Regional Development Fund (ERDF), which is spent mainly on underdeveloped areas (particularly those affected by the decline of traditional industries such as coal, steel and textiles) and inner cities.
- The Cohesion Fund, set up under the terms of Maastricht, targets member states with a per capita GDP of less than 90 per cent of the EU average (that is, Greece, Portugal, Spain and Ireland). It is aimed at helping to compensate these states for the additional costs incurred by the tightening of environmental regulations. It also provides financial assistance for transport projects.

The roots of European regional policy lie in the provisions made by the European Coal and Steel Community for grants to depressed areas for industrial conversion and retraining. The Common Agricultural Policy introduced a welfare element in the sense that funds could be used to upgrade farms and farming equipment, improve farming methods and provide benefits to farmers. Broader regional disparities were not addressed until 1969, however, when the Commission proposed a common regional policy, including the creation of a regional development fund, but the idea was met with little enthusiasm in Germany and France, which were already concerned, respectively, about the costs of CAP and the surrender of further powers to the EC.

Little more was done until the first round of enlargement in the early 1970s, when a complex pattern of political and economic interests came together to make the idea of a regional policy more palatable. Most importantly, the 'rich man's club' of the 1950s (Italy excepted) had been joined by Britain and Ireland, two countries with regional problems. Their accession not only widened the economic disparities within the EEC, but strengthened Italy's demands for a regional policy. The Commission-sponsored Thomson Report argued in 1973 that regional imbalances were acting as a barrier to one of the goals of the Treaty of Rome ('a continuous and balanced expansion' in economic activity), threatened to undermine plans for economic and monetary union, and could even pose a threat to the common market (Commission, 1979). Agreement was reached to create a European Regional Development Fund in 1972, but its launch was delayed until 1975 by the energy crisis of 1973–74. The fund originally accounted for about 5 per cent of the EEC budget, but spending was doubled in 1977 and has grown steadily since then, reaching nearly 14 billion ecu in 1998 (just over 15 per cent of the EU budget).

Funds were at first distributed by a system of national quotas, worked out during the negotiations leading up to the creation of the ERDF. The largest net beneficiaries were Britain, Ireland, France and Italy, although the balance later changed with the accession of Greece, Spain and Portugal. The ERDF was not to be used in place of existing national development spending, but was to provide matching grants of up to 50 per cent, supplemented by loans from the European Investment Bank (EIB). The requests had to come from the member states, and funds could only be spent on industrial and service sector projects aimed at creating new jobs or protecting existing ones, or on infrastructure related to industry or in areas such as remote or mountainous regions.

A major problem with the ERDF is that the definition of 'region' and of priority areas is left to the discretion of the member states. Each has different kinds of administrative units, ranging from the *lander* of Austria and Germany, which have a range of powers independent of those of their federal governments, to the *departements* of France and the counties of Britain, which have few independent powers and are governed in very different ways. This has meant that member states have always had different ideas about how to justify ERDF spending, which has tended to be based less on real 'need' (however that is defined) than on the relative political and economic influence member states can bring to bear on regional policy negotiations; the structural funds have always skirted with the danger of promoting pork barrel politics in the European Union.

It has been argued that politics enters the equation in at least two ways (Coombes and Rees, 1991, pp. 209–11). First, member states have been reluctant to give the EU powers over industrial development, employment and social security because this would reduce the control they have over domestic economic policy. Second, member states have been unwilling to transfer powers without the promise of net gains to themselves. They have always looked for some kind of compensation, and have placed national interests above European interests. The structural funds have routinely been seen as a way of compensating for the uneven distribution of agricultural spending – in that sense they have become a form of institutionalized bribery.

Reforms in the late 1970s led to the introduction of a small 'non-quota' element in the ERDF – 5 per cent of the total could be determined by the Commission on the basis of need – and suggestions that the richer countries should give up their quotas altogether on the ground that they could afford their own internal development costs. From being a passive recipient of requests for aid, the EC adopted a more active approach to the problem of regional disparity. Reforms in 1984 led to a tighter definition of the parts of the EC most in need of help, pushed up the non-quota segment to 20 per cent, and replaced the fixed quotas with minimum and maximum limits. Britain, for example, could receive anything between 14.5 per cent and 19.3 per cent, while the maximums for Germany and France were lower (3.4 per cent and nearly 10 per cent, respectively) and those for Spain and Italy were higher (about 24 per cent and 29 per cent, respectively).

The SEA brought new attention to the regional issue, introducing a new Title V on Economic and Social Cohesion, and arguing the need to 'clarify and rationalize' the use of the structural funds. Further reforms, agreed in 1988, were based on a Britain's insistence on reduced spending under CAP and increased spending under the structural funds to 25 per cent of the EC budget by 1993 (in the event they reached nearly 32 per cent of spending). The 1988 reforms were also aimed at improving the efficiency of regional policy by setting up Community Support Frameworks under which the Commission, the member states and the regions would work more closely together on agreeing the means to achieve regional development planning goals.

The most recent changes to regional policy came with Maastricht, under which a Committee of the Regions was created to give regional authorities a greater say in European policy, and the Cohesion Fund was created. The latter grew out of concern that economic and monetary union might worsen regional disparities, particularly given that poorer countries were going to be handicapped by the requirement (as a prelude to the single currency – see Chapter 7) for member states to limit their budget deficits to 3 per cent of GDP.

Regional policy is today one of the primary concerns of the European Union. In 1975 structural fund spending accounted for less than 5 per cent of the EEC budget, but in 1998 it amounted to more than one third of all EU spending (more than 33 billion ecu) and more than 50 per cent of EU citizens now benefit from projects paid for by the structural funds. It has even been suggested (Marks, 1993) that collaboration on the management of the structural funds between the European Commission, national planning authorities, and regional and local bodies has led to the emergence of a form of multilevel government in the EU. Others (Hooghe and Keating, 1994) have argued that most of this activity is symbolic and that the national governments have lost very little of their power.

There is little doubt, however, that regional policy is helping to close the gap between richer and poorer member states, and that the balance of economic power among them is changing. There is still a substantial gap in per capita GDP between the richest (Luxembourg) and the poorest (Greece), but most member states have seen their per capita GDP move towards the EU average – all but Greece, Spain, Ireland and Portugal are within ten percentage points of the average. One of the biggest success stories has been Ireland, whose per capita GDP has grown since 1960 from 60 per cent of the EU average to more than 82 per cent. Changes of this kind have created new opportunities in the poorer parts of the EU that discourage the outflow of labour, generate new sources of wealth and develop new markets for the rest of Europe.

Improving environmental quality

The process of European integration was long driven by matters relating to quantity. Efficiency, economic expansion and profit were at the heart of the construction of the common market, the agreement of a customs union and the development of the Common Agricultural Policy. Although the Treaty of Rome mentioned the need for 'an accelerated raising of the standard of living', qualitative issues were of relatively minor importance in the early years of the Community. The EEC agreed several pieces of environmental law in the 1960s, but they came out of the drive to build a common market and were incidental to the overriding economic goals (McGrory, 1990, p. 304); environmental policy was driven less by concern about environmental quality than about the extent to which different environmental standards were distorting competition and complicating progress towards the common market.

By the early 1970s the emphasis had begun to change. There was a public reaction in industrialized states against what was widely seen as uncaring affluence, generated by a combination of improved scientific

Box 5.3 European environmental policy

The goals of EU environmental policy are outlined in the SEA and the Environmental Action Programmes (with changes introduced by Maastricht and Amsterdam), but remain broad and generalized. They include the promotion of 'a harmonious and balanced development of economic activities, sustainable and non-inflationary growth respecting the environment . . . preserving, protecting and improving the quality of the environment . . . [and] prudent and rational utilization of natural resources'.

While these goals can be interpreted in many ways, EU policy has so far tended to focus on problems that are better dealt with jointly than nationally, such as the control of chemicals in the environment, the control of air and water pollution and the control of wastes. The EU has also been active in areas not normally defined as 'environmental' at the national level, including noise pollution and the control of genetically modified organisms. It has been less involved in the protection of ecosystems, natural habitats and wildlife, the management of natural resources such as forests, fisheries and soil, and the promotion of energy conservation and alternative sources of energy. Among the underlying principles of EU policy are the following:

- Integration, meaning that environmental protection must be a component of all EU policies that might have an environmental impact. This principle applies in only three other EU policy areas: culture, human health protection and consumer protection.
- Prevention, meaning that the EU emphasizes action to prevent the emergence of environmental problems, rather than just responding to problems when they arise.
- Subsidiarity, meaning that the EU must restrict itself to dealing with issues that are best dealt with jointly, leaving the rest to be addressed by the member states.
- Derogation, meaning that member states unable to bear the substantial economic burden of environmental protection are given longer deadlines, lower targets or financial assistance.

understanding, several headline-making environmental disasters and new affluence among the Western middle classes (McCormick, 1995, ch. 3). The EEC could not avoid being caught up in the growing demand for a response, and began to develop greater policy consistency and direction with the launch in 1973 of the first in a series of Environmental Action Programmes. Subsequent programmes combined with the SEA, Maastricht and Amsterdam gradually to switch the emphasis of policy towards sustainable development and environmental protection as an essential part of 'harmonious and balanced' economic growth. The SEA gave the environment legal status as an EC policy concern, while subsequent institutional changes gave public opinion (through the European Parliament) a greater role in environmental policy making, and introduced qualified majority voting on most issues related to environmental law and policy.

A multinational response to environmental problems makes sense because the latter do not respect national frontiers. Growing scientific and political awareness of this has led in the last twenty years to international action on such problems as air pollution and the management of shared rivers. However national governments have been slow to take unilateral action for fear of losing comparative economic advantage, and have been unwilling to give significant powers to international environmental organizations such as the United Nations Environment Programme, which is underfunded and has no direct powers of coercion.

Regional integration offers a way out of both dilemmas. As states become more dependent on trade and foreign investment, and the barriers to trade come down, so parochial worries about loss of comparative economic advantage become less important. At the same time, different environmental standards can create trade distortions, so national governments may be more inclined to take collective action and to agree common policies. In the case of the EU, this has already happened; it has been at the heart of the most concerted programme ever to replace national environmental controls with uniform multinational regulations.

Community policy was initially based on taking preventive action and working to ensure that divergent national policies did not act as barriers to the formation of the common market, a problem noted by the Court of Justice in 1980 when it argued that competition could be 'appreciably distorted' in the absence of harmonized environmental regulations (Commission versus Italy, Case 91/79). States with weak pollution laws, for example, had less of a financial or regulatory burden than those with stricter ones, and might attract corporations that wanted to build new factories with a minimum of built-in environmental safeguards. By the early 1980s the Community had switched to a focus on environmental management as the basis of economic and social development. For the first time environmental factors were consciously considered in other policy areas, notably agriculture, industry, energy and transport. Environmental concerns were no longer subordinate to the goal of building a common market (Hildebrand, 1993, pp. 20–2).

All these changes took place without any amendments being made to the Treaty of Rome, so EC environmental policy lacked a clear legal basis and was technically unauthorized by the member states (Rehbinder and Stewart, 1985, p. 19). The Community also expanded in the 1980s to include Greece, Spain and Portugal, whose industries were underdeveloped and pollutive, and whose environmental standards were relatively low.

The threat these changes posed to the EC's environmental activities were finally addressed by the SEA, which gave legal basis to Community environmental policy, made environmental protection a component of all the EC's other policies, outlined the underlying principles and goals of environmental policy, and included the environment on the list of policy areas subject to the cooperation procedure in the European Parliament.

At the same time, though, the SEA muddied the waters by noting that environmental policy would be based on the principle of subsidiarity: 'The Community shall take action relating to the environment to the extent to which the [policy] objectives . . . can be attained better at the Community level than at the level of the individual Member States' (Article 130r(4)). This heightened the possibility of member states challenging EC law by arguing about competence. States with weaker environmental laws could also challenge steps taken by other states to strengthen their laws; the SEA noted that Community measures would not prevent member states from imposing stronger measures of their own, but that they could not amount to discrimination or a disguised restriction on trade (Article 130t). Arguments about which laws were discriminatory and which were not could go either way. Maastricht helped clarify the issue by making the environment more obviously a priority policy area for the EU. It introduced qualified majority voting in the Council of Ministers for most environmental issues, thereby making it more difficult for reluctant member states to avoid toeing the line, and added the environment to the list of topics subject to codecision by the European Parliament.

Another boost was given by public support for environmental protection. Eurobarometer polls have found that most Europeans rank the environment above finance, defence or employment as an issue of EU concern, that most feel pollution is an 'urgent and immediate problem', and that most agree that environmental protection is a policy area better addressed jointly by EU states than by member states alone. Meanwhile green parties have won growing support in most member states: 30 green members were returned by seven EC states in the 1989 European Parliament elections (the number fell to 23 in the 1994 elections), and by the mid-1990s green members were sitting in the national legislatures of ten EU member states: Austria, Belgium, Finland, Germany, Greece, Ireland, Italy, Luxembourg, Portugal and Sweden.

More than 700 environmental laws have now been agreed by the EU, covering everything from environmental impact assessment to controls on lead in fuel, sulphur dioxide and suspended particulates, lead in air, pollutants from industrial plants and large combustion plants, nitrogen dioxide, and vehicle exhaust emissions. Five action programmes have been published (the fifth covers the period 1993–2000), a plethora of green and white papers has generated discussion on a wide range of issues, and the goals of EU policy have been given new definition since 1995 by the work of the European Environment Agency (EEA), a data-gathering agency that provides information to the other EU institutions. The EEA was involved in the publication in 1995 of the first regional assessment of the state of the European environment, which was followed up by a second report in 1998.

Although there has been progress on environmental policy making, the record on implementation is not so good. This can be explained in part by the limited ability of the Commission to ensure that member states implement EU law, the long-term lack of a legal basis to EU environmental policy, and the pressure on the Commission to maintain the impetus on new legislation, all of which have combined to encourage EU policymakers to focus on policy formulation at the expense of implementation (Collins and Earnshaw, 1993, p. 213; Macrory, 1992). Another problem relates to differences between the regulatory programmes and systems of the member states. For example Greece and Spain have had more infringement proceedings begun against them than most other EU states, mainly because local government in both states is relatively poorly organized and under-equipped. Germany and the Netherlands also have a bad record on implementation, but that is because they both have a sophisticated system of domestic environmental law, and lack the motivation to fully adapt their own measures to EU requirements. Meanwhile Denmark has a good record on implementation, helped by a high degree of public and official environmental awareness, effective monitoring systems and the involvement of the Danish parliament in negotiating new environmental law (Collins and Earnshaw, 1993).

Poor implementation has also been blamed on the lack of financial and technical resources, organizational problems within EU institutions, the fact that most EU law has focused on developing policies rather than the means of implementing and enforcing them, and on the failure of all the parties involved in making policy to recognize the difficulty of meeting the goals they have set (that is, they are too ambitious). It has been argued that the Commission – through the EEA – should be given the power to carry out inspections and ensure compliance, but this would raise fundamental questions about sovereignty and the 'interference' of the Commission in the domestic affairs of the member states. Besides, effective inspections would require a huge new staff: even the Environmental Protection Agency in the United States – with a staff of 18 000 and a multibillion dollar budget – is hard-pressed to keep up with everything it is expected to do. For the foreseeable future the Commission will have to continue to rely on whistle-blowing by interest groups, and on cases being brought before national courts and the European Court of Justice.

Regional cooperation among countries promises a quicker and more effective resolution of transnational environmental problems than any other approach, at least among countries with similar political systems and similar levels of economic development. Isolated national approaches may be handicapped by the fear of reduced competitive advantage; bilateral or multilateral approaches have worked only when limited to selected issues of mutual concern, such as the management of shared rivers, lakes or oceans; broader global approaches are handicapped by the increased likelihood of disagreement and deadlock and by the lack of competent authorities with the power to promote and enforce regulation. Given the extent to which the causes and effects of environmental problems do not respect national frontiers, the EU model may provide the only effective response to such problems, in large part because it encourages different states to cooperate rather than to adopt potentially conflicting objectives.

An emerging European civil society

The examples of regional and environmental policy suggest that European states have shifted increasingly from separate national approaches to common problems towards joint approaches. They have done this in part through strengthening pan-EU institutions and policymaking, harmonizing policy goals and methods, and developing common goals and standards. However, while the member states have been the major actors in this process, it would be wrong to think that the process of integration had been unidimensional, and that the EU was founded solely on the compromises worked out among the leaders of the member states. European integration has also led to the emergence of a European civil society, or a framework outside the formal structures of government in which people interact and associate with each other. While leaders have negotiated with their national interests to the fore, non-governmental organizations – or interest groups – have cut across national frontiers to promote the shared sectoral interests of communities in multiple member states.

As the EU has involved itself in a growing number of policy areas, so the number and the range of interest groups has grown. They have not always simply followed the evolution of the EU, going wherever new opportunities for influence have presented themselves, but have often been actively involved in pushing the EU in new directions. Business leaders, for example, were champions of the single market, arguing that competition among European corporations was a handicap to their ability to take on the Americans and the Japanese. At the same time, the European

Commission in particular has encouraged interest group activity, helping open channels for the participation of Europe-wide groups at almost every stage of policy making. This may have slowed down the policy process, but it has also reduced the Commission's workload, provided a ready source of expertise and helped the Commission monitor the compliance records of member states. By the early 1990s, the Commission estimated that there were about 3000 interest groups based in Brussels trying to influence EU affairs, and covering a wide variety of issues, from business to labour and professional interests, from consumer matters to environmental protection, and from the broadest kinds of interests to the most narrow and specialized.

Historically, business and labour groups have dominated European-level interest representation, mainly because the process of integration has been driven for so long by economic issues (Greenwood, 1997, p. 101). As the EU has extered greater power and influence since the mid-1980s over competition, mergers, the movement of workers, and related matters, so business and labour groups have turned their attention to activities in the Commission and the Council of Ministers. Not only are individual corporations represented either directly or through lobbying firms in Brussels, but a number of cross-sectoral federations have been created to represent the interests of a broader membership. Notable among these are the Union of Industrial and Employers' Confederations of Europe (UNICE) which was created in 1958 and now represents 32 national business federations from 22 countries. Meanwhile, the European Round Table of Industrialists brings together the chief executives of major European corporations, such as Fiat, Philips, ICI and Siemens, and the EU Committee of the American Chamber of Commerce represents the interests of American firms active in Europe

European labour is also represented in Brussels, most notably through groups such as the European Trade Union Confederation (ETUC), which was founded in 1972 and whose membership consists of a combination of European-level industry federations and national labour federations, such as Britain's TUC or Germany's DGB. At the same time, professional interests are represented by groups such as the Council of European Professional and Managerial Staff (EUROCADRES), and by associations representing everything from architects to dentists, journalists, opticians and vets. Several Brussels-based interest groups include member organizations from outside the EU, a reflection of the extent to which the EU has come to matter to business and labour throughout Europe.

Recent years have also seen a rise in the activities of groups representing public (or non-producer) interests, such as consumer issues and the environment. The latter provides a good example of an issue that has attracted growing attention among groups as the EU has become more involved in matters about which they care. Particularly until the 1970s, most of the pressure for domestic environmental regulation in industrialized countries came from environmental interest groups; they not only provided the pressure for policy change, but also the ideas and the scientific data upon which change was based. Among EC member states, there was initially little inclination for those groups to lobby Community institutions, because most environmental policy was still made at the national level, and the priorities varied from one member state to another.

However, interest groups have since become increasingly active at the European level since the mid-1980s, in part because the development of an expanding body of European environmental laws and policies has made EU institutions (notably the Commission) a more profitable target for interest group pressure, but also because these institutions lack the resources to collect information or to enforce laws, and welcome the input of interest groups. The change was reflected in the opening of offices in Brussels in the second half of the 1980s by such groups as Friends of the Earth, Greenpeace and the World Wide Fund for Nature, while many other groups employed full-time lobbyists. It has also been reflected in the increased activities of groups representing the industrial perspective on environmental issues, such as the European Chemical Industry Council, Eurelectric and the European Crop Protection Association.

Increased access to EU policy makers has led in turn to a more systematic approach among environmental groups to Euro-lobbying, and a clear trend towards approaching domestic environmental problems as EU-wide problems. The complexity of those problems has encouraged domestic groups to work more closely together and to form transnational coalitions, the best known of which is the European Environmental Bureau (EEB). Founded in 1974 with the encouragement of the Commission, the EEB is an umbrella body for national interest groups in the EU, and acts as a conduit for the representation of those groups in the EU institutions, particularly the Commission. The Bureau now claims to represent more than 130 national environmental groups with a combined membership of 23 million.

The activities of interest groups have helped offset the problem of the democratic deficit (see Chapter 6) by offering Europeans channels outside the formal structure of EU institutions which they can use to influence EU policy. They have also helped focus the attention of the members of interest groups on the expanding significance of the EU on the policies that affect their lives, have helped draw them more actively into the process by which the EU makes its decisions, and have encouraged them to bypass their national governments and to focus their attention on European responses to shared and common problems.

The changing character of the EU

Changes in the relationship among the member states of the EU have complicated discussions about the character and effects of international relations, because the EU only partly fits with conventional ideas about the ways in which societies organize and govern themselves.

Most political scientists agree that the EU is not a 'state' because it lacks many of the conventional features of a state, including a strong and separate legal identity, political unity and sovereignty, powers of coercion, and significant financial independence. At the same time it has some of the features of an international organization and it has developed unprecedented levels of power and influence over its members. This has led some scholars to argue that the EU is not really an institution, but is better understood as an ideal, a process, a regime, or even a network that has involved not so much a transfer of powers as a pooling of sovereignty (Keohane and Hoffmann, 1991, p. 10).

Jean Monnet argued in 1975 that he saw no point in trying to imagine what political form the United States of Europe would take, and that 'the words about which people argue – federation or confederation – are inadequate and imprecise' (Monnet, 1978, p. 523). He and his contemporaries might have been able to avoid the question then, but it is less easily avoided today. The idea of Europe has taken on new substance, making it essential better to understand the relationship between the EU and its member states. The process of integration has effectively gone beyond the point of no return, and the ties that Europeans have built over the last fifty years are too tightly knotted to be easily undone. The views of Eurosceptics notwithstanding, political union is now spoken of less in terms of 'if' than in terms of 'when' and 'how'. Hence we must think more actively about the form that 'union' might take, and what it will mean for the member states.

There have been at least five different sets of forces at work in European integration, pulling the member states in several directions:

● *Intergovernmental versus supranational.* One of the fundamental tensions in the process of European integration has been that between, on the one hand, member-state governments trying to preserve their sovereignty by relating to each other as equals, and, on the other hand, the forces and impulses that compel or encourage them to transfer sovereignty to a new supranational authority. In some respects the European Union remains a pact among independent states, whose leaders make most of the key decisions, but in other respects the balance of power has shifted to European institutions.

- *Independence versus dependence.* After the Second World War Europe consisted of several legally independent polities, but they were bound more closely than some of them cared to admit by history, culture and shared political and economic interests. The process of integration has strengthened those ties and given them clearer definition, so that the member states have moved along a path from considerable independence towards extensive mutual dependence. This is particularly true in the economic sphere, with increased investment and trade flows, and the creation of pan-European industries and corporations.

- *Competition versus cooperation.* Until 1945 the history of Europe was one of competition, conflict and constantly changing alliances and balances of power. Some of those conflicts persist, and the balance of power continues to change, but it does so inclusively rather than exclusively, and out of a sense of both cooperation and competition. The conflicting goals of separate states have been replaced by the promotion of mutual interests, and European states work increasingly closely in a variety of policy areas.

- *Autonomy versus unity.* The process of integration has reduced the freedom of action of the member states and steadily pushed them along the road to unity as they pull down the structural, political, technical, physical, fiscal and attitudinal barriers that have long divided them. As their autonomy declines, so does their freedom of movement, and the possibility of European political union becomes more real.

- *Elitism versus democracy.* The citizens of western Europe have had relatively little input into the development of the EU because most of the initiatives have come from political, economic and social elites. The balance is changing, though, as citizens are becoming more interested and involved in EU policy (see Chapter 6.)

Where the member states now sit on these five different continua is debatable, but it could be argued that integration has moved them more towards supranationalism, dependence, cooperation, unity and democracy. What are the features of the European Union at the turn of the millennium?

First, it has far more powers than any international organization that has ever existed, and has developed an unprecedented degree of authority over its member states. It is not yet a federation, nor even a confederation, and although it has several different 'governing' institutions, it is not yet a government in itself; it is more like a network of institutions and national governments, all of which are still jostling to define their powers relative to the other institutions and member states. While 'supranationalism' may describe the political process of the EU, it has been argued that the EU has always rested ultimately on a set of intergovernmental bargains (Keohane

Box 5.4 Intergovernmental conferences

The extent to which decisionmaking in the EU is still intergovernmental rather than supranational is reflected in the way that many of the key decisions of recent years have come out of intergovernmental conferences (IGCs), convened outside the formal framework of the EU's institutions to allow negotiations among the governments of the member states. Even as the powers of those institutions have grown, so the IGC has become an increasingly common event on the EU calendar; there have been six IGCs since 1950, but four of them have been held since 1985.

The first IGC was opened in May 1950, was chaired by Jean Monnet, and led to the creation of the ECSC and the signing of the Treaty of Paris. The second was opened at Messina in April 1955, and led to the creation of the EEC and Euratom and the signing of the Treaties of Rome. Perhaps because national leaders were focused on building the three Communities and the common market, because of the intergovernmental nature of Community decisionmaking in the early years, and because of the fallout from the energy crises of the 1970s, it was to be another 27 years before another IGC was convened. Concerned about the lack of progress on integration and Europe's declining economic performance in relation to the United States and Japan, the third IGC was launched in September 1985, and by December had outlined the framework of what was eventually to become the Single European Act.

Two more IGCs met during 1991 to look at political union and monetary union, their outcome being the Treaty on European Union. A sixth IGC was launched in 1996 with institutional reform and preparations for eastward enlargement at the top of its agenda, the product of which was the Treaty of Amsterdam. Even before the treaty was ratified and came into force in 1999, however, talk had already begun of the need for a seventh IGC that could plan a complete overhaul of the EU institutions in the event of the expansion of EU membership to twenty states or more.

The IGCs since 1985 have been negotiated by a combination of national government ministers and permanent representatives, and have continued to symbolize the extent to which decisionmaking on the big initiatives of the EU still rests with the member states. While there is nothing in the founding treaties about IGCs, they have become a normal part of the calendar of European integration, and all have so far resulted in landmark decisions on the development of the EU.

and Hoffmann, 1991, p. 10). Opinion is divided about the extent to which it has moved beyond such bargains; realists argue that the member states are still the key actors, and that integration progresses according to the decisions they take, while neofunctionalists argue that integration has its own expansive logic, and has taken on an irresistible life and momentum of its own.

Second, while the EU has its own bureaucracy, a growing body of treaties and laws, and a court that can adjudicate disputes between its member states, it has limited institutional independence and limited powers of coercion. EU institutions lack the power to raise taxes and implement laws, have neither the power nor the personnel directly to enforce the law, and must rely almost entirely on the voluntary compliance of the member states. Europe still lacks a common police force, a common tax agency, a regional postal and telecommunications service, and a common defence force.

Finally, although the EU does not yet have exclusive responsibility for any single policy area, it has effectively taken over most or all responsibility from the member states for making (or at least coordinating) policy on external and internal trade and agriculture. In other areas (such as the environment) the trend is in favour of the EU, while issues such as education, policing and criminal law still rest largely with the member states. The EU has also gone well beyond focusing on economic integration and moved into the realms of social integration and political integration. Amendments to the treaties since the SEA have resulted in the accelerated transfer (or pooling) of policy responsibility, and the introduction of the single currency will provide the final step in the integration of economic policy. Economic union will in turn provide irresistible pressure to complete the integration of other internal policy issues.

All of this still begs the question of just what kind of polity the European Union has become. Most people like to use labels to help them understand their environment, but there are no such easy labels for the EU, or at least none on which most scholars can agree. Europeans are well aware of the dangers of the divisions they are leaving behind, but are much less clear about the features of the unity towards which they are moving. As Benjamin Franklin argued after trying to find a model upon which the new American republic could be based, history consists only of beacon lights 'which give warning of the course to be shunned, without pointing out that which ought to be pursued' (Franklin, in *Federalist*, no. 37).

The European Union is distinctive and unique, and cannot neatly be slotted into any of the usual ideas about government. 'Boundaries are difficult to draw in a world of complex interdependence', argue Keohane and Hoffmann (1991, p. 12); 'because relationships cross boundaries and coalitional patterns vary from issue to issue, it is never possible to classify all actors neatly into mutually exclusive categories'. The EU has many intergovernmental characteristics, but over time they have given way to a growing emphasis on supranationalism. The member states are increasingly answering to a higher authority, with some of the features of confederalism and some of the features of federalism. Both these concepts take many different forms, and for Eurosceptics to talk about federalism as some kind of hell towards which Europe should not travel is too simplistic. The European brand of federalism already has several unique features, and once it achieves some kind of regularity, those features will look very different from most of the characteristics we usually associate with federalism.

Conclusions

While debates rage about the powers and nature of the European Union, and while there is widespread resistance to the expansion of EU powers and responsibilities, there is no question that its member states have lost powers to the EU and now have less political and economic independence than they did even twenty years ago. Integration has redefined the relationship among EU member states at several levels: there has been a reduction in economic differences, a harmonization of standards, laws and regulations, and removal of the physical and fiscal barriers that have differentiated the member states from one another. The EU record on regional and environmental policy provides an indication of the kinds of forces that are at work in this process.

Regional development has meant an attempt to help the poorer regions catch up with their richer neighbours, with the utopian goal of encouraging an equitable distribution of the benefits of regional integration. The EU has tended to equate development with growth, but whether quantity and quality go hand in hand has long been debatable. It is also debatable whether the free market can ever entirely eliminate inequalities of opportunity, which is why regional policy has been based on a kind of grand welfare system that sees the redistribution of wealth as a means of encouraging equal opportunity. It remains to be seen how long it will take to bring the different parts of the EU to the same economic level (assuming this is even possible).

In the case of the environment, there is little question that international cooperation is desirable and even inevitable. Problems such as air and water pollution ignore national boundaries, and there are repeated examples from around the world of one state being a producer and down-wind or down-stream states being recipients.

As the global economy advances, a new dimension is added by the barriers posed to trade by different environmental standards. There will always be strong ideological disagreement about the extent to which the state should manage natural resources and regulate industry, but there is a strong internal logic to international cooperation on environmental management. There is an emerging consensus that the EU has been a positive force in environmental protection, and that European environmental problems are better dealt with at the EU level than at the national or local level.

There is also an emerging consensus that cooperation in a variety of other areas makes better sense than independent action, which can lead to unnecessary competition and duplication of effort. It is still far too early to talk about the creation of a federal relationship among the member states, and between them and the EU institutions, but the trend is undoubtedly in that direction. Several levels of government are being created, all with independent powers. How far European cooperation will go depends on how we choose to define subsidiarity, but while this is moving higher up the agenda of EU negotiations, the definition of which issues are best dealt with at the level of the member state and which at the level of Europe remains fluid.

Chapter 6

The EU and its Citizens

Public opinion and the democratic deficit
The people's Europe
Social policy
Improving accountability
Conclusions

According to the Maastricht treaty, the goal of European integration is to create 'an ever closer union among the peoples of Europe, in which decisions are taken as closely as possible to the citizen'. Even the most ardent supporters of integration will admit, however, that integration has been less a popular movement for change than a process begun and largely sustained by elites. The limited ability of Europeans to influence the work of the major EU institutions is a problem that has become so entrenched as to merit its own label: the democratic deficit.

Except through the occasional referendum, the European people have rarely been asked directly for their opinion on the changes agreed in their collective name. Most notably, public opinion played only a marginal role (at best) in the negotiations leading up to the six major treaties and in the decision to proceed with the single currency. Meanwhile the channels through which Europeans are able to express themselves directly on European issues are few and insubstantial. Voters may have an indirect influence on the deliberations of the Council of Ministers, but ministers are appointed officials accountable to national governments rather than the European electorate. Similarly the only institution in which the views of Europeans on Europe are directly represented – the European Parliament – has a relatively minor influence on the process of integration.

'What about us?', the European public might reasonably ask. 'Is anyone in Brussels really listening?' It sometimes seems as though integration is proceeding *despite* public opinion, which is often confused about the changes that have taken place, is sometimes doubtful about those changes, and in many cases is actively hostile. Public apathy has played its part, as reflected in the poor turnout at European elections and the low levels of understanding among Europeans about how the EU works, but whether this apathy has been a cause or an effect of the elitist nature of European leadership is debatable. The European Council decided in 1984 to begin promoting 'a people's Europe' in an attempt to make Europe more 'real' to

147

its people, and changes have been made to the treaties in order to promote 'transparency' (making the deliberations of the EU institutions more open to scrutiny), but the argument that public enthusiasm can somehow be encouraged by public policy is fundamentally flawed.

The development of the European Union has changed the way that Europeans relate to each other, in many different ways. Some of the changes have come as a direct consequence of policy decisions such as the removal of border controls and the expansion of opportunities under the single market programme. Other changes have been an indirect consequence, growing out of the realization among Europeans that they are involved in a communal exercise with implications for them all. Under the circumstances it has become vital for leaders to make more of an effort to refer to public opinion, and for citizens to make more of an effort to understand what is being done in their name and to play a more active role in the making of decisions at the European level.

This chapter asks what integration has meant for Europeans, and for the nature of democracy in the European Union. It begins with an assessment of the problems arising from the democratic deficit, and looks at the relationship between public opinion and the decisions taken by national leaders. It then looks at some of the specific policy areas in which the EU has focused on the needs and priorities of Europeans: the People's Europe, the concept of European citizenship, cultural issues and social policy. It ends with a discussion about the kind of changes that need to be made to bring Europe closer to its citizens.

Public opinion and the democratic deficit

The EU has a public opinion survey system known as Eurobarometer, which regularly measures public opinion on a wide variety of issues relating to European integration, ranging from views on the entire process to those on specific programmes and undertakings. The autumn 1997 survey (*Eurobarometer*, 48) found that most Europeans were either supportive of EU membership or felt neutral about it, but also revealed a recent fall in the level of support. Support grew from 50 per cent in 1980 to 71 per cent in 1990, but fell in Germany after reunification, and then more widely throughout the EU in the wake of the controversy over Maastricht. By 1997 only 47 per cent of Europeans supported membership, although only about 10–15 per cent were opposed to it. Support for the EU tends to be most enthusiastic in poorer member states such as Ireland, Greece and Portugal, while scepticism is greater in newer and wealthier member states such as Denmark, Sweden, Austria and the Britain (see Figure 6.1).

Figure 6.1   *Public opinion on EU membership*

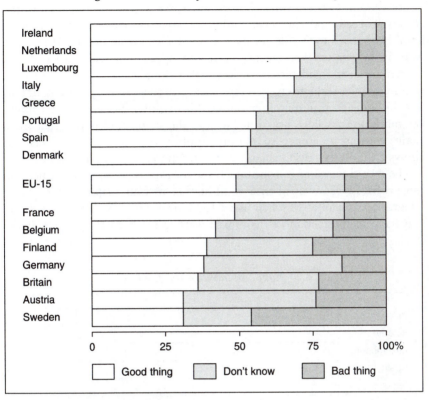

Source: *Eurobarometer*, 48 (Autumn 1997).

When interviewees were asked which issues they felt were priorities for the EU, there was majority support (65–90 per cent) for EU action on unemployment and poverty, fighting organized crime and drug trafficking, protecting the environment, protecting consumers, a common defence policy, a common foreign policy, common rules on political asylum and immigration, social policy based on a set of common fundamental principles, and greater influence for the regions in EU decision making. There was less support (45–50 per cent) for increasing the powers of the Commission, the single European currency and giving Europeans the right to vote in local elections wherever they live. Expanding EU membership was considered a priority by only 24 per cent of respondents. The 1997 poll also revealed that the majority felt that issues such as drug control, foreign policy, the environment, regional support and unemployment would be better addressed by joint EU action, while workers' rights, education, and health and social welfare are better left to the member states.

One issue on which there is a clear divergence between public and political opinion is the single European currency. The development of the euro is proceeding despite every indication that many Europeans are either actively opposed to the idea or have mixed feelings at best; only 51 per cent were in favour in 1997 (Figure 6.2), and opposition had hardened still further by 1998. Undeterred, in May 1998 the leaders of eleven member states committed themselves to the single currency, in every case failing to put the issue to a public referendum. Meanwhile, the leaders of Britain, Denmark, and Sweden opted not to join the single currency at that time, again without reference to national public opinion. (Greece was not allowed to join because it had not met the necessary conditions.)

The mixed views of Europeans on the idea of integration or unification can probably be ascribed to a combination of four major factors. First, integration is a relatively new issue for Europeans. The Treaty of Rome may have been signed more than forty years ago, but it has only been in the

Figure 6.2   *Public opinon on the single currency*

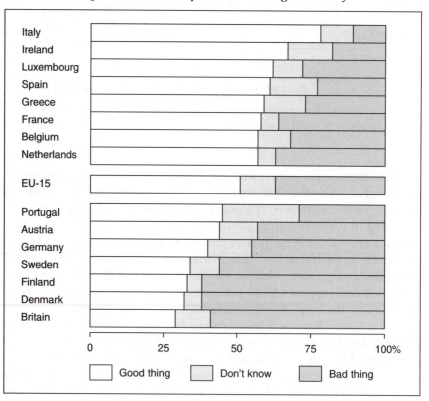

Source: Eurobarometer, 48 (Autumn 1997).

last 10–15 years that Europeans have really begun to feel the effects of integration, and to be regularly reminded of the work of the EU. One result is that very few have fully weighed up the costs and benefits of integration. When opinions are discussed and expressed, they are often driven by narrow interests – many Europeans are familiar with the effects of European policy and law in some particular area that interests them, but few are familiar with the broader arguments about integration (see Chapter 2).

Second, it is clear that Europeans have been marginalized in the decision-making process, and that the actions of national leaders often fail to gel with public opinion. The Danish people's rejection of Maastricht in June 1992 came as a shock not just to the Danish government, but to all European governments. It certainly raised questions about just how many other initiatives might have been rejected – or passed by small majorities – if put to a national referendum in any of the member states. For example it is almost certain that the single currency would have been rejected by German voters if put to the test in 1998, because polls indicated that more than 60 per cent were opposed to the idea. Given the essential role of Germany in the single currency, such a result would have brought an end to the programme.

Third, national leaders, European institutions, the media and academic experts have done a poor job of explaining the implications and the costs and benefits of integration. To be fair, the process is enormously complex and changes constantly, and the implications of the steps taken have not always been fully understood – every new venture has produced unanticipated effects (the single market programme being a prime example) and the single currency is a leap into the unknown. Nonetheless the growing volume of information on the EU tends to focus on the minutiae of the treaties and European law, media coverage in the more eurosceptical member states tends to emphasize the negative at the expense of the positive, and the average European remains confused (Box 6.1).

Finally, and perhaps most fundamentally, there is the problem of the democratic deficit. This is commonly defined in terms of the unequal powers of the European Parliament relative to the other EU institutions. For example it is defined by Williams (1991, p. 162) as 'the gap between the powers transferred to the Community level and the control of the elected Parliament over them', and by Archer and Butler (1996, p. 58) as 'the shift in decision-making powers from the national to the EU level, without accompanying strengthening of parliamentary control of executive bodies'. Such definitions seem to suggest that the democratic credentials of the EU institutions would be improved if representation of the interests of EU citizens was strengthened *indirectly* by giving Parliament greater powers. Yet there is also a case to be made for improving the ability of citizens *directly* to influence the work of EU institutions by being allowed, for example, to elect the president of the Commission, who might then be allowed to appoint Commissioners instead of relying on the governments of the member states.

A more universal definition of the democratic deficit might be the gap between the powers held by European institutions and the ability of European citizens to influence the work and decisions of those institutions. However it is defined, the democratic deficit represents a damaging psychological barrier between Europeans and the EU. It reminds Europeans that there are few ways in which they can directly influence the EU decision-making process, and also serves to prevent the development of the ties that must exist between leaders and citizens in order for a system of government to work.

The deficit takes several different forms:

- The leaders of the member states, meeting as the European Council, reach decisions on important policy matters without always referring them to their electorates. A prime case in point was the Maastricht treaty, which was negotiated largely behind closed doors, poorly explained to the European public and – despite the important changes it would make to the structure and goals of the EU – put to the test of a referendum in only three member states. Similarly, membership of the EC/EU was put to a national vote in less than half the 15 member states, and approval of the single currency in none at all (although it was subject to debate and a vote in several national legislatures).
- Despite its considerable powers to propose and develop new European laws, the European Commission is subject to little direct or even indirect public accountability. Commissioners are appointed without reference to the people. The president of the Commission is appointed as a result of a strange and informal little power dance among the leaders of the member states, he (to date all presidents have been male) represents the views of the EU in several international fora without a mandate from the people, and his tenure is subject only to the whims of the national leaders. Furthermore there is little opportunity for members of the public to take part in or contribute to the deliberations of the Commission, and limited (albeit improving) opportunity for the European Parliament to hold it accountable for its initiatives and decisions.
- Meetings of the Council of Ministers and the permanent representatives in Brussels are closed, despite the fact that many of the most important decisions on the content of new laws and policies, and on their acceptance or rejection, are taken there. At the national level, decisions such as these are taken by elected representatives.

- The European Parliament – the only democratically elected institution in the EU system – lacks most of the powers of a true legislature: it cannot raise revenues, introduce and develop new laws or take a final vote on whether or not a proposal will become law, and has only a limited ability to hold senior bureaucrats in the Commission accountable for their decisions. It has worked long and hard to win new powers for itself, but the key decisions on EU law and policy are taken elsewhere, notably in the Commission and the Council of Ministers.

- Voters have a very limited impact on the EU policy-making process. By voting in the European parliamentary elections they determine the composition of Parliament, but their interests are still better represented in national legislatures, and there is no change of government at stake (Franklin, 1996, p. 187). They have no say in the composition of the Council of Ministers or the European Commission, and they have little influence on appointments to or the work of the College of Commissioners.

- The Court of Justice is arguably the institution that best champions the cause of individual Europeans, being the final court of appeal for anyone who feels they have been hurt by European law, by its non-appliance, or by contradictions between European and national law. However Europeans have no say in appointments to the Court, nor will they until the kind of legislative confirmation that is used for courts in many member states is adopted by the EU, and prospective Court of Justice appointees are subject to investigation and confirmation by the European Parliament.

- The formal rights of Europeans relative to the EU are modest: they have the right to vote in European elections, to petition Parliament or the European ombudsman if they feel their rights or interests have been violated (see below), to gain access to the documents of EU institutions (within certain limits), and to diplomatic representation outside the EU by any member state, provided their own country has no local representation.

Under the circumstances it is hardly surprising that Europeans have so little psychological attachment to the EU institutions. It is also hardly surprising that the anti-European media are able to generate so much public distrust and resentment towards these institutions, which appear distant and mysterious to many Europeans. The relationship between the public and the Commission is symptomatic of the broader problem. The Commission is a small and extremely productive institution, and while it can only propose and oversee the implementation of new laws, it is often portrayed as powerful, overpaid, unaccountable and secretive. It is helped

Box 6.1 The knowledge deficit

No matter how much the European Commission tries to make Europe seem more real to its citizens, and no matter how often the European Council talks about the importance of transparency, one fundamental problem remains: the average European knows little about how the EU works.

This has been made very clear by the results of recent Eurobarometer surveys. In late 1997, for example, respondents were asked how much they felt they knew about the EU, its policies and its institutions, and to give themselves a score out of 10, with 10 meaning they knew a great deal and 1 meaning they knew little. While 13 per cent admitted they knew nothing at all, just 6 per cent gave themselves scores of 8 or higher. No less than 75 per cent of respondents gave themselves scores of 5 or less, and the average for the sample worked out at 4.01.

Those who felt they knew the most included managers, people with a university education, people who used the media regularly and those in the age range of 25–54. Those with the lowest levels of knowledge included manual workers, retirees and people with a high school education or lower. In descending order, the Austrians, the Danes, the Germans, the Dutch and the Finns felt they knew the most, while the Italians, the Irish, the Spanish, the British and the Portuguese knew the least.

On more specific issues, the same survey found a low degree of knowledge about the Amsterdam treaty and the single currency. When asked if they had simply heard of the treaty, 53 per cent admitted they had not. Awareness was highest in Denmark (91 per cent), thanks mainly to extensive media coverage of the treaty, and lowest (67–70 per cent had not heard of it) in Ireland, Germany, Britain and Greece. On the single currency, more than 70 per cent of Europeans admitted they were not very well or not at all informed about the euro (although this was an improvement on the results of a 1996 survey). Ironically, while so many pleaded ignorance, this did not prevent 51 per cent of respondents saying they were in favour of the single currency and 37 per cent saying they were opposed (*Eurobarometer*, 48, autumn 1997).

These are not encouraging figures. It will be difficult for Europeans to develop a sense of belonging to the European Union if they continue to know so little about it, and as long as they know so little, they will not make their views known about its work. This will perpetuate the democratic deficit, and decisions will continue to be taken by national leaders and Eurocrats. Ironically, the lack of public knowledge persists despite attempts by the Commission to make its work more accessible through printed and audiovisual media and the internet.

little by the fact that most of its staff occupy a series of anonymous buildings spread around the suburbs of Brussels, and that access to those buildings by ordinary Europeans is heavily restricted.

While there is little question that further reforms are needed to make the EU institutions more accountable and democratic, moves in this direction usually come up against the resistance of national governments: to make these institutions more democratic would involve reducing the control that national governments currently exert over them. The Treaty of Amsterdam emphasized the need to make the work of the EU comprehensible and 'transparent', but while it established the right of Europeans to greater access to European documents, this is not the same as affording them a greater opportunity to influence the content of those documents.

Under the circumstances, one of the most hopeful short-term channels for the democratization of the European Union lies with the growth in the activity of interest groups working at the European level. Such groups not only contribute to the development of a European civil society (as noted in Chapter 5), but also provide Europeans with important channels for political pressure. There are a number of European bodies that look much like interest groups, but are in fact part of the formal EU structure, including the Economic and Social Committee and the Committee of the Regions (see Box 4.3). Beyond these, the last 10–15 years have seen the growth of hundreds of non-governmental organizations that represent the views of a wide variety of sectional interests with a stake in the content of EU policy and law. Many are an outgrowth of preexisting national groups, others have been set up specifically to respond to European issues, and an increasing number have opened offices in Brussels so as to be close to the Commission and the Council of Ministers.

The growth in interest group activity at the European level has paralleled the growth of the power and influence of the EU institutions, or the 'Europeanization' of policy areas that were previously the exclusive province of national governments (Mazey and Richardson, 1996, p. 200). Studies indicate that there are nearly 700 groups working to influence decisions taken at the European level, about two thirds of which have existed since 1980 or earlier. Just over 60 per cent are business groups, 21 per cent deal with public interest issues and 16 per cent are professional organizations (Aspinwall and Greenwood, 1998). Examples of business groups include the European Roundtable of Industrialists, the EU Committee of the American Chamber of Commerce, organizations representing specific issues such as the plastics, chemicals and paper industries, and the offices of multinational corporations. Public interest groups include the European Bureau of Consumer Unions, Amnesty International and environmental groups such as Greenpeace and Friends of the Earth.

The methods that Euro groups use are similar to those used by groups at any level: promoting public awareness in support of their cause, building membership numbers in order to increase their influence and credibility, representing the views of their members, forming networks with other interest groups, providing information to the EU institutions, meeting with EU law makers in an attempt to influence the content of law, and monitoring the implementation of EU law at the national level.

Aspinwall and Greenwood (1998) argue that the representation of interests at the European level has become more diversified and specialized, and that Euro groups are becoming protagonists – they now try to influence policy rather than simply to monitor events, using increasingly sophisticated means to attract allegiance. Something of a symbiotic relationship has developed between the Commission and interest groups, with the former actively supporting the work of many groups and giving them access to its advisory committee meetings, and the latter doing what they can to influence the content and development of policy and legislative proposals as they work their way through the Commission.

The work of interest groups, however, does not remove the problem of the democratic deficit. Franklin (1996, p. 197) describes the lack of proper democratic accountability in the EU as 'a crisis of legitimacy'. It is unlikely that the essential psychological link between EU institutions and EU citizens will be made until such time as the European Parliament becomes a true legislature, national political parties form pan-European federations and run for election as such, and the outcome of European elections has a direct effect on the content and performance of the Commission and the Council of Ministers. However this will not happen as long as the governments of the member states feel the need to use the Council of Ministers as the guarantor of national interests.

The people's Europe

It took nearly thirty years for the leaders of the member states to begin asking the people of Europe what they thought about the process of integration. In 1975 a report drawn up at the request of the European Council by Leo Tindemans, prime minister of Belgium, investigated the steps that might be taken to achieve a more integrated Europe that was 'closer' to its citizens. However nothing more was done until June 1984, when the EEC heads of government, meeting in Fontainebleu and spending most of their time agreeing reforms to the Community budget, briefly turned their attention to the idea of a 'people's Europe'. Pietro Adonnino, a former Italian MEP, was hired to chair a committee to put forward suggestions on how the EEC could be brought more closely in touch with its citizens. Those suggestions fell into four categories.

Box 6.2 European cultural policy

A critical element in the evolution of a nation-state is that its people have a shared sense of common history and common culture. Where this exists, the state enjoys a high degree of legitimacy (public acceptance), which breeds stability and longevity. Where it does not exist, and where there are significant social divisions, there is more likely to be instability and a weak sense of common identity. The United States is an example of the former, while former Yugoslavia is an extreme example of the latter.

When Europeans think of European history they are more likely to think of the wars and divisions that have plagued the continent than of any common experiences or heritage. While the idea that the European Union should promote the idea of European culture might be anathema to many (how can culture be legislated or 'promoted'?) it has nevertheless done so. Maastricht introduced a Title IX to the Treaty of Rome, committing the EU to 'contribute to the flowering of the culture of the Member States' with a view to improving knowledge about and dissemination of the culture and history of Europe, conserving the European cultural heritage, and supporting and supplementing non-commercial cultural exchanges and 'artistic and literary creation'.

What this has so far meant in practice has been to spend money on restoring the architectural heritage, contributing to training schemes in conservation and restoration, helping to meet the costs of translating works by European authors (particularly into less widely spoken languages) and supporting cultural events. For example, the EU has funded a Youth Orchestra and a Baroque Orchestra to bring young musicians together, declared European 'Cities of Culture' (Thessaloniki in 1997, Stockholm in 1998 and Weimar in 1999) and established a European Cultural Month (Ljubljana in 1997, Linz and Valetta in 1998 and Plovdiv in 1999).

While the sentiments behind such projects are laudable, it is difficult to see how cultural exchanges and the development of a European cultural identity can really work unless they are taken on board by Europeans themselves. While it is relatively easy to argue that Shakespeare, Michelangelo, Voltaire, Goethe, Charlemagne and Mozart are all part of the heritage of Europe, it is much more difficult to promote the idea of a present-day pan-European popular culture. Even the most mobile of art forms – film and rock music – come up against the barrier of national preferences, and almost nothing that is not produced in English enjoys commercial success outside its home market.

Changes already begun

The committee endorsed arrangements that had already been made for a European passport and a European flag. All national passports have since been replaced by a standardized burgundy-coloured 'European' passport bearing the words 'European Community' in the appropriate national language, and the name of the holder's home state. This ensures that Europeans are given equal treatment by the customs and immigration authorities of other countries, and also helps give them a sense of belonging to the EU.

Meanwhile the European Commission decided to declare the anniversary of the Schuman Declaration (9 May) 'Europe Day', to adopt as the official anthem of Europe Schiller's 'Ode to Joy', sung to the final movement of Beethoven's 9th Symphony, and, most importantly, to adopt as its own the flag that had been used by the Council of Europe since 1955 – a circle of twelve gold stars on a blue background. The flag, which was designed by Paul Levy, director of information for the Council of Europe, was chosen in preference to several other designs (Bainbridge and Teasdale, 1995, p. 188–9) and can now be seen flying on public buildings and hotels throughout the EU. (It was popularly thought that the 12 stars represented the 12 member states but the number was coincidental and the design has not been changed as membership of the EU has grown.)

Changes introduced by the Single European Act

The most important of these involved the easing of restrictions on the free movement of people. It had been understood as early as the signing of the Treaty of Rome that an open labour market would be an essential part of a true single market, and while Article 8a gave all citizens of the Community the right to 'move and reside freely' within the territory of the member states, Article 48 made this subject to 'limitations justified on grounds of public policy, public security or public health'. The movement of workers was initially seen mainly in economic terms, and hence the emphasis was placed on removing the barriers for those EU citizens who were economically active. Migration was at first limited because of employment opportunities within the home states (governments were protecting themselves against the possibility of a shortage of skilled workers), and subsequently because of the lack of opportunities in the target states (Barnes and Barnes, 1995, p. 108).

More recently free movement has been granted to all EU nationals, whether or not they are economically active. Hence changes arising from the SEA made it possible for EU citizens to move and live anywhere in the

EU, provided they are covered by health insurance and have sufficient income to avoid being a 'burden' on the welfare system of the country in which they live. The concerns of national governments have been twofold: to control the effects of economic pressures that encourage workers to leave the poorer parts of the EU for the richer parts, thereby destabilizing the employment situation and increasing welfare spending in the richer parts, and to control the movement of non-EU citizens, notably nationals of Turkey and North African countries. At the heart of the debate about free movement has been concern about differences in welfare laws, which is why the harmonization of social policies has been given high priority (see below), and why there has been a particular focus on meeting the needs of younger and older people.

There is no question that Europeans have become much more mobile in the last 10–15 years, and the number of non-nationals living in member states has also grown: there were five million immigrants in 1950, ten million in 1970 and probably close to fifteen million today (although the growing porosity of borders makes it increasingly difficult to be sure). Meanwhile an estimated 550 000 Europeans have been posted temporarily to another member state by their employers. While the flow of immigration was initially from the south to the north, and consisted largely of workers from Mediterranean states seeking employment, and then sending for their families to join them, immigration flows in recent years have become much more complex and there has been an increase in the movement of professionals and managers (Romero, 1992). In other words there has been a trend away from economically motivated migration and towards voluntary migration by people wanting to move to a different environment for a variety of reasons.

This movement has been helped by another element of the Adonnino report that was formalized by the SEA: arrangements for the mutual recognition of professional qualifications. Although the basic training for most health workers (doctors, nurses, dentists and so on) was harmonized relatively early and they were quickly given the right to work in any EC member state, progress in other areas was much slower. The initial strategy of the Commission was to work on each profession in turn, to reach agreement on the requirements, and to propose a new law. This was extremely time-consuming, however, and it took 17 years to harmonize the requirements for architects, for example, and 16 years for pharmacists. Progress was made in 1988 with agreement of the general systems directive, under which the member states agreed (effective as of 1991) to trust the adequacy of qualifications that require at least three years of professional training in other member states (Orzak, 1991). The list of mutually recognized professions is growing, and now includes accountants, librarians, architects, engineers and – since 1998 – lawyers. The Commission has meanwhile published a comparative guide to national qualifications for more than 200 occupations, helping employers work out equivalencies across the member states.

An important element in worker mobility is education and youth training, in which the EU has become more involved since Maastricht by encouraging educational exchanges and addressing the knotty problem of language training. Language differences pose a barrier to the free movement of workers, and stand as a potent reminder of the differences among Europeans. Hence member states are taking additional steps to encourage educational exchanges and training in second and even third languages, including the following programmes:

- ERASMUS, a programme to encourage student and faculty exchanges among colleges and universities, and to make it easier for students to transfer credits. About 60 000 students currently attend non-home-state universities with the help of ERASMUS, and the goal is eventually to push this figure to 150 000.
- LINGUA, which encourages training in second and third languages.
- TEMPUS, which links universities in the United States and western and eastern Europe by promoting joint research projects.
- COMETT, which encourages universities and industry to work together on training projects.
- PETRA, which is aimed at modernizing vocational training.

The EU now has 11 official languages: Danish, Dutch, English, Finnish, French, German, Greek, Italian, Portuguese, Spanish and Swedish. Almost all EU business is conducted in English and French, although Germany is keen to make sure that German is not forgotten; one of the consequences of the eastward expansion of the EU will be an increase in the number of Europeans who speak German, which will alter the linguistic balance of power in the EU. Almost all secondary school pupils in the EU learn at least one foreign language, but the record varies from one state to another. The British have the worst record, but have been spoiled by the steady growth of English as the international language of commerce and entertainment, and by the fact that a growing number of continental Europeans speak English: more than 90 per cent of secondary school pupils in Germany, Spain, the Netherlands and Denmark learn it as a second language. Meanwhile only 33 per cent of Italian pupils and 23 per cent of German pupils are learning French (Eurostat figures, 1995).

The issue of language cuts to the very core of national pride, and particularly upsets the French, who have done everything they can to stop the perfidious spread of 'franglais' – the use of English words in French, for example 'le jumbo jet' (officially *le gros porteur*) and 'le fast food' (officially *pret-à-manger*). In an attempt to prevent any one language winning out over the others it has been suggested that all Europeans should learn Esperanto, an artificial international language developed in 1887, or even that Latin should be revived for the purpose. Despite the number of EU employees who work as translators, the publication of all EU documents in all 11 official languages, and the attempts by France to stave off the inroads being made by English and Anglo-American culture, it seems almost inevitable that English – with the help of American, Japanese and German business – will continue its steady progress towards becoming the common language of Europe.

While tourism, the removal of technical barriers to movement and the promotion of language training all have their place, the treaties say nothing directly about social barriers to free movement: differences in the routine of daily existence that pose a psychological barrier to the concept of doing business in or moving to another culture. Americans can readily travel from one state to another in search of jobs or to improve the quality of their lives, but will find that their daily routine is much the same; they will find the same shops, the same banking system, the same money, the same programmes on television and so on. In contrast, Europeans not only face a different language, but must also become used to social and functional differences. For example, they must learn new sets of social norms and new sets of road signs and traffic regulations, as well as accustom themselves to the different processes involved in renting or buying a home, taking out car insurance or opening a bank account. It is psychologically difficult enough for an American family to uproot itself and move hundreds of miles away, but while an Italian moving to Denmark or a Swede moving to Ireland can eventually learn how things are done locally, it involves a complex and perhaps lengthy process of acculturation. This is not the kind of problem that can be addressed by new EU laws.

Changes introduced by the Maastricht Treaty

The most notable of these was the promotion of the concept of European 'citizenship'. While this term is applied differently in different societies, in democracies it is usually taken to mean full and responsible membership of a state. This has been described by some social scientists as including the right to equality before the law, the right to own property, the right to freedom of speech and the right to a minimum standard of economic and social welfare. However these are all rights that legal non-citizens of democracies also enjoy.

What makes a citizen different from a non-citizen in practical terms is that a citizen can vote and run for elective office in his or her home state, can serve on a jury in that state, is eligible to serve in the armed forces of that state, can move freely throughout the territory of that state, cannot be forcibly removed from that state to another, owes allegiance to and has the right to receive protection from the state when outside its borders, is recognized as a member of that state by other governments, and must usually obtain the permission of other governments to travel through or live in their territory.

According to Maastricht 'every person holding the nationality of a Member State shall be a citizen of the Union', but given the features listed above, Europeans still have some way to go before they can truly be considered citizens of Europe. A step in that direction was taken with the agreement that citizens of a member state finding themselves in need in a non-European country where their home state has no diplomatic representation can receive protection from the diplomatic and consular authorities of any EU member that has a local office. However, while the limitations on voting and running for office have been eased, Europeans can only vote and stand for municipal and European Parliamentary elections outside their home states, and in some member states they are not even allowed to do that. Also, there are still limitations on the movement of Europeans within the EU – national laws prevent people with limited means from settling in another member state and drawing welfare benefits in that state, travellers still have to take some form of identification with them when they cross borders, and Europeans can still be deported to their 'home' state, as English football hooligans discovered during the 1998 World Cup in France.

Another change introduced by Maastricht was the creation of an ombudsman. If a citizen or a legal resident of any member state feels that any of the EU institutions (other than the Court of Justice and the Court of First Instance) is guilty of 'maladministration', and can put forward a compelling case, the European Parliament is required to ask the office of the European ombudsman to review the complaint, and if appropriate to carry out an investigation. The ombudsman, who is appointed for a five-year term that runs concurrently with the term of Parliament, is expected to be both impartial and independent of any government. The first ombudsman – Jacob Söderman – was appointed in 1995, and dealt with a growing number of complaints: nearly 300 in 1995, more than 840 in 1996 and more than 1400 in 1997. The Commission has been the target of most of the complaints, which have included charges that it has failed to carry out its responsibilities as guardian of the treaties, that it lacks sufficient transparency and that it has abused its power. The growing number of complaints is probably less a sign that things are getting worse than a sign that more people are becoming aware of the work of the ombudsman.

Changes not made

Some of the Adonnino committee's recommendations have yet to be implemented, including the creation of a European lottery, the introduction of common postage stamps and the establishment of a uniform electoral procedure for European elections. The latter idea was first outlined in the Treaty of Paris, repeated in the Treaty of Rome and raised again on several subsequent occasions, but little has been achieved in practical terms. Even the definition of the word 'uniform' in this context is debatable, and while a decision was taken at the 1974 Paris summit that the goal would be met if European elections were secret, direct, based on universal suffrage and held on the same day, this has not been the end of the story.

The most obvious structural problems with European elections are (1) they are not held on the same day in all the member states, (2) countries such as Germany use different electoral systems for national and European elections and (3) the member states use different forms of proportional representation (PR). For example, while Italy, Ireland and Belgium use regional lists and divide themselves into multiple constituencies, Denmark, France, Portugal and Spain use national lists and treat the whole country as one constituency. (Britain long used the same first-past-the-post system used for national and local elections, but adopted PR with effect from 1999 in order to fall into line with the rest of Europe.)

Dabbling with the structure of European elections does not really address the most fundamental weakness in the People's Europe programme: the absence of an electoral system that truly holds the institutions of the EU accountable to the wishes of the electorate. European elections are now held on a fixed five-year rotation, but the membership of neither the Commission nor the Council of Ministers changes as a result of the elections, the parties contesting the elections are still essentially national parties running on national platforms and using European elections to test their popularity at the national level, and while there are party groups within Parliament, there are still no truly pan-European parties.

* * *

The changes that have come out of the Adonnino committee's report have had an important effect on the psychological relationship between Europeans and the EU institutions, and have helped build a European identity that has made the EU more real to Europeans. Icons are an important element of 'belonging', and the European flag has played an important role in giving the EU a personality that goes beyond the work of its bureaucrats. Leaders have spoken of the need to promote the 'transparency' of European institutions, agreement of a uniform voting procedure is now an official EU goal and the Amsterdam treaty provides for greater access to the documents of EU institutions.

However a 'People's Europe' cannot be legislated. The idea that the citizens of the member states also belong to larger communal entity must take root and grow in their minds if it is to be at all effective. They must understand the implications of integration, they must see and directly experience the benefits of integration, and they must feel that they can have a real impact on the decisions of the European institutions through meaningful participation before the EU can have real significance in their lives.

Social policy

Full economic integration demands social cohesion, which requires investment not only in agriculture, industry and services, but also in social issues such as workers' rights, women's rights and improved working and living conditions (Box 6.3). The poorer European states have been concerned about new competition from economic powers such as Germany, while those with less progressive employment laws have worried that jobs will be lost to those with more progressive laws. Social policies are not only an outcome of the long history of welfare promotion in individual western European states, but are an important part of the drive to build a single market by ensuring equal opportunities and working conditions. They are also another channel through which the EU can reach its citizens, making more real to them the implications of European integration.

At the same time, social issues have proved controversial, and have led to some of the most bruising political battles the EU has witnessed since its foundation. While there is little question that one of the foundations of a workable single market is equal pay, equal working conditions and the provision of the kind of education and training that can help promote worker mobility, social policy treads on sensitive ideological and cultural toes. Conservatives and liberals will never agree on the best way of building a level social playing field, and programmes that may be seen as progressive by one member state may be seen as a threat to cultural identity by another. Generally speaking, national labour unions are in favour of EU social policy, as are the Commission and Parliament (dominated as it is by social democratic parties), while business interests and conservative political parties are opposed, arguing that social policy could make European companies less competitive in the global market (Geyer and Springer, 1998, p. 208).

Box 6.3 European social policy

The core of European social policy is contained in the Social Charter, which has brought together all the social policy goals mentioned at earlier stages in the life of the Community, but emphasizes general goals at the expense of specifics. An action programme lists 47 separate measures that needed to be taken to achieve the goals of the Charter, categorized under the following headings:

1. Improvement of living and working conditions.
2. The right to freedom of movement, including entitlement to equal treatment and the harmonization of conditions of residence.
3. The right to exercise any trade or occupation on the same terms as those applied to nationals of the host state, and to enjoy the same social protection as nationals of the host state in gainful employment.
4. Fair remuneration for all employment.
5. The right to social protection, including a minimum income for those unable to find employment or no longer entitled to employment benefits.
6. The right to freedom of association and collective bargaining.
7. The right to vocational training throughout a worker's working life.
8. The right of men and women to equal treatment.
9. The right to information, consultation and worker participation.
10. The right to health, safety and protection in the workplace.
11. A minimum working age of 16, protection of children and adolescents, and special vocational training for them.
12. A retirement income that is suffcient to allow a reasonable standard of living.
13. The best possible integration of disabled people into working life.

About half of these require legislation, but by the end of 1998 only four had been enacted: a directive that works councils for informing and consulting employees be set up in companies with more than 1000 employees and based in at least two member states, a directive prohibiting discrimination against part-time workers, and directives on parental leave and sex discrimination.

Social policy can be broadly defined as policy relating to the rights, opportunities and benefits provided to potential, actual or former workers. Relatively little attention was paid to such questions in the early days of the EEC: even though worker mobility and expansion of the skilled labour force were important parts of the idea of constructing a common market, concern about the competitive implications of different levels of social security payments and labour costs encouraged the EEC Six to avoid addressing social issues head-on during the negotiations leading up to the Treaty of Rome. The treaty ended up being based on the naive assumption that the benefits of the common market would improve life for all

European workers. That proved true to the extent that it helped increase wages, but market forces failed to deal with gender and age discrimination, wage disparities, different levels of unemployment, and safety and health in the workplace.

The Treaty of Rome made it the Community's business to deal with such issues as the free movement of workers, equal pay for equal work, working conditions, and social security for migrant workers, and Article 123 set the goal of creating a European Social Fund that would help promote worker mobility. However, social issues were pushed down the EEC agenda while it concentrated on completing the common market and resolving battles over agricultural policy, and the movement of workers was heavily restricted. Restrictions began to be eased so that labour shortages in the larger northern economies could be overcome. This led to an influx of immigrants from southern Europe, mostly from non-EC states such as Turkey, Yugoslavia, Greece, Portugal and Spain. By the early 1990s there were an estimated four million foreign workers in the 12 EU member states, about half of whom came from other EU states.

The worsening of economic disparities brought on by EEC enlargement in 1973 pushed social issues back up the agenda, and the first in a series of four-year Social Action Programmes (SAPs) was launched in 1974, aimed at developing a plan of action to achieve full employment, improved living and working conditions, and gender equality. A combination of recession and ideological resistance from several European leaders ensured that words failed to be translated into deeds, but the EEC did establish the European Social Fund (ESF) in 1974 to address long-term unemployment and create jobs and training schemes for young people. Spending under the ESF grew rapidly during the 1980s, the major recipients being Ireland, Greece, Spain and Britain. By 1998 the fund accounted for nearly 10 per cent of the EU budget (or just over 8.6 billion ecu).

One of the goals of the Single European Act was to enable Europeans to live and work wherever they liked in the EC, so the importance of social policy was underlined once again as questions were raised about the mobility of workers and about 'social dumping', a phenomenon in which money, services and businesses move to those parts of the EU with the lowest wages and social security costs. The Commission began to promote social policy more actively and tried to focus the attention of national governments on the 'social dimension' of the single market. However economic recession made sure that the SEA initially lacked such a dimension, encouraging Commission president Jacques Delors – a moderate socialist – to launch an attempt in 1988 to draw more attention to the social consequences of the single market.

The idea of a charter of basic social rights had been introduced by the Belgian presidency of the Council of Ministers in 1987, modelled on

Belgium's own new national charter. The idea was taken up by Jacques Delors in 1989, and was given a helping hand by the determination of the socialist government of François Mitterrand to promote social policy during the French presidency of the EC. Germany was also in favour, even though it was led by the moderate conservative government of Helmut Kohl, as were states with socialist governments, such as Spain and Greece. However the conservative Margaret Thatcher was vehemently opposed: she considered it 'quite inappropriate' for laws on working regulations and welfare benefits to be set at the Community level, and saw the Social Charter as 'a socialist charter – devised by socialists in the Commission and favoured predominantly by socialist member states' (Thatcher, 1993, p. 750). In the event, the Community Charter of Fundamental Social Rights of Workers (or the Social Charter) was adopted at the 1989 Strasbourg summit by 11 of the 12 member states, Britain refusing to go along.

The need for unanimity in the Council of Ministers on social legislation has meant that little progress has so far been made on turning principles into law. Britain under the Major government was usually painted as the key opponent of the Social Charter, but there have been heated debates involving several member states about issues such as working hours, maternity leave and employment benefits for part-time workers. There were plans to incorporate the Social Charter into Maastricht, but the Major government again refused to go along, so a compromise was reached whereby it was attached to the treaty as a social protocol. Britain was excluded from voting in the Council on social issues while the other 11 member states formed their own *ad hoc* Social Community. This all changed in 1997 when the newly elected Blair government committed Britain to the goals of the social protocol, and it was incorporated into the Treaty of Amsterdam.

Despite all the rhetoric about social issues, since 1991 most attention has been focused on just one problem: the failure of the EU to ease unemployment, the persistence of which was once described as equivalent to the persistence of poverty in the United States (Dahrendorf, 1988, p. 149). The single market has not been able to generate enough jobs for Europeans, and while unemployment in the United States and Japan hovered around 4 per cent in mid-1998, in the EU it ranged from about 4.5–7 per cent in the Netherlands, Britain and Denmark, to 11–12 per cent in France, Germany, Italy and Belgium, to a high of nearly 20 per cent in Spain (*The Economist*, June 1998). The average figure for the EU as a whole was just over 10 per cent, and while this was an improvement on 1997, more than 18 million Europeans were still out of work.

The reason why unemployment has remained so high is not clear, but at least part of the problem has been the relative weakness of trade unions and the relative ease with which workers can be laid off. Another factor is the size of the informal labour market in Europe, which accounts for as much as 15–30 per cent of GNP in some states (Krause, 1991, p. 82) and is all but institutionalized in southern Italy, where it overlaps with the destructive power of organized crime. The EU has launched a host of retraining programmes, and is shifting resources to the poorer parts of the EU through various regional and social programmes, but with mixed results. Geyer and Springer (1998, p. 210) argue that EU employment policy has had 'high visibility but little focus', and that the search for solutions is hampered by a lack of support in the member states, traditionally responsible for employment policy. They also note that the EU has the problem of trying to create jobs through increased competitiveness while preserving the traditional rights of employees.

The Amsterdam treaty introduced a new employment chapter that called on the member states to 'work towards developing a coordinated strategy for employment', but it only requires the Commission and the member states to report to each other, and leaves most of the responsibility for employment policy with the member states. In November 1997 the European Council met with unemployment as the sole item on its agenda, and agreed common guidelines on employment policy, including a fresh start for the young and the long-term unemployed, and simplified rules for small and medium-sized enterprises. Although millions of new jobs have been created in the EU over the last decade, nearly half are temporary or part-time jobs, many of them are in the service sector, and because most are being filled by men and women new to the job market, they have done little to help ease long-term unemployment.

Another issue on the social agenda has been an improvement in the status of women. Overall, the position of women in politics and the workforce in the EU is not that different from their relative position in other liberal democracies, but the situation varies from one member state to another, giving added significance to EU social policy and the goal of building economic and social cohesion. In general, women are in a better position in progressive northern European states such as Denmark, Finland and Sweden, and relatively worse off in poorer southern states such as Portugal, Spain and Greece.

Women make up about one third of the workforce in the EU. Nonetheless career options are still relatively limited, proportionately more women than men are employed in part-time jobs, and women are more likely to work in traditionally feminized jobs – such as nursing and teaching – than in management, and in the less well paid and more labour-intensive sectors of industry (Springer, 1992, p. 66). Unemployment figures are higher for women than for men in most EU states, and women are also paid less than men for comparable work – about 80 per cent of the

Box 6.4 European consumer protection policy

The EU began to concern itself with consumer issues in the mid-1970s, but consumer protection remained submerged under the economic goals of the single market programme until it was made an EU policy goal in its own right by Maastricht. Even then, however, it was agreed that initiatives by the EU must complement rather than replace national law, and member states are allowed to implement stronger regulations provided they do not pose a barrier to trade.

The major goals are to ensure that consumer interests are taken into account in the development of other policies, to improve the safety of consumer products and services, to improve consumer confidence and to strengthen the links between the Commission and consumer organizations. The earliest pieces of European law were aimed at the safety of cosmetics, the labelling of foodstuffs, misleading advertising (allowing consumers to complain to courts, which can then make advertisers prove the accuracy of their claims), product liability and the provision of consumer credit. With the single market programme, the generation of new laws increased, focusing on such issues as safety standards for toys and building materials, and new labelling requirements for food and agricultural products.

Notable recent EU initiatives include the following:

- A major 1993 amendment to a 1976 directive banning the marketing of cosmetics that contain ingredients tested on animals; however, because of the slowness of testing methods, it will not come into force until 2000.
- A 1995 directive removing barriers to the free movement of personal data but establishing common standards to protect individual rights and privacy.
- A 1997 directive allowing comparative advertising throughout the EU, thereby expanding a practice already allowed in Britain to member states such as Belgium, France and Germany.
- A 1997 directive requiring retailers clearly to indicate both the absolute price and the unit price of all products, which enables consumers to compare costs more easily. Until then, only France and Sweden had similar legislation.
- A general ban on tobacco advertising, first proposed in 1989, was finally made law in 1998, although Germany planned to challenge the law before the Court of Justice, claiming that it was a health measure rather than a single market measure, and hence did not come under the EU's remit (*European Policy Analyst*, 3rd quarter 1998).

wages earned by a man. On the plus side, about 75 per cent of working women are employed in the expanding service sector, all EU member states are legally obliged to provide maternity leave, several member states offer parental leave, and the public provision of child care is improving.

Although the rights of working women were mentioned in the Treaty of Rome (Article 119, for example, establishes the principle of equal pay for men and women), it was not until the EEC began to look more actively at social policy in the 1970s that women's issues began to be addressed. The 1974 SAP included the goal of achieving gender equality in access to employment and vocational training, and equal rights at work were promoted by new laws such as the 1975 equal pay directive and the 1976 equal treatment directive. Even though direct and indirect gender discrimination are illegal under EU law, however, women still face invisible barriers and glass ceilings.

The SEA and Maastricht were both more concerned with broad institutional reform than with human rights, and did little in specific terms to address gender imbalances. Springer (1992, pp. 72–3) argues that the single market may actually pose a threat both to the jobs that women hold and to the laws that protect them; little was done in the planning stages to anticipate how the changes would affect women, and not all the proposals made under the SAPs or related Commission white papers have the force of law, so compliance is voluntary.

Elitism and gender bias in the EU are exemplified by imbalances in the staffing of the major EU institutions. There were five women on the Commission in 1995–2000, but there had been none at all until the appointment of Vasso Papandreou of Greece in 1991. There are many more men than women in the more senior bureaucratic positions in the Commission and many more women than men in secretarial and clerical positions, the 1995–99 European Parliament had about 170 women MEPs (nearly 27 per cent of the total), there has never been a woman judge in the Court of Justice, and only two women – Margaret Thatcher and former French Prime Minister Edith Cresson – have ever taken part in meetings of the European Council.

Improving accountability

European integration began as an agreement among governments to cooperate in selected areas, and for much of its early life remained a process in which the power of decision making was restricted to those governments. As its effects began to spread, however, and to affect a growing number of people, it could no longer remain so limited a process. Nonetheless governments continue to move ahead with their decisions on

Europe using a decision-making structure that remains out of step with new realities. As Featherstone (1994, p. 168) puts it, the elitist and technocratic character of institution-building might have served its purpose in the 1950s, 'but its continuation in the 1990s threatens instability and an increasing lack of legitimacy in the system'.

Reformation of the European institutions has been on the agenda of a number of European Council meetings, but progress to date has been limited by the desire of the governments of the member states to keep as much control as possible over the decisions taken in the name of European integration. The discussions leading up to the Amsterdam treaty were an opportunity to address the problem, but they resulted in little substantial change: the equal roles of Parliament and the Council of Ministers in the legislative process were recognized, the legislative process in Parliament was simplified, the membership of Parliament was capped at 700, the powers of the Court of Justice were extended with regard to issues such as asylum, immigration and cooperation in police and judicial matters, and the powers of the Court of Auditors and the Committee of the Regions were increased.

Given that integration is having so much more impact on the lives of Europeans, it is arguably time for a new effort to be made to improve public understanding of the structure of the EU, and to strengthen the channels through which public opinion can be gauged and expressed. A useful place to start might be the development of a European constitution. One of the conclusions reached at Amsterdam was that the agreements underlying the EU had become increasingly complex and difficult to understand, consisting as they now do of a dozen basic treaties and acts, and protocols containing nearly 800 articles. However it was also decided that codifying the treaties without modifying everything that had already been agreed would be too complicated, and that an 'unofficial consolidation' would be more practical. This, however, was to avoid the issue.

By definition a constitution is a contract between a government and its citizens, outlining their relative powers, obligations and responsibilities. Every modern democratic state has a constitution, but they vary in terms of the extent to which they are followed and respected, and the extent to which they actually make sense; human society is so full of ambiguities and contradictions that constitutions need constant refinement to keep them efficient and relevant. To have any meaning a constitution must be respected, have stability and permanence, be comprehensible, be capable of being enforced and be grounded in the political and social character of the state or body to which it applies; the larger the gap between constitutional principles and political reality, the weaker the constitution.

The extent to which the EU treaties and laws meet these conditions is questionable. The European Court of Justice has helped 'constitutionalize' the founding treaties by trying to remove the differences between the Treaty of Rome and a conventional constitution, notably the lack of safeguards for individual rights, and the absence of a constitutional right to European citizenship (Mancini, 1991). However, each new treaty that is agreed and each new law that is passed makes the European 'constitution' increasingly messy. The main barrier to agreeing a constitution is that the EU is still evolving – constitutions work best when the system of government that is being committed to paper has achieved a high degree of stability and permanence, which is not the case in Europe; the EU institutions are a work in progress.

Nonetheless it could be argued that the long-term benefits of actively addressing the democratic deficit outweigh short-term concerns about the stage that EU institutions have reached in their evolution. The exercise of developing a European constitution may help focus the minds of leaders and citizens alike, and force them to think more actively about the nature of the entity they are building. Furthermore, democratic constitutions are never the final word, and can be amended and fine-tuned by changes in the law and judgements of a constitutional court. To date the powers of EU institutions have been allowed to grow in response to the evolving interests of the EU, but as Europeans better understand the impact that integration is having on their lives, public pressure for institutional reform will inevitably grow. Possible reforms include the following:

- The European Parliament might become a true legislature. For this to happen the power to initiate the law-making process would have to shift from the Commission to Parliament, the power to take final decisions on the adoption or rejection of new laws would have to shift from the Council of Ministers to Parliament, and Parliament would have to be given greater power over decisions on the EU budget. It should also be sited exclusively and permanently in Brussels, so that it is close to the Commission and the Council of Ministers.
- A second, upper chamber of Parliament might be created, providing a different level of representation from that offered by the present chamber. It might be something like the United States Senate, where every state has the same number of representatives, irrespective of size, or the German Bundesrat, where the number of representatives varies roughly according the population of each state. It would be difficult to justify giving 420 000 Luxembourgers the same representation as 82 million Germans, so the upper chamber might be based instead on providing representation to the more than 200 regions of the member states, or it might be based on sectoral interests, such as industry and the professions. The former have already been given advisory powers through the Committee of the Regions, and the latter through the

Economic and Social Committee, so the new chamber might evolve out of one or both of these committees. However the upper chamber is structured, it should have the same powers over legislation as the lower – all proposals would have to go through the same process of introduction, discussion, amendment and adoption before they could become law.

- The president of the European Commission could be directly elected by all eligible voters for a limited number of terms, and could have the right to appoint his or her own Commissioners, either from inside Parliament or – with Parliamentary approval – from outside. The Amsterdam treaty included an agreement that the president be given greater powers over selecting commissioners and exercising policy leadership, but future agreements will almost certainly lead to the president eventually being given similar executive powers to those of the president of the United States.
- The power of the European Commission could be restricted to policy implementation. In other words, it would have the same role as a conventional bureaucracy.
- Key appointments – such as those to the Court of Justice and senior positions in the Commission – could be made subject to parliamentary approval. Similarly, commissioners and directors-general could be called more often before Parliamentary committees to answer for their policy decisions and the performance of their departments.

The Amsterdam treaty fell short of meeting its primary objective of overhauling EU institutions in preparation for an expansion of membership. However it includes the agreement that at least one year before the membership of the EU grows to 20 states, an intergovernmental conference will be convened to carry out a 'comprehensive' review of the provisions of the treaties on the composition and powers of the institutions. Negotiations are already under way with six aspirant new members, so that figure will probably be reached – and passed – very soon. If past form is any indication, however, the desire of the leaders of the member states to keep their hands on the reins of power will ensure that the changes will be minimal.

Conclusions

The European Union has helped redefine the relationship among Europeans. Where they have long identified themselves in national terms, and have been tied economically, legally and culturally to one nation-state or another, the reduction of the barriers to trade and to movement over the past decade has encouraged the inhabitants of the European Union to think of themselves as part of a larger entity. Common social policies have resulted in key powers over the lives of individual Europeans shifting to Brussels, so that an increasing number of Europeans feel the effect of decisions made at the EU level. Personal mobility has increased and, cultural barriers aside, Europeans have taken more interest in neighbours who have long been considered as 'foreign', rivals and occasionally a direct threat to their own national interests.

However, while this horizontal integration has been taking place, the ability of Europeans directly to influence the European Union has lagged. European integration has been driven by the priorities and the values of the leaders of the member states, who have made the majority of their decisions with limited reference to their citizens. The result has been the creation of a European governing structure that is only indirectly accountable to the views of the vast majority of people who live within it. European law is proposed and implemented by unelected bureaucrats in the European Commission, decisions are taken by elected national representatives meeting either as the European Council or as the Council of Ministers, and the only institution that represents European citizens – the European Parliament – has limited powers over the other institutions.

As European leaders struggle to sell the concept of European integration to their citizens, they handicap themselves by failing to provide effective channels of accountability, and by perpetuating the democratic deficit. Changes made under the People's Europe programme and as a result of changes to the Treaty of Rome have made Europe more real to its citizens, but uniform passports, a European flag and student exchange programmes fall far short of the kinds of change needed to make Europeans feel as though they are truly connected to the EU, rather than connected only through their national governments. The democratic deficit can only be addressed by a wholesale reform of the EU institutions aimed at making them accountable to the citizens of Europe instead of to the leaders of the member states.

Chapter 7

Economic Integration

Completing the single market
Effects of the single market
Agriculture in Europe
Towards a single currency
Conclusions

For most of its short life, the European Union has been driven mainly by the goal of economic integration. Its members set out with the narrow goal of cooperating on coal and steel production, worked in the 1960s to complete a customs union and build a common agricultural policy, wrestled during the 1970s with attempts to agree common economic policies and achieve exchange rate stability, focused in the late 1980s on completing the single market, and are now working on their most ambitious project to date: replacing their national currencies with a single European currency, the euro.

The priority given to economic integration was made clear from the outset in three of the primary goals of the Treaty of Rome. The first was the creation of a customs union, whereby all tariff barriers and other obstacles to trade among EEC members would be removed, and agreement reached on a common external tariff so that all goods coming into the EEC – irrespective of their point of entry – would be subject to exactly the same costs and controls. A related goal was the agreement of a common commercial policy towards third countries (see Chapter 8).

The second major goal of the Treaty of Rome was the creation of a European common market, meaning the agreement of rules that would allow the free movement of people, goods, services and money among the members of the Community. In order to achieve this, the member states had to develop a common competition policy by minimizing or abolishing state aid and subsidies to national industries so as to avoid economic distortions, break down monopolies and cartels and harmonize national health and safety standards. Finally, the member states also agreed to develop a common agricultural policy by ensuring that farmers were paid guaranteed prices for their produce, and that agricultural markets were stabilized and food supplies assured.

The customs union was completed without much fanfare with the agreement of a common external tariff in 1968, but non-tariff barriers to trade persisted, including variations in technical standards and quality controls, different health and safety standards and different rates of indirect taxation. The gap between the dream and the reality of the common market widened in the mid-1970s as recession encouraged member states to think more about protecting their national markets than about building a European market. Meanwhile the common agricultural policy soaked up more and more Community funds and led to massive overproduction by European farmers.

The mood changed in the 1980s with the sense that something radical needed to be done to reverse the EC's relative economic decline, and a new sense of direction needed to be given to the common market programme in order to respond to the superiority of the United States and Japan in high technology industries. It was considered essential for the Community to exploit the potential of its own market, which had almost as many consumers as the United States and Japan combined. Reducing duplication of effort, encouraging joint research, paving the way for trans-European corporate mergers and removing the final barriers to European companies doing business in all the member states would reduce costs and improve efficiency and competitiveness (Cecchini, 1988). It was this change of thinking that produced the Single European Act (SEA), which led to reforms in the Common Agricultural Policy (CAP) and attempts to build exchange rate stability in the EU as a prelude to the creation of a single European currency.

Completing the single market

The Cockfield report of 1985 provided a list of specific steps that needed to be taken to complete the internal market (Commission, 1985). As discussed in Chapter 3, this became the basis of the Single European Act of 1986, which came into force in 1987. Its goal was to remove the remaining non-tariff barriers to the free movement of people, goods, services and capital within five years. Those barriers took three main forms: physical, fiscal and technical.

Physical barriers

Customs and border checks persisted at the EC's internal frontiers because national governments wanted to control the movement of people (especially illegal immigrants), to collect tax and excise duty on goods being moved from one state to another, and to enforce differing health standards. Not only did these barriers continue to remind Europeans of their differences, thereby posing a psychological block to integration, but they were also a significant economic constraint, a problem that was compounded by inconsistencies in border checks. Anyone driving from one Benelux country to another, for example, simply had to slow down as they crossed the border, and customs officials would decide on the spot whether or not a check was needed. Meanwhile train travellers could be vetted by customs and police officials, while air travellers went through rigorous security controls.

Barriers to the movement of goods were removed in stages. Despite the 1968 agreement on customs union, most goods remained subject to cross-border checks in the interests of enforcing trade quotas, controlling banned products, collecting taxes and preventing the spread of plant and animal diseases. These checks were costly and time-consuming. The first step towards simplifying the process came in 1988 with a decision to do away with administrative checks at internal frontiers by agreeing common laws as quickly as possible. A second step was taken with the consolidation of paperwork; the more than 130 different forms used by different customs authorities were replaced between 1985 and 1988 by a Single Administrative Document (SAD), the use of which was in turn almost entirely abandoned in January 1993.

One troublesome issue remains the control of drug trafficking and terrorism. Terrorist groups operating in Britain, France, Germany and Italy have long had informal links with each other, which to some extent have been made controllable by the existence of national frontiers. The SEA does not affect the right of member states to take whatever action they think necessary to control terrorism, drugs trafficking, trade in arts and antiques and immigration from outside the EU as this does not interfere with trade. At the same time, the member states are working towards common measures on visas, immigration, extradition and political asylum. The goal is not so much to stop terrorists moving from one member state to another as to halt them at the EU's external borders. This means ensuring that border controls are equally effective; in the past, terrorists have found it easier to enter countries such as Greece and Portugal than Britain or Germany.

A 'fast-track' for the removal of border controls was launched in 1985 with the signature of the Schengen Agreement by France, Germany and the Benelux countries. Named after the town in Luxembourg near which it was signed, the agreement came into force in 1995 but remained informal until the Treaty of Amsterdam brought it under the umbrella of the EU. However, the removal of controls has taken longer than originally hoped. Thanks mainly to problems with the setting up of the computerized Schengen Information System, which provides police and customs officials with access to a database of undesirables whose entry into 'Schengenland' they want to control, it was not until March 1995 that almost all customs and passport controls were finally eliminated by France, Germany, Spain, Portugal and the Benelux countries. This has meant the free circulation of EU and non-EU citizens, common rules on asylum, the right of hot pursuit across frontiers, and steps towards a common policy on visas. Among other things, airline passengers flying between the Schengen states now leave from domestic rather than international airport terminals and do not have to go through customs or passport controls.

Britain has so far refused to join the agreement, citing its concern about security and the particular requirements of an island state, and Ireland has been unable to join because of its customs arrangements with Britain. Meanwhile agreement has been reached to combine the passport union of Denmark, Finland, Iceland, Norway, and Sweden with Schengenland, so that passport-free travel will now be possible from the Mediterranean to the Arctic (although all travellers still need to carry some form of identification).

In order to help deal with concerns arising from the removal of internal border controls, the EU is also working towards intra-EU police cooperation, to which end the European Police Office (Europol) was created in 1995. Based in The Hague, Europol's initial role was as an intelligence service, gathering and analysing information to support the work of national police forces. The priorities agreed among the EU member states were to deal with drug trafficking, illicit trafficking in radioactive and nuclear materials, illegal immigration, money laundering and organized crime, not only from internal sources, but from Turkey, Poland, Russia and Colombia. By 1997 Europol's interests had expanded to include terrorist activities. Modelled in part on Interpol, the global police organization, Europol is building a computer database that can be accessed by its liaison offices in the member states, and by national police forces in the interests of building cooperation across borders.

Fiscal barriers

Indirect taxation causes distortion of competition and artificial price differences, and as such constitutes a barrier to trade. Thanks in part to the influence of the EEC, all member states introduced value added tax (VAT) in the 1970s, but rates in the 1980s varied from as low as 12 per cent in Luxembourg to as high as 22 per cent in Denmark. This was one reason why border controls on the movement of goods persisted; because VAT was paid at the point of purchase, refunds could be claimed for exported goods and imports could be subject to additional charges.

Excise duties also varied, reflecting the different degrees of national concern about human health. Smokers in France, for example, paid nearly twice as much duty on cigarettes as those in Spain, smokers in Ireland four times as much and smokers in Denmark six times as much. Travellers felt the effects of the varying levels of indirect taxation when they tried to take home alcohol, tobacco products and other consumer items bought duty-free en route or duty-paid in another country. For example, British visitors to France could buy French wine much more cheaply than at home, but were allowed to take back only limited quantities into Britain – excess quantities were subject to duty.

Agreement was reached in 1991 on a minimum VAT rate of 15 per cent, with lower rates on basic necessities such as food, and in 1992 various minimum rates were agreed on excise duties. In July 1993 an agreement came into force whereby VAT was collected at the local rate in the country to which the goods and services were going. Agreement has since been reached on an EU-wide VAT system in which tax is collected only in the country of origin, the ultimate goal being a single rate of VAT, or at least variations within a very narrow band. Controversially, duty-free sales have been abolished for those travelling within the EU, effective as of July 1999; critics have charged that the benefits for the single market will be marginal, while the costs in terms of lost jobs and reduced sales will be substantial.

Technical barriers

The EEC was able to do little to address the persistence of different technical regulations and standards among the member states, a problem that seemed to pose an almost insurmountable barrier to the single market. Most of these regulations were based on different safety, health, environmental and consumer protection standards, and many seemed petty and inconsequential: for example the low cocoa butter content in British chocolate prevented it from being sold as such in many member states, and Germany insisted that no beer could be sold in Germany that did not meet the local 'purity laws'. At one level, technical standards were in the interests of consumer safety; at another they amounted to economic protectionism. There was an attempt to remove technical barriers by developing EC-wide standards and encouraging the member states to conform, but this was a time-consuming and tedious task and did little to discourage the common image of interfering Eurocrats.

Three breakthroughs helped simplify the process. First, the 1979 Cassis de Dijon decision by the Court of Justice established the principle of mutual recognition. West Germany had prevented the importation of a French blackcurrant liqueur, Cassis de Dijon, on the ground that its alcohol content was below the minimum set by the West German government for fruit liqueurs. The importer charged that this represented a restriction on imports of the kind prohibited under the Treaty of Rome. The Court of Justice agreed, and thereafter member states had to accept products from other states that met the domestic technical standards of those states. With regard to trade in foodstuffs, for example, the implication was that a member state could not block imports from another member state on the basis of local health regulations. This helped clear the way for the free movement of goods and services where there is no specific EU law, although the Commission still receives about 300 complaints a year about obstacles to trade.

Second, the 1983 mutual information directive required member states to inform the Commission and the other member states of their intention to introduce new domestic technical regulations, and to allow the others three months to respond if they felt these would create new barriers to trade. Finally, the Cockfield report included a 'new approach' to technical regulation: instead of the Commission trying to work out agreements on every rule and regulation, the Council of Ministers would agree laws with general objectives, and detailed specifications could then be drawn up by existing private standards institutes, such as the European Standardization Committee (CEN) or the European Electrotechnical Standardization Committee (CENELEC)

These three arrangements helped clear away many bureaucratic and political hurdles. Progress has been made on regulations for road vehicles, for example, where nearly 50 directives have been agreed on everything from the brilliance of headlights to the depth of tyre treads and limits on exhaust emissions. There is also greater agreement on food content, and since 1990 food manufacturers in all EU member states have had to print details about the nutritional content of their products on the packaging.

There has been less progress in other areas however. The pharmaceuticals industry (with more than $30 billion in sales per year) is still fragmented, although the work of the European Agency for the Evaluation of Medicinal Products is helping the process of harmonization. Free trade also continues to be handicapped by technical differences that the marketplace is powerless to overcome. For example television systems are different throughout the EU, obliging manufacturers to make eight different kinds of television set. Most member states use the German PAL system of TV broadcasting, but the French use their own, called SECAM. Similarly, the design of electrical plugs and sockets differs from one member state to another, forcing travellers to take an adapter with them wherever they go. In 1992 CENELEC announced that it planned to begin developing a common plug, and put the total cost of rewiring homes and businesses at $1.2 billion, a figure that will probably prove hopelessly conservative.

Effects of the single market

The Single European Act was the most radical of all the steps taken in the process of European integration since the signing of the treaties of Paris and Rome. As well as accelerating economic integration, it has also had a number of more tangible effects on the lives of Europeans.

Right of residence

As noted in Chapter 6, the Treaty of Rome allowed Europeans only a limited right to stay for any length of time in EEC countries other than their own, seeing migration mainly in terms of its economic benefits. In other words, migration was tied to occupation, and individuals who wanted to take up residence in another country were assessed on the basis of the skills they brought with them. In the last few years, however, this right has been expanded to the point where almost any resident of an EU member state can now live and work in any other EU member state, open a bank account, take out a mortgage, transfer unlimited amounts of capital and even vote (in some countries) in local and European elections. A few restrictions remain, but they are relatively minor. For example students must obtain annual residence permits, must be enrolled in a college and must be able to support themselves. Retirees and people of independent means are given five-year renewable residence permits, and pensions are not yet entirely transferable to other countries, although work is under way on making it possible for workers to move their pensions with them.

Joint ventures and corporate mergers

European corporations have a long history of transnational mergers, producing such giants as Unilever, Royal Dutch Shell (both Anglo-Dutch) and Asea Brown Boveri (Sweden and Switzerland). Despite this, between 1950 and the early 1980s European companies lost markets at home and abroad to competitors first from the United States and then from Japan. With the revival of competitiveness pushed to the top of the EC agenda, the Commission became actively involved in trying to overcome market fragmentation and the emphasis placed by national governments on promoting the interests of (often state-owned) 'national champions'. The EC also launched new programmes aimed at encouraging research on information technology, advanced communications, industrial technologies and weapons manufacture (Tsoukalis, 1993, pp. 49–51).

Among the more notable joint ventures have been those between Thompson of France and Philips of the Netherlands on high-definition television, Pirelli of Italy and Dunlop of Britain on tyres, BMW and

Box 7.1 European cooperation and the aerospace industry

The possibilities and potential benefits of multinational cooperation among Europeans – and the nature of European economic integration itself – are well illustrated by the aerospace industry. Western Europe has long been a major producer of civilian and military aircraft, and was once home to some of the greatest names in aircraft production, including Vickers, Hawker Siddeley, Messerschmitt and Dassault. But rationalization, competition and other economic pressures led to mergers and closures, and many of the old manufacturers became part of massive new national corporations. In Britain, for example, by 1986 the 19 aircraft producers of the 1940s had been whittled down to just one, British Aerospace (Owen and Dynes, 1992, pp. 162–3). At the same time the United States and the USSR were producing most of the world's military aircraft, and the civilian airliner market was dominated by Boeing, McDonnell-Douglas and Lockheed.

One of the earliest European joint ventures in civil aircraft resulted in the Anglo-French Concorde, a high-technology product but a commercial disappointment. A less ambitious and much more successful joint venture has been gaining ground since 1970 in the form of Airbus Industrie, a European consortium that has become the only significant competitor in the civil aircraft market dominated by the United States, and which turns in healthy profits. The Airbus consortium is made up of Aérospatiale of France and DaimlerChrysler Aerospace (Dasa) of Germany (37.9 per cent each), British Aerospace (20 per cent) and CASA of Spain (4.2 per cent). It produces seven different airliners, which between them have captured 30 per cent of the

→

Rolls-Royce on aeroengines, and among the 14 states collaborating in the European Space Agency (ESA), set up in 1973 to promote European cooperation in space research (see also Box 7.1). ESA members include Switzerland, Norway and all the EU member states except Greece, Luxembourg and Portugal. The largest shares of its budget come from France (21.5 per cent), Germany (17.2 per cent), Italy (11.3 per cent) and Britain (4.9 per cent). Twelve European countries have also cooperated in the development of Arianespace, a space-launch consortium owned by governments and state-owned companies (France has a stake of just over 50 per cent). Since the launch of the first in its series of Ariane rockets in 1979 from Kourou in French Guiana, Arianespace has won more than half the global market for commercial satellite launching, eating into a business long dominated by the United States.

The single market has also helped encourage the growth of new pan-European businesses seeking to profit from the opportunities it offers, and looking to create 'world-size' companies to compete more effectively with

→

global market for passenger aircraft with more than 100 seats (Airbus Industrie Homepage, 1998). It also has plans to build the world's largest aircraft, the 550–seat A3XX, although feedback from potential customers has been discouraging.

Discussions are currently under way that may lead to the merger of Aérospatiale, Dasa and British Aerospace, and the creation of what is already being called the European Aerospace and Defence Company. The idea was prompted by the argument that economies of scale give US corporations such as Boeing and Lockheed an advantage over the big three European industries, whose national markets are too small to sustain them. Agreement has been reached in principle on the merger, but the stumbling block remains the unwillingness of the French government to reduce its stake in Aérospatiale (currently just under 50 per cent).

Meanwhile Europeans have also made significant strides in the market for military aircraft. Individual member states still make competitive products, for example France's Mirage jet fighters, and Britain's Harrier jump jets, but are finding that it makes better commercial sense to pool their resources. One of the most successful European collaborations to date has been the profitable Tornado fighter-bomber (a British–German–Italian collaboration), which played a critical role in the 1990–91 Gulf War. Another project, which has been in the pipeline since 1985, is the Typhoon (formerly Eurofighter, a British–German–Italian–Spanish joint venture). The Europeans have also been dipping their toes in the market for military transport aircraft, currently dominated by the United States with planes such as the Hercules, made by Lockheed.

the United States and Japan. The last ten years have seen an unprecedented surge of mergers and acquisitions, notably in the chemicals, pharmaceuticals and electronics industries. In 1989–90 there were 622 mergers and acquisitions in the EC, and for the first time the number of intra-EC mergers overtook the number of national mergers (Owen and Dynes, 1992, p. 222). In 1996 the value of cross-border mergers reached a record $253 billion; the European mergers and acquisitions market is now about two thirds the size of that in the United States, and is likely to overtake the US market in the next few years. The following are notable recent examples: the 1992 purchase by Air France of a 37.5 per cent stake in the Belgian airline Sabena; the merger between Zurich Group and the insurance operations of British American Tobacco to create a new $36 billion insurance company; the 1996 merger between Ciba-Geigy and Sandoz to create Novartis (the world's second largest drug group), and the takeover by BMW of the British car manufacturers Rover Group and Rolls-Royce in 1994 and 1998, respectively.

At the same time there has been a concern about large corporations developing monopolies and overwhelming smaller businesses, so the EU has developed a controversial competition policy to prevent abuses such as price fixing, and to monitor potential 'abuses of a dominant position' by bigger companies (Cini and McGowan, 1998). The 1989 merger regulation allows the European Commission to scrutinize all large mergers (even those involving companies based outside the EU that might have an effect on EU business), and the Commission also keeps an eye on the effect of state subsidies on competition in trade (Allen, 1996b).

A European transport system

Markets are only as close as the ties that bind them, and one of the priorities of economic policy in the EU has been to build Trans-European Networks (TENs) aimed at integrating 15 different transport, energy supply and telecommunications systems, thereby pulling the EU together and promoting mobility. Until 1987, harmonization of the transport sector was one of the great failures of the common market – little of substance had been done to deal with problems such as an airline industry split along national lines (see below), time-consuming cross-border checks on trucks, national systems of motorways that do not connect with each other, air traffic control systems using 20 different operating systems and 70 computer programming languages, and telephone lines incapable of carrying advanced electronic communications. Two phenomena have begun to make a difference.

First, there has been a dramatic increase in tourism. Not only is Europe the biggest tourist destination in the world, capturing nearly 60 per cent of the world tourist trade (World Trade Organization, 1996), but Europeans are now travelling in much greater numbers to each other's countries, which has helped break down prejudices, made Europeans more familiar with each other, and encouraged greater cooperation on transportation by increasing the demand for cheap and easy access. Tourism now employs an estimated 35 million Europeans (more than 8 per cent of the workforce), accounts for about 6 per cent of the EU GDP and has brought economic development to rural areas (Hall, 1998, pp. 311–12). The six major tourist destinations in 1997 were France, Italy, Spain, Britain, Germany and Austria, which between them earned nearly 105 billion ecu from tourism.

Second, the rail industry has been revitalized as a cost-efficient and environmentally friendly alternative to road and air transport. The EU has hopes of developing a 35 000km, high-speed train (HST) network connecting Europe's major cities; the building of the $15 billion Eurotunnel under the channel between Britain and France and of a bridge between Sjaelland and Fyn in Denmark have been important pieces in the jigsaw. France has led the way in new technology with its high-speed TGV, which needs special new track, and Germany with its ICE network, which can use existing track. With trains travelling at 200–300 kph (some of them with coaches finished to luxury standard), the HST system has cut travel times considerably. Germany even has a long-term plan to replace the bulk of domestic air services with a system of very high-speed trains (VHSTs), based in part on floating maglev technology. Among the possible hurdles to the development of a European HST system are the high costs involved, the fact that most national rail companies are state-owned monopolies that plan in national rather than EU terms, and the tension between centralizing and decentralizing decision making in the EU (Magiera, 1991).

The development of TENs is now one of the priorities of the EU, and the European Commission has proposed a programme aimed at improving transport links within the EU; it will cost a projected 400 billion ecu by 2010, and will involve the building of 70 000km of railway track (including 22 000km of new and upgraded track for HSTs) and 15 000km of new roads, mainly on the outer edges of the EU. Among the priority projects identified by the European Council are a 20 billion ecu North–South HST link between Berlin and Verona, a 13 billion ecu HST link between Paris, Brussels, Cologne, Amsterdam and London, new motorways for Greece, a motorway link between Portugal and Spain, a rail/road link between Denmark and Sweden, and a 1400-km Ireland–UK–Benelux road link.

Open skies over Europe

One of the most notable changes in the European marketplace since the 1980s has been the loosening of regulations on air transport (see Armstrong and Bulmer, 1998, ch.7). Because most European states are too small to support a significant domestic industry, the majority of air traffic in Europe is international. Until the 1980s most European countries had their own state-owned carriers (for example Air France, Lufthansa and Alitalia) which played an influential part in the making of national air transport policy and had a national monopoly over most of the international routes they flew. The result was that air transport was highly regulated and very expensive to consumers.

Changes began in the mid-1980s when the Thatcher government launched a liberalization programme in Britain (leading to the privatiza- tion of British Airways in 1987) and negotiated bilateral agreements with several other EU member states. Meanwhile the European Civil Aviation Conference recommended liberalization, as did a number of national and European interest groups (notably those representing consumers) and the idea was taken up by the European Commission and incorporated into the

Cockfield report. Britain was most actively in favour, Germany and France provided limited support, and states with smaller or less efficient national carriers – such as Spain, Italy and Denmark – were opposed.

Against this background, three packages of laws and regulations worked their way through the EU institutions in 1987–92. These substantially opened up the market and led to a restructuring of the air transport market. Large carriers have taken over smaller ones, national carriers have created international alliances, and there has been a growth in the number of cut-price operators such as Virgin. More importantly, consumers now have greater choice and can fly much more cheaply than before; happily the days when it was cheaper to fly from London to Madrid via New York (Owen and Dynes, 1992, p. 208) are gone.

Broadcasting, the film industry and telecommunications

The mass media play an important role in shaping and determining the extent to which people feel they belong to a community with common interests. The building of European media as a contribution towards the creation of a European identity has moved slowly up the EU agenda, but has so far achieved little. An attempt was made in the mid-1980s to launch a daily European newspaper, *The European*, but it was published in Britain in English. The five-nation Europa-TV consortium, which hoped to transmit multilingual TV broadcasts to five million homes in the EC, collapsed in 1986 after amassing huge debts. More recently, Euronews was created in 1993 as a multilingual European response to CNN, but its record to date has not been hopeful. (Headquartered in France, it is owned jointly by 18 European broadcasters.)

A 'Television Without Borders' directive was agreed in 1989 in an attempt to promote the development of a single market in TV broad-casting, which the Commission saw as an important part of the broader single market project that would provide for minimum standards on advertising, the protection of minors and right of reply. The Commission has also tried to become involved in the regulation of satellite broad-casting, but has found the technology developing faster than the Commission could respond and its involvement has also been criticized by several member states, which have argued that it has no competence in that area.

The biggest problem is market fragmentation. The volume of produc-tion is not in doubt – nearly 670 films were produced in the EU in 1996, compared with just 421 in the United States (Eurostat, 30 March 1998) – but European film producers tend to focus on their own national markets. This makes them too small to compete on the European or international markets, which are dominated by productions coming out of the United

States, Britain and other English-speaking countries. Coproductions occasionally succeed – usually those made in English.

In an attempt – probably a futile one – to control the cultural inroads of Anglo-American broadcasting, and to protect the European cinema and electronics industries from American and Japanese competition, a directive was adopted in 1989 on television broadcasting to ensure that broadcasters, 'where practicable', use a majority of European programming. This has been criticized as being contrary to the European tradition of encouraging cultural interaction with other parts of the world, and as preventing freedom of expression and information (Fratianni and von Hagen, 1992, pp. 30–1). It faces other problems as well: for example American TV shows are more popular on the continent than much of the locally produced material, which is why US programme sales grew from $330 million in 1984 to nearly $6 billion in 1996. At the same time, Europeans tend not to much like each other's programming (the French, the Germans and the British, for example, have very different senses of humour). Finally, the twin assault of American programming provided by CNN and MTV, and of Anglo-American programming provided by British satellite companies such as Sky TV and British Satellite Broadcasting, is a difficult one to beat.

While the film and TV markets will probably remain fragmented for cultural reasons, the telecommunications market is rapidly integrating for commercial reasons. In an effort to improve trans-European links and to pave the way for increased traffic, basic telephone services have been liberalized in every member state except Spain, Portugal, Ireland and Greece (which have been given a deadline of 2003), work is under way on an Integrated Service Digital Network (ISDN), which will allow the transmission of voice, data and images through telephone lines, and member states are being encouraged to remove the need for different sets of licences and regulatory approval, and to end monopolies on mobile phone services.

While considerable progress has been made since 1987 on completion of the single market, work still remains to be done. In June 1997 the Commission launched a Single Market Action Plan aimed at encouraging a political commitment to completion of the single market by January 1999. This divided the remaining requirements into three groups: those that could be quickly implemented because they did not need new EU legislation, those that had already been proposed but still needed approval from Parliament and the Council of Ministers, and those that were more complex, such as the reworking of the VAT system. As of November 1997 about 27 per cent of the nearly 1340 existing single-market-related directives had still not been implemented in all member states (*Eurecom*, December 1997).

Agriculture in Europe

Agriculture is a low priority for most Western governments, and draws much less public attention than economic or foreign policy. However it has long been a headline issue in the European Union (although perhaps less today than a few years ago). It employs just 5 per cent of the workforce and accounts for just 3 per cent of EU GDP, yet it has variously been the biggest, most expensive, most complex and sometimes most contentious of all the policy areas in which the EU has become involved. The EU has more powers over agriculture than over any other policy area, it has passed more legislation on agriculture than on any other single policy area, almost as much of the EU budget is spent on agriculture as on all other policy areas combined, and there is more political activity on agriculture than on almost any other policy area. Only the foreign ministers meet more often than the agriculture ministers, for example, and the Commission's agricultural office (DGVI) is the second biggest of all its directorates-general.

Agricultural policy is also different from other EU policy areas in two more important respects. First, while barriers have been removed and markets opened up in almost every area of EU economic activity, agriculture remains heavily interventionist. The EU has taken a hands-on approach to keeping agricultural prices high, drawing criticism not only from within the EU but from the EU's major trading partners. Second, unlike most other EU policy areas, agricultural policy was built in to the Treaty of Rome, where the commitment to a Common Agricultural Policy (CAP) was spelt out more clearly than was the case for any other policy area, although the details were only agreed in the 1960s. Why does agriculture have such a high profile?

The main reason is that, at the time the Treaties of Rome were being negotiated, agriculture sat high on the agendas of European governments; it was important to their economies and to their cultures. The Second World War had made Europeans aware of just how much they depended on imported food, and just how prone those imports were to disruption. Furthermore, agriculture still accounted for about 12 per cent of the GNP of the Six, and about one fifth of employment. Agricultural intensification after the war led to a big fall in agricultural imports from outside western Europe and a growth in trade among Community members, but the drive for self-sufficiency had a key formative influence on agricultural policy and its affects have not yet gone away.

Second, it was a key element in the trade-off between Germany and France when the EEC was first discussed (Grant, 1997, pp. 63–8). France was concerned that the common market would benefit German industry while providing the French economy with relatively few benefits. France had a large and efficient agricultural sector in the mid-1950s, accounting for 12 per cent of GNP and employing about 25 per cent of the French workforce (von der Groeben, 1987, pp. 71–2). Concern that the common market would hurt its farmers encouraged the French government to insist on a protectionist system. Even though this was to prove expensive, any mention of changing the system brought (and still brings) protesting French farmers out in their thousands.

Third, agricultural prices are more subject to fluctuation than prices on most other goods, and since Europeans spend about a quarter of their incomes on food, those fluctuations can have knock-on effects throughout the economy. Price increases can contribute to inflation, while price decreases can force farmers to go deeper into debt, perhaps leading to bankruptcy and unemployment. The problem of maintaining minimum incomes has been exacerbated by mechanization, which has led to fewer people working in farming in Europe. European governments felt that subsidies could help prevent or offset some of these problems and encourage people to stay in rural areas rather than move to towns and cities, perhaps adding to unemployment problems.

Finally, farmers in the richer EU states have traditionally had strong unions working for them. As well as national unions, more than 150 EU-wide agricultural organizations have been formed, many of which directly lobby the EU. Among these is the Committee of Professional Agricultural Organizations (COPA), which represents farmers on a wide range of issues. Not only are farmers an influential lobby in the EU, but there are many other people who live in rural areas, and many rurally based services. Farmers and the residents of small towns and villages add up to a sizable proportion of the population, and of the vote. No political party can afford to ignore that vote, especially as there is little organized resistance to the agricultural and rural lobbies, either at the national or at the EU level.

No discussion of EU agricultural policy would be complete without mentioning the special case of France. French farmers account for barely one in 35 French workers (or about 0.4 per cent of the total EU population), yet they have enormous influence over the French government, which goes out to bat on their behalf in the halls and corridors of Brussels, helping underpin the centrality of agricultural spending in the EU budget, and causing spillover effects on other EU policy areas. In large part the farming lobby owes its influence to economic factors: more than 20 per cent of all EU agricultural produce comes from France, it is the world's second largest exporter of food after the United States, and subsidies account for more than one third of French farmers' incomes (Grant, 1997, p. 48).

However some of the explanation also lies in the role the countryside plays in the French national psyche. Even though three in every four

French citizens live in towns or cities, the rural idyll still has a strong nostalgic hold on the sentiments of many, as does the idea that France is still a great power. The Italian journalist Luigi Barzini once argued that 'foreigners have to remind themselves that they are not dealing with a country that really exists . . . but with a country that most Frenchmen dream still exists. The gap between the two is a large one, but the French indefatigably try to ignore it or forget it' (Barzini, 1983, p. 124). CAP provided a captive market for French agricultural products, and attempts to reform it have always been seen as a direct threat to the rural sector in France. Even urban voters are prepared to come to the defence of their rural compatriots, and this is where the real political significance of the French rural lobby comes into play.

Box 7.2 The Common Fisheries Policy

The EU has a Common Fisheries Policy (CFP), the main goal of which has been to resolve conflicts over territorial fishing rights and prevent overfishing by setting catch quotas. Even though fishing employs just 0.2 per cent of the EU workforce, the state of the fishing industry has implications for coastal communities all around the EU. Disputes over fishing grounds in European waters have occasionally led to bitter confrontation between EU partners and their neighbours, for example the infamous cod wars of the 1960s between Britain and Iceland over access to fisheries in the north Atlantic. Similarly, in 1984 French patrol boats fired on Spanish trawlers operating inside the Community's 200-mile limit, and more than two dozen Spanish trawlers were intercepted off the coast of Ireland. Spain's fishing fleet was bigger than that of the entire EC fleet at the time, and fishing rights were a major issue in Spain's negotiations to join the EC. More recently, Spanish fishing boats became an issue in domestic British politics when Eurosceptics in the Major government quoted their presence in traditional British waters as one of the many deleterious effects of British membership of the EU.

The attempts to resolve competing claims to fishing grounds and develop an equitable management plan for Community fisheries were bitter and controversial, but they resulted in agreement on the CFP in 1983. The CFP regulates fisheries in four main ways. First, all the waters within the EU's 200-mile limit are open to all EU fishing boats, but member states have the right to restrict access to fishing grounds within 12 miles of their shores. Second, it prevents overfishing by imposing national quotas (or 'total allowable catches') on the landing of Atlantic and North Sea fish, and by regulating fishing areas and equipment, for example by setting standards on the mesh size of fishing nets. Third, it set up a market organization to oversee prices, quality, marketing and external trade. Finally, it guides negotiations with other countries on access to waters and the conservation of fisheries.

The Common Agricultural Policy

The foundation of agricultural policy in the EU is the Common Agricultural Policy. The underlying principles of CAP – which were worked out at a landmark conference convened in Stresa, Italy, in July 1958 – are the promotion of a common market in agricultural produce, 'Community preference' (a polite term for protectionism aimed at giving priority to EU produce over imported produce) and joint financing, meaning that the costs of CAP are shared equitably by all the member states. The goals of CAP include increased agricultural productivity, a 'fair' standard of living for the farming community, stable markets, assured food supplies and 'reasonable' prices for consumers. In short, all EU farmers are guaranteed the same minimum price for their produce, irrespective of how much they produce, world prices and the prevailing levels of supply and demand. Meanwhile the EU's internal market is protected from imports by tariffs. The member states share the financial burden of making all this possible.

The specifics of how CAP would work were agreed in the early 1960s, and resulted not so much in a common agricultural policy as a common agricultural price support system, which works as follows. Annual prices are fixed for all agricultural products by the agriculture ministers meeting in the spring (usually April or May). On the basis of discussions and negotiations that have usually been going on since the previous September and have involved the Commission, the Agriculture Council, interest groups and national governments, the ministers set three kinds of price:

- *Target prices*, or the prices they hope farmers will receive on the open market in order to receive a fair return on their investments.
- *Threshold prices*, or the prices to which EU imports will be raised if world prices are lower than those in the EU.
- *Guaranteed (or intervention) prices*, or the prices the Commission will pay as a last resort to take produce off the market if it is not meeting the target price. The EU will buy produce from farmers and place it in storage, thereby reducing the supply and pushing up demand and prices. If prices go above the target price, the EU will sell some of its stored produce until the price has levelled out again, although in practice it has never had to do this because the target prices have always been set high enough to encourage farmers to produce more than the market needs.

This arrangement became increasingly expensive and complex as EU farmers produced more and more, exceeding the demands of consumers for commodities such as butter, cereals, beef and sugar. The EU was forced to buy up the surplus, some of which was stored in warehouses strung across the EU. The rest was either sold outside the EU, given as food aid to poorer countries or 'denatured', that is, destroyed or converted into another product. For example excess wine was distilled into spirits, and thus took up less space, or even turned into heating fuel. The EU tried to discourage production by subsidizing exports (thereby upsetting other agricultural producers, such as the United States) or paying farmers not to produce food, which encouraged new golf courses to sprout up in various parts of the EU as farmers turned their land to other uses. The OECD estimated that full-time farmers were being paid an average subsidy of $21 000 in 1995, compared with $12 000 in 1986–88 (figures quoted in Grant, 1997, p. 183).

The costs of CAP are borne by the European Agricultural Guidance and Guarantee Fund (EAGGF), which was created in 1962 and has since been the largest item on the EU budget, although overall agricultural spending has fallen from about 85 per cent of the budget in 1970 to slightly less than 50 per cent today. The bulk of the funds (about 46 billion ecu in 1998, or nearly 42 per cent of the EU budget) are spent under the Guarantee Section to buy and store surplus produce and encourage agricultural exports. Most of the money goes to the producers of dairy products (the EU accounts for 60 per cent of global dairy production) and the producers of cereals, oils and fats, beef, veal and sugar. The Guidance Section of the EAGGF is one of the elements that makes up the EU's structural funds (see Chapter 5), and is used to improve agriculture by investing in new equipment and technology and helping those working in agriculture with pensions, sickness benefits, and other support.

The CAP has been a huge success in terms of increasing productivity, stabilizing markets, securing supplies and protecting European farmers from fluctuations in world market prices. The EU is the world's largest exporter of sugar, eggs, poultry and dairy products, and accounts for nearly 20 per cent of world food exports. Encouraged by guaranteed prices, European farmers have produced as much as possible from their land, with the result not only that production has gone up in virtually every area, but also that the EU now produces far more butter, cereals, beef and sugar than it needs. The EU is now self-sufficient in almost every product it can grow or produce in its climate, including wheat, barley, wine, meat, vegetables and dairy products. These successes have come partly through intensification and partly from the increased use of fertilizers – EU farmers now use nearly 2.5 times as much fertilizer per hectare of land as US farmers.

At the same time, member states have tended to specialize in various products, so duplication has been reduced. For example permanent crop-land is now concentrated in the southern states, and most livestock is raised in the northern states. CAP has also helped make farmers wealthier, and helped make their livelihoods more predictable and stable – while unemployment in the EU has grown, farm employment and farm incomes have generally remained steady.

Unfortunately, CAP has also created problems:

- As discussed above, EU farmers produce far more than the market can bear. Surplus products are stockpiled throughout the EU, and in the past warehouses have been packed full of surplus cereal, powdered milk, beef, olive oil, raisins, figs and even manure. By the late 1990s the stockpiles had largely disappeared, but there were warnings that rising world prices could lead to their reappearance unless the EU acted to reform the agricultural price structure.

- Stories of fraud and the abuse of CAP funds abound. Differences between EU prices and world prices have meant high refunds that provide an irresistible temptation for less honest farmers and – in Italy – organized crime (Grant, 1997, pp. 99–101).

- CAP has created economic dependency because many farmers would undoubtedly go out of business if it was abandoned. Furthermore it has pushed up the price of agricultural land and failed to close the income gap between rich and poor farmers. While mechanization and intensification have brought new profits to farmers in states with efficient agricultural sectors, such as Denmark, the Netherlands and France, those in less efficient states, such as Greece, Italy and Portugal, remain relatively poor. To make matters worse, spending on productive northern farmers eats into the funds that could be going to less productive southern farmers, undermining attempts to encourage them to stay on the land (Shackleton, 1990, pp. 38–40).

- Environmentalists have been unhappy about the way CAP has encouraged the increased use of chemical fertilizers and herbicides, and encouraged farmers to cut down hedges and trees and 'reclaim' wetlands in the interests of making their farms bigger and more efficient.

- CAP has upset consumers forced to pay inflated prices for food despite production that is often surplus to needs; the contradiction between high prices and warehouses full of stored food has been a major source of public scepticism about the wisdom and benefits of European integration.

- As if all this is not bad enough, CAP has distorted world agricultural prices, soured EU relations with its major trading partners, and perpetuated the idea of a protectionist European Union that cannot seem to get its priorities and values straight.

Several attempts have been made to reform EU agricultural policy, with varying degrees of success. The first came at the end of the 1960s, when growing concern about the cost of price supports prompted the Commission to suggest that small farmers be encouraged to leave the land, and that farms be amalgamated into larger and more efficient units. This was vehemently opposed by small farmers in France and Germany.

In the wake of several other failed attempts to reform the system, Agriculture Commissioner Ray MacSharry took up the banner in 1991 to warn of the rising volume of stored agricultural produce. He proposed moving away from guaranteed prices, reducing subsidies on grain, beef and butter, and encouraging farmers to take land out of production. Despite the opposition of many farmers and their unions, the proposals were finally approved by the Agriculture Council in May 1992 after 18 months of talks. Although they initially made CAP more expensive than before and led to a warning from the Court of Auditors that they increased the likelihood of fraudulent claims, the changes promised to lead to a medium-term reduction in surpluses, lower food prices for consumers and – in the longer term – better use of the money spent on CAP.

In recent years, food surpluses have diminished, farm incomes have risen and the rise in world cereal prices has helped negate the effect on farmers of CAP price cuts. Proposals were made in 1998 by Agriculture Commissioner Franz Fischler for price cuts on cereals, beef and milk, for more arable land to be set aside, for additional environmental management conditions to be attached to payments to farmers, and for more investment in rural development generally. These would continue to build on the EU agricultural reforms as pressure grew on the EU from global trade negotiations under the auspices of the World Trade Organization. Grant argues that agricultural policy might now be considered as a policy of the past rather than of the future of the EU. It was once perhaps the only example of a 'working' Community policy in the sense that it influenced decisions taken by farmers, but its share of the EU budget has fallen as Europe has focused more on other policy areas (Grant, 1997, p. 2). However, while it has certainly slipped down the list of media and public concerns in the EU, this does not mean that it has gone away, and it may move back up the agenda as membership of the EU expands eastwards.

Towards a single currency

Few aspects of European integration have been as controversial as the idea of a single currency, yet few barriers to the creation of a true single market are so fundamental as the existence of 15 different currencies with fluctuating exchange rates. The latest – and perhaps riskiest – step in the

process of European integration was taken in Jar
member states locked in their exchange rates as a
2002 to a single European currency. The issue of
the heart of sovereignty and independenc
relinquishes control over its national curre
control over all significant domestic econom
freedom to adjust interest rates. The creation oi
seen by its detractors as a significant step towards a
government. Whether or not it will lead to a United States oi L
debatable point, but it certainly promises completely to change the w
that Europeans do business with each other.

Economic union implies agreement on economic policies (which in practice means the establishment of a single market), while monetary union means the agreement of fixed exchange rates and a single currency. Whether economic union is a necessary precondition for monetary union, or vice versa, has long been a bone of contention, but attempts to achieve fixed (or at least stable) exchange rates failed during the early 1970s, contributing to the shift of focus towards establishment of the single market.

Stable exchange rates were identified by European leaders as early as the 1950s as being central to the building of a common market, but the postwar system of fixed exchange rates took care of most of their concerns. It was only when this system began to crumble in the late 1960s, and finally collapsed with the US decision in 1971 to abandon the gold standard, that European leaders paid more attention to the idea of monetary union. The first attempt to plan the transition to a single currency was made in 1969–70 by a committee headed by Luxembourg Prime Minister Pierre Werner. Its proposal for a single currency to be introduced by 1980 was approved by Community heads of government, but was largely derailed by international currency turbulence in the wake of the energy crises of the 1970s. The EEC states tried linking their currencies to the German deutschmark in a system known as the 'snake in the tunnel', but it proved unsatisfactory.

The European Monetary System (EMS) followed in 1979 (see Chapter 3), its goal being to create a zone of exchange rate stability and to keep inflation under control. Economic and financial policies were coordinated through an Exchange Rate Mechanism (ERM), designed to reduce the fluctuation of EC currencies relative to each other. The ERM was centred on the European Currency Unit (ecu). Although several member states found it difficult to keep their currencies stable relative to the ecu, the EMS contributed to exchange rate stability in Europe in the 1980s and to the longest period of sustained economic expansion since the war. The Delors plan in 1989 focused new attention on monetary union, and despite its

llapse in 1992–93 when Britain and Italy left the ERM and several
countries had to devalue their currencies, the Maastricht treaty
rmed the basic principles of the plan. All EU member states who wished
take part in the single currency would have to meet four 'convergence
criteria' that were considered essential prerequisites:

- A national budget deficit of 3 per cent or less of GDP. The average
  deficit in the member states fell from 6.1 per cent of GDP in 1993 to 2.4
  per cent in 1997.
- A public debt of less than 60 per cent of GDP.
- A consumer inflation rate within 1.5 per cent of the average in the three
  countries with the lowest rates.
- A long-term interest rate within 2 per cent of the average in the three
  countries with the lowest rates.

At the Madrid European Council in December 1995, the EU leaders
decided to call the new currency the euro, and agreed to introduce it in
three stages. The first stage came in May 1998 when it was determined
which countries were ready: all member states had met the budget deficit
goal, but Greece had not been able to reduce its interest rates sufficiently,
Germany and Ireland had not met the inflation reduction target, and only
seven member states had met the debt target (*The Economist*, 11 April
1998). Maastricht, however, included a clause that allowed countries to
qualify if their debt-to-GDP ratio was 'sufficiently diminishing and
approaching the reference value at a satisfactory pace'. In the event, despite
the fact that the national debt in Belgium and Italy was nearly twice the
target, all but Britain, Denmark (both of which had met all four criteria),
Greece and Sweden signed on to the euro. This raised a question in the
minds of Eurosceptics about the seriousness with which member states
were approaching the convergence criteria, the wisdom of which had
already been questioned by many economists (*The Economist*, 5 August
1995). Questions were raised in particular about the extent to which efforts
by governments to meet the criteria had contributed to the economic
problems of several EU states (notably Germany), and therefore about the
strength of the foundations upon which the euro was built.

Pressing on regardless, the second stage began on 1 January 1999, when
the participating countries fixed their exchange rates and the new
European Central Bank (ECB, see Box 7.3) began to oversee the single
monetary policy. All its dealings with commercial banks and all its foreign
exchange activities are now transacted in euros, which is quoted against
the yen and the US dollar. The next stage is due to start on 1 January 2002,
when – if all goes to plan – euro coins and notes will become available.
Europeans will then be given six months to make the final transition from

their national currencies to the euro, and national currencies will cease to be legal tender by 1 July 2002 at the latest.

One result of the adoption of the euro has been the decision to create a series of new pan-European stockmarket indices. The euro is already the main currency quoted on 17 stockmarkets, but an agreement signed between the Paris, Frankfurt and Zurich Stock Exchanges promises to take this much further. With the help of Dow Jones in the United States, the Dow Jones Stoxx and the Euro Stoxx will be created, based respectively on 665 and 326 companies in the EU member states that are part of the euro, together with Switzerland. Two more specialized indices will follow, called the Dow Jones Stoxx 50 and the Euro Stoxx 50. The four are expected to replace national indices such as the CAC 40 in Paris and the DAX 30 in Frankfurt, and will (it is hoped) simplify trades and generate an inflow of international investment.

Pros and cons of the single currency

The development of the single currency has proved both complex and controversial. The project has been nearly thirty years in the making, and yet – even as the date for its completion nears – many doubts remain about its underlying wisdom. The opinions both of European citizens and their governments are divided about its implications, and it is probably safe to say that no one chapter in the history of European integration has been approached with so many doubts remaining. It raises questions about the long-term economic effects for Europe, few of which are fully understood, even by economists.

First, some of the advantages:

- There are few things that remind people quite so visibly and so potently of the differences between them as having to change currencies when they travel from one country to another, and having to pay for goods and services with unfamiliar banknotes and coins. The single currency will remove that reminder and help make the citizens of the EU feel more connected to one another. On a larger scale, the same will be true when Europeans realize that changes in economic health will have repercussions for them all.
- Backed by the credibility of the large European market, the euro will be more stable against speculation than the individual currencies of EU member states. Currency instability within the participating countries should decline, as should instability relative to outside currencies. This will help exporters project future markets with greater confidence, promoting economic growth.

Box 7.3 The European Central Bank

Although the ECB, until recently, has been one of the least known of the EU institutions, it will play an increasingly important role in the development of the euro, and in the lives of Europeans. As it has become increasingly involved in the direction of European monetary policy, worrying questions have been raised about its powers, and about the lack of an effective check on those powers.

First proposed in 1988, the framework of the bank was described in the Maastricht treaty, it was founded in 1994 as the European Monetary Institute (EMI) and it was finally established in June 1998 as the European Central Bank. Based in Frankfurt, its main job is to ensure monetary stability by setting interest rates. It has a governing body consisting of the central bank governors from each state participating in the single currency, and a six-member, full-time executive board. Directors serve non-renewable terms of eight years and can only be removed by their peers or by an order from the European Court of Justice. The ECB also has links to non-participating countries through a general council composed of the central bank governors of all EU member states. A new exchange rate mechanism (ERM II) links the euro with the national currencies of non-participating countries, and the ECB is allowed to take action to support non-participating countries as long as this does not conflict with its primary task of maintaining monetary stability among the participating countries.

Concerned about the need to convince the sceptical German public that the new European currency would be as strong as the deutschmark (Daltrop, 1987, pp. 175–6), Helmut Kohl insisted that the ECB should be an almost direct copy of the famously independent German Bundesbank. In fact it makes the Bundesbank seem quite restricted by comparison, and – in the words of *European Voice* (April 1998) – has already become 'the most powerful single monetary authority in the world'. Neither national nor EU leaders are allowed to try to influence the bank, its board, or its constituent national central banks, and the only body that can act as a watchdog over the bank is the monetary subcommittee of the European Parliament, but it so far lacks the resources to be able to hold the ECB or its president – Wim Duisenberg of the Netherlands – accountable. This makes it very different from its US equivalent, the Federal Reserve (the Fed), whose chairman regularly has to appear before the banking committee of the US Senate to account for Fed policies.

- Businesses will not have to pay hedging costs to insure themselves against the possibility of currency fluctuations.
- Travellers will not have to worry about changing money, there will be fewer bureaucratic barriers to the transfer of large sums of money across borders, and businesses will no longer have to worry about the time and accounting costs involved in changing currency. This will save everyone – particularly travellers – a lot of money in transaction costs, and will take the guessing game out of buying goods and services in different countries.
- The credibility of the deutschmark should help lower interest rates across the EU, and improved fiscal responsibility across the EU (as agreed by the European Council at its December 1996 summit in Dublin) should then help build the international credibility of the euro. Many European leaders hope and believe that it will become a world-class currency in the same league as the US dollar and the Japanese yen. If this happens, the EU will have more power to influence global economic policy, rather than having to react to developments in the US and Japan.

Arguments levelled against the single currency include the following:

- There is the threat of the unknown. Never before has a group of sovereign states with a long history of independence tried to combine their currencies into one. The risks are significantly greater than those involved in completing the single market.
- Unless Europeans learn each other's languages and are able to move freely in search of jobs, the single currency could perpetuate the pockets of poverty and wealth that already exist across the EU, thereby interfering with the development of a true single market. Having a common currency in a country as large as the United States works mainly because people can move freely – this is not true of the EU, where there are still physical, fiscal, technical and social barriers to movement.
- Different countries have different economic cycles, and having separate currencies allows them to devalue, borrow, adjust interest rates and take other measures in response to changed economic circumstances. Such flexibility will not be possible with a single currency, and the European Central Bank will not be able to follow different fiscal policies for different parts of the EU.
- Switching to the new currency – although it will only happen once – will be expensive. The 13 billion notes and 76 billion coins currently in circulation will have to be collected and replaced with comparable numbers of new euro notes and coins (which will need to be printed/minted), consumers and retail staff will need to be trained, tills, parking

meters and dispensing machines will have to be redesigned, and in some cases replaced altogether, computer software will have to be changed as will all signs showing costs in national currencies, and banks will need to prepare for the switch.

- There are widely voiced concerns about loss of sovereignty, and there is also considerable public resistance to the idea. In *Eurobarometer* polls in 1997–98 the majority of German, British, Danish, Swedish, and Finnish respondents were opposed to the single currency and barely half the EU population as a whole was in favour. Furthermore, four of the 15 member states did not take part in the first round. This was hardly a vote of confidence, and stood in stark contrast to the support for – or at least absence of strong opposition to – the single market programme.
- Some economists were concerned about underlying weaknesses in the EU economies in 1997–98, and questioned the extent to which figures relating to the convergence criteria were being fudged to allow countries that had not met those criteria to take part. Some feared that these weaknesses could result in the high-credibility deutschmark being replaced by a low-credibility euro, undermining economic health throughout the EU. The most sceptical express doubt that all the countries that have signed up for the euro will be able to see it through, and that the domestic economic problems of some participants will cause them to fall by the wayside before 2002.

One of the principle motives behind European integration has been the argument that Europe must create the conditions in which it can meet external economic threats without being undermined by internal divisions. For many, the single currency – if it succeeds – will represent the crowning achievement of exactly fifty years' worth of effort (1952–2002) to remove the barriers to trade among Europeans and to construct a single market that will allow Europe to compete on the global stage from a position of strength. It has been argued that European monetary integration has been driven in large part by external forces and the pressures of an international monetary system dominated by the US dollar (Loedel, 1998). While its effects on the domestic economies of Europe are debatable, there is little question that the successful adoption of the euro will make the EU a substantial new actor in that international system.

Conclusions

Although the work of the European Union has been driven most obviously by economic factors – most notably the goal of free trade in a single market – European leaders have found, through neofunctionalist logic, that economic integration has had a spillover effect on many other policy areas. In particular, completion of the single market turned out to be a much more complex process than originally expected. The primary objective of the single market was to remove tariffs and non-tariff barriers to trade, but behind that seemingly harmless term – non-tariff barriers – lay a multitude of problems, handicaps and obstacles.

Among other things, economic integration meant removing cross-border checks on people and goods, controlling the movement of drugs and terrorists, agreeing standard levels of taxation, harmonizing technical standards on thousands of goods and services, agreeing regulations in the interests of consumer safety, reaching agreement on professional qualifications, allowing Europeans to take capital and pensions with them when they move to another country, opening up the European market for joint ventures and corporate mergers, developing trans-European transport and energy supply networks, providing the means by which Europeans can communicate with each other electronically, developing common approaches to working conditions, establishing common European environmental standards, promoting the development of poorer rural and urban areas in order to avoid trade distortions, and creating an equitable and efficient agricultural sector.

In a sense, however, everything that was agreed during the 1960s, 1970s, and 1980s – the thousands of decisions taken by prime ministers, chancellors, presidents, ministers and European bureaucrats, and the thousands of directives, regulations and decisions developed and approved by the different EU institutions – was simply a prelude to the biggest project of all, conversion to a single currency. As this book went to press, 11 EU member states had signed on for the euro, and four remained outside, at least temporarily. Many questions remained about the wisdom of the positions taken both by the supporters of the idea and the doubters. Have France and Germany been too hasty in their decision to press on, regardless of their domestic economic problems? Are Britain and Denmark being wisely cautious or typically Eurosceptic in their decision to wait and see? Will the creation of the single currency turn out to be a disruptive step too far, or one of the most farsighted and creative decisions ever taken by Europe's leaders?

Whatever happens over the next few years, the single market has had radical and irreversible implications for everyone living in the European Union, and for all the EU's trading partners. It has helped create new wealth and opportunity, has brought down many of the economic barriers that for decades divided Europeans, and has paved the way for the creation of trans-European economic ties that have reduced national differences and promoted the idea of Europe as a powerful new actor on the world stage.

Chapter 8

The EU and the World

Foreign policy cooperation: from EPC to CFSP
The WEU and European defence
Europe as an economic superpower
Relations with the United States
Relations with eastern Europe
Development cooperation
Conclusions

The world does not yet quite know what to make of the European Union, in large part because the European Union does not yet quite know what to make of itself. The core problem is one of definition: the EU is neither a state nor a superstate, and yet it is much more than a conventional international organization. There are elements of confederalism in its structure, but in some areas the relationship among the member states and the major EU institutions has gone much further. There are also elements of federalism in its structure, but the idea of a federal Europe is so troubling to many Europeans that the two words are rarely spoken together, except as a warning.

To further confuse the issue, the member states present multiple personalities to the rest of the world. When trade negotiations are on the agenda, for example, governments outside the EU are obliged to deal with the member states as a group, but when it comes to defence and security interests they are usually obliged to deal with them individually. The lack of focus and the absence of leadership on foreign policy was neatly encapsulated in a question once posed by former US Secretary of State Henry Kissinger: 'When I want to speak to Europe, whom do I call?'

If Europe was a military union, its combined armed forces would make it one of the two biggest powers on earth. But it does not yet have a common defence policy, and those armed forces are divided among a group of countries with often different priorities. This became particularly obvious during the 1991 Gulf War and the crises in Iraq in 1998, when the member states adopted very different policy positions. It has also been obvious in the divided opinions about how to respond to the various problems in the Balkans, from Bosnia in the early 1990s to Kosovo in 1998. The seeds of a common defence force have been planted in the Eurocorps, founded by France and Germany in 1992, and the Western European Union may eventually become a pan-European defence organization, but

202

much work remains to be done before Europe can present a common face to the rest of the world on security matters.

In contrast, few doubts remain about the new status of the European Union as an economic superpower, and it is exerting its influence over global trade issues with growing confidence. It is the world's richest marketplace, accounting for more than 28 per cent of global GNP and 36 per cent of global imports and exports. Its influence over the global economy will grow even further if the single currency succeeds, because the US dollar and the Japanese yen will then face some formidable competition, and there will be greater coordination on EU economic policy.

Europe may have been unprepared for the crises in the Gulf and the Balkans, lacking both political unanimity and military preparedness, but there has been progress on the development of common foreign policies. As Christopher Hill (1992, pp. 135–6) puts it, setbacks have produced renewed efforts at policy cooperation, which has followed a path of 'peaks and troughs along a gradual upward gradient . . . (and) consensus has become more habit-forming'. This chapter looks at the reasons for those peaks and troughs, and at how the role of the EU as an actor on the global stage has changed. It shows how European integration has moved beyond economic issues, and how western Europe – once a bystander in the cold war – has recently exerted a new influence over international affairs.

Foreign policy cooperation: from EPC to CFSP

The development of a common European foreign policy has always been one of those issues – like the single currency – that Eurosceptics believe will lead inexorably to the surrender of national sovereignty and the creation of a European federation. In their attempts to work together, EU leaders have found themselves being pulled in two directions. On the one hand it is clear that the member states will have more power and influence in the world if they act as a group rather than independently. On the other hand there is the fear that coordination will interfere with the freedom of member states to address matters of national rather than of European interest. The tension between these two views has interfered from the beginning with attempts to build common policy positions, let alone a common foreign policy.

The Treaties of Rome make no mention of foreign policy, and the EEC long focused on domestic economic policy, although the logic of spillover implied that it would become increasingly difficult to ignore the need to develop common external economic policies. There were several abortive attempts to implement common foreign and security policies in the early years of integration, including the European Defence Community (EDC)

Box 8.1 The EC/EU and the Balkans

The outbreak of civil war near the EC's back porch in 1991 provided a demanding test of its foreign policy capacity. While the result was abysmal failure – German chancellor Helmut Kohl described the situation as 'Europe's shame' – the crisis did serve to spur the development of EC foreign policy, and in fairness the EC was neither politically nor militarily prepared for a problem of such proportions. Ironically, the fact that the Community was so roundly criticized by the United States for the weakness of its response suggests just how much was coming to be expected of the EU as a political entity.

The creation of Yugoslavia was one of the outcomes of the First World War, and brought together several independent states whose internal ethnic, religious and nationalist tensions were kept in check after the Second World War only by the power of the Tito regime (1944–80). The end of the cold war allowed those tensions to be brought into the open, resulting in the June 1991 declaration of independence by Slovenia and Croatia. Serbs living in Croatia rejected secession and seized control of the region. When Bosnia voted for independence in 1992, Serbian troops based in the province refused to accept the decision, declared a 'Serbian Republic' and launched a programme of 'ethnic cleansing' against Muslims and Croats.

The EC's position had initially been to try to keep Yugoslavia intact, but under German pressure it recognized Slovenia and Croatia in January 1992, undermining its credibility with the Serbs. The EU then tried without success to broker a ceasefire (sending in negotiators such as Lord Carrington and Lord Owen, both former British foreign secretaries). It also sent in unarmed monitors in an attempt to keep the warring factions apart, imposed sanctions on Serbia, supported an embargo on arms sales to Bosnian Muslims in the hope of reducing hostilities, and contributed most of the UN peacekeeping forces deployed in the area. Ambivalence on both sides of the Atlantic about how to respond to the Bosnian civil war led to one of the most serious disagreements ever between the United States and its NATO allies in Europe.

Despite the obvious attempts by Serbs to expand their territory and eradicate Bosnia's Muslims, the EU was concerned about becoming directly involved in the hostilities and about the implications of Russia's historical ties with the Serbs. At the same time the EU faced political pressure to address the flagrant disregard for human rights in the conflict, and to assuage charges by Muslim states that it was biased. In the end, peace came to Bosnia only after US-led NATO airstrikes in 1995, and the US-brokered peace accords signed in Dayton, Ohio, which built on the foundations of earlier European initiatives. Once the political agreement had been reached the EU came into its own – it now provides just over two thirds of the 36 500 peacekeeping forces in Bosnia. All 15 EU states are involved, including traditionally neutral Austria, Finland, Ireland and Sweden.

and the European Political Community, and Charles de Gaulle's plans for regular meetings among the leaders of the Six to coordinate foreign policy. The EDC was proposed in 1950, was pursued most actively by the French, and was to have been built on the foundations of a common European army and a European 'minister of defence'. However Britain was opposed to the idea, preferring to pursue the goals of the Treaty of Brussels (see below) and to bring Italy and West Germany into the fold. All prospects of an EDC finally died in 1954 when it was turned down by the French National Assembly (Urwin, 1995, pp. 60–8).

European integration was subsequently focused on building the common market, and it was only at the 1969 Hague summit that Community leaders decided to look again at the question of political union. They agreed in 1970 to promote European Political Cooperation (EPC), a process whereby the six foreign ministers would meet to discuss and coordinate foreign policy positions. However EPC was not incorporated into the founding treaties; it remained a loose and voluntary arrangement outside the Community, no laws were adopted on foreign policy, each of the member states could still act independently, most of the key decisions on foreign policy had to be arrived at unanimously, and no new institutions were to be created, although the European Council was launched in 1974 in part to bring leaders of the member states together to coordinate policies.

EPC was originally concerned more with how foreign policy should be agreed than with what that policy should be. The need to develop common positions was helped by the creation in 1975 of the Conference on Security and Cooperation in Europe (CSCE). Although Community member states acted as a group in the CSCE, and subsequently consulted with each other on virtually every aspect of foreign policy, they remained reluctant to give up too many of their independent powers. Nevertheless EPC was given formal recognition with the Single European Act, which confirmed under Title III that the member states would 'endeavour jointly to formulate and implement a European foreign policy'.

The main goal of EPC was to coordinate the foreign policies of the member states, on the basis that the EC as a whole could achieve more than its individual members acting alone. The EPC process was strictly intergovernmental, and was overseen by the foreign ministers meeting as the Council of Ministers, with overall leadership subsequently coming from the European Council. Continuity was provided by regular meetings of senior officials from all the foreign ministries, and a small secretariat was set up in Brussels to help the country holding the presidency of the Council of Ministers, which provided most of the momentum. Larger or more active states such as Britain and France had few problems providing leadership, but policy coordination put a strain on smaller and/or neutral countries such as Luxembourg and Ireland. The shifting of responsibilities every six months gave each member state its turn at the helm, but complicated life for non-EU states, which had to switch their attention from one member state to another, and to establish contacts with ministers and bureaucrats in six, then nine, then 12 capital cities.

A new sense of urgency was provided by the end of the cold war, the rapid changes in eastern Europe and the former USSR in 1989–91 and, most obviously, the confused European response to the Gulf crisis. Following the August 1990 Iraqi invasion of Kuwait, the United States orchestrated a multinational campaign involving 13 countries in the defence of Saudi Arabia, a six-week air war against Iraq, and a four-day ground war in February 1991. The EU states took significantly different positions on the crisis (van Eekelen, 1990; Anderson, 1992):

- Britain was strongly in favour of using force, and placed a substantial military contingent under US operational command; France also made a large military commitment, but put more emphasis on diplomatic resolution in order to maintain good relations with Arab oil producers and protect its arms.
- Germany was constrained by a strong postwar tradition of pacifism and constitutional limits on the deployment of the German troops.
- Out of fear of retribution, Belgium refused to sell ammunition to Britain and, along with Spain and Portugal, refused to allow its naval vessels to be involved in anything other than minesweeping or enforcing the blockade of Iraq. Ireland, meanwhile, maintained its neutrality.

For the Luxembourg foreign minister the EC's response underlined 'the political insignificance of Europe'. For the Belgian foreign minister, it showed that the Community was 'an economic giant, a political dwarf, and a military worm' (*New York Times*, 25 January 1991). More significantly the divisions underlined the need for Europe to address its foreign policy more forcefully, and political pressure began to grow for a review of EPC. Commission President Jacques Delors noted that while the member states had taken a firm line against Iraq with regard to sanctions, once it became obvious that the situation would have to be resolved by force, the EC realized that it had neither the institutional machinery nor the military force to allow it act as one (Delors, 1991).

Integrationist states now began to press for the use of qualified majority voting on foreign policy issues, and for new emphasis to be placed on the development of a common defence policy. The result was the decision under the terms of Maastricht to replace the EPC with a Common Foreign and Security Policy (CFSP), which became one of the three pillars that now make up the European Union. The goals of the CFSP are only very loosely defined, with vague talk about the need to safeguard 'common values' and 'fundamental interests', 'to preserve peace and strengthen international security', and to 'promote international cooperation'. The result has been little real change in the practice of European foreign policy. Smith (1998) identifies just four differences between EPC and the CFSP: the CFSP represents a stronger commitment to common policies, joint action can be initiated and/or implemented by qualified majority voting in the Council (although unanimity is the norm), security issues are fully included in the CFSP, and the CFSP is part of the institutional structure of the EU.

Overall the record on common European foreign policy has been mixed. On the one hand there has been a steady convergence of positions among the member states on key international issues, helped by the fact that their ambassadors to the United Nations meet every week to coordinate policy, and the EU states vote together on about 75 per cent of resolutions in the Security Council, where the EU – through Britain and France – holds two of the five permanent seats. Among the recent results has been 'common positions' on relations with Ukraine, Rwanda and Burundi, and a number of 'joint actions', such as transporting humanitarian aid to Bosnia and sending observers to elections in Russia and South Africa. The EU has also flexed its economic muscle to political ends, cutting all aid to China in 1989 in protest at the Tiananmen Square massacre, blocking $1 billion in aid to the USSR in 1991 in protest at a crackdown on pro-independence groups in the Baltic states, and being highly critical of US attempts in the late 1990s to penalize companies profiting from property seized by the Castro regime in Cuba (see below).

The EU also coordinates Western aid to eastern Europe, Russia and the former Soviet republics, has become a major supplier of aid to developing countries, and has been a magnet for foreign investment from the United States and Japan. The president of the European Commission attends meetings of the G7 alongside the leaders of Russia and the seven most industrialized countries, four of which are EU member states. The significance of the EU as an actor on the global stage is also reflected in the fact that almost every country in the world now has diplomatic representation in Brussels (both for Belgium and for the EU), and that the Commission has opened more than 120 overseas delegations.

On the other hand there are many examples of weakness and division, including the failure of the EC to broker peace in Bosnia (a job subsequently completed under US leadership – see Box 8.1, p. 204), and its failure to act on a 1996 dispute between Greece and Turkey over an uninhabited Aegean island, which prompted Richard Holbrooke, the US assistant secretary of state for European affairs, to accuse the EU of 'literally sleeping through the night'. Perhaps the most serious recent example of EU hesitancy was its feeble response in 1997–98 to the crisis in the Yugoslav province of Kosovo. Most of the inhabitants of Kosovo are ethnic Albanians, and in mid-1998 began agitating for independence from Serb-dominated Yugoslavia. The government of Slobodan Milosevic responded with force, and by August 1998 there was an enormous refugee problem in the province, and growing reports of massacres of both Kosovars and Muslims. The West's position on the conflict seemed to be aimed at discouraging separatism rather than stopping the violence, and the Milosevic government took this as a signal to continue its offensive. Meanwhile the EU stood by while the United States took the initiative on prompting a response under the auspices of NATO.

There are also repeated instances of individual member states taking action on foreign policy issues without reference to their EU partners. For example the Kohl government in Germany took a unilateral decision to reunite East and West Germany in 1989–90 and to recognize Croatia in 1991. Greece unilaterally imposed a blockade on the former Yugoslav republic of Macedonia in 1994, wanting to punish it for using an Hellenic name and Hellenic symbols, and accusing it of having designs on the neighbouring Greek province of Macedonia. When Saddam Hussein tried to interfere with the work of UN arms inspectors in Iraq in 1997–98, Britain was the only EU country to support the US threat to attack the Iraqi regime.

The problems have stemmed in part from differences in culture and historical interests, and in part from an inability to demonstrate a common political will, but they have also been a consequence of weaknesses in the institutional machinery of the EU. For example, while trade negotiations are carried out by the Commission on behalf of the EU as a whole, discussions on the CFSP rest more firmly with the Council of Ministers, and are thus more intergovernmental. Some of these problems may be addressed as a result of changes made to the CFSP by the Treaty of Amsterdam. As well as opening the possibility of limited majority voting on foreign policy issues, the rotation of countries holding the presidency of the EU has been changed; this was previously arranged in alphabetical order by the name of each member state in its national language, but it is now arranged so that large member states alternate with small ones, thereby more effectively balancing the leaderships of large and small states.

The institutional changes brought by Amsterdam are twofold. First, a Policy Planning and Early Warning Unit (PPEWU) has been set up in Brussels to help the EU anticipate foreign crises. It consists of 20 members: one each from the member states, the Western European Union and the European Commission, and three from the Council of Ministers. Second, rather than distributing external relations portfolios in the European Commission (among four different commissioners and the president – see Table 4.1), these now go to the holder of a new foreign policy post, with the rank of vice-president. Structural changes such as these will be useful, but only if the member states develop the political will to use them, and only if they work more aggressively on agreeing common foreign policy positions.

Ironically, while the leaders of the member states have had difficulty reaching common positions, and are divided on the idea of relinquishing more powers over foreign policy to the EU institutions, there is considerable public support for the idea of common European foreign and defence policies. Eurobarometer polls in recent years have found that about 68–75 per cent of Europeans favour a common defence policy, and 63–69 per cent favour a common foreign policy. Italians generally show the most enthusiasm (as high as 74 per cent in favour and only 11 per cent against), about two thirds of Germans, French, Dutch and Belgians are in favour, and there is even strong support in neutral Ireland (more than half in favour and only about one fifth against). Among the British, about half are in favour and about one third against.

The WEU and European defence

The EU will continue to work with one arm tied behind its back on most foreign policy issues until it has the ability to back up its words with military action. Together the 15 member states constitute a formidable military power: they have more than two million troops, 22 000 tanks, 21 000 artillery pieces and 6300 combat aircraft, and between them account for 85–95 per cent of the military capacity of western Europe. Britain and France are both nuclear powers, and the European corporate world includes some of the biggest arms manufacturers in the world, such as British Aerospace and Matra-Défense of France, which merged their missile production units in 1996 to create an industry with a $1.7 billion turnover. However, European governments tend to have independent opinions and priorities when it comes to committing their forces, there is still only limited coordination on policy, and progress on setting up a European defence force has been slow.

The fundamental problem lies in a philosophical division between Atlanticists such as Britain, the Netherlands and Portugal, which emphasize the importance of continuing the security relationship with the United States, and Europeanists such as France, Italy, Spain and sometimes Germany, which look more towards European independence. The Atlanticists have had the advantage to date, but may lose influence in the wake of changes in US policy. President Kennedy spoke during his inauguration of the willingness of the United States to 'bear any burden' and 'meet any hardship . . . to assure the survival and success of liberty', but American public opinion is increasingly turning against such an idea. The term 'burden sharing' has become more and more common in transatlantic discussions in recent years, with demands for the EU to take on greater responsibility for addressing its own security threats. The EU has shouldered an increased share of the burden of global economic development by providing additional aid to Russia and eastern Europe as they make the transition to market economics, sharing the costs of maintaining US troops in Germany and becoming the world's largest provider of foreign aid. However its military response to security threats has been inadequate, a problem that has become more critical over the last ten years as US defence expenditure has fallen (Barber, 1998).

During the cold war (1945–91) defence was pushed down the agenda of European integration by the emphasis on economic policies, the failure of the European Defence Community, the very different positions and capacities of the member states, and the fact that the main defence issue was security against a Soviet attack, something that fell squarely under the remit of the US-dominated North Atlantic Treaty Organization (NATO). The British and the French had their own special interests in their colonies and former colonies, the Germans and the Dutch saw their armed forces as very much part of the broader NATO system, and several countries – notably Ireland – were protective of their neutrality. Nevertheless the Europeans became used to coordinating their defence policies within the NATO framework, guided by US leadership.

Maastricht states that one of the goals of the EU should be 'to assert its identity on the international scene, in particular through the implementation of a common foreign and security policy including the eventual framing of a common defence policy' (Article B). While the CFSP moved defence more squarely onto the EU agenda, Article J.4(1) provided a loophole that could be used to slow down the development of common defence policy: it committed member states to defining and implementing a common policy that 'shall include all questions related to the security of the Union, including the *eventual* framing of a common defence policy, *which might in time* lead to a common defence' (emphasis added).

There are two critical elements missing from the development of a European defence capability. First, there is no European defence policy. Nothing illustrates this quite so much as the independent stance taken by France over the years. Since withdrawing its forces from the integrated NATO military command in 1966, France has more often preferred to go its own way rather than cooperate with either NATO or its European partners. Driven by a combination of its concern about US influence in Europe through NATO, and its own political marginalization, it has adopted policy positions that have often run counter to those of its neighbours, and of the EU as a whole. For example, it tried to prevent the creation of a new consultative council bringing together NATO countries and former Warsaw Pact members, it refused to place its warships under NATO command during the blockade of Serbia and Montenegro, it has pursued its own independent interests in its former African colonies, and it unilaterally resumed nuclear testing in the Pacific in 1995.

Second, Europe lacks the necessary institutional machinery to manage a defence capability, and there is nothing within the existing EU structure to provide the seed of such machinery. However, the growing sense that the Europeans should be taking care of their own defence, independently of NATO, has led to the revival of a long-moribund organization, the Western European Union (WEU). Maastricht elevated the WEU to being 'an integral part of the development of the Union' (which can be taken to mean several things), and stipulated that it should 'elaborate and implement decisions and actions' of the EU that have defence implications, although it was left to the EU Council of Ministers to 'adopt the necessary practical arrangements'.

The history of the WEU dates back to the Brussels Treaty for collective self-defence, signed by Britain, France and the Benelux in 1948 and creating the Western Union. It was quickly overtaken by the 1949 treaty creating NATO, and the Western Union's defence functions were shifted to NATO so as to avoid duplication of effort. The Brussels Treaty remained in force, however, and the Western Union became the WEU in 1954 when Germany and Italy joined. Its political objective was to help Germany contribute to the defence of western Europe without taking part in the kind of European army envisioned by the European Defence Community. NATO was clearly the major actor in European defence, however, and while the foreign and defence ministers of the WEU continued to meet, it was sidelined and – as one diplomat put it – became 'a place where you found jobs for retired Italian admirals' (*The Economist*, 2 February 1991).

It was only in 1984, following the failure of a plan to give EPC a security dimension (van Eekelen, 1990), that the cobwebs were dusted off and the WEU was slowly reactivated. It passed its first modest test in 1987–90 when it coordinated minesweeping by its members in the Persian Gulf during the Iran–Iraq war, but the 1990–91 Gulf War stretched it beyond its limits. Coincidentally, the end of the cold war brought a redefinition of NATO's role and of the US attitude towards the defence of western Europe. In 1991, NATO ministers welcomed the development of the CFSP and the reinforced role of the WEU as 'the defence component of the process of European unification and as a means of strengthening the European pillar of [NATO]'.

With its membership expanding (Spain and Portugal joined in 1990, and Greece in 1995) and the acknowledgement under the terms of Maastricht that it was 'an integral part of the development of the [European] Union', the WEU underwent a substantial overhaul. It now has ten full members: Belgium, France, Germany, Greece, Italy, Luxembourg, the Netherlands, Portugal, Spain and Britain. In addition, Austria, Denmark, Finland, Ireland and Sweden are observers, Iceland, Norway and Turkey are associate members, and ten eastern European states are 'associate partners'. In order to improve liaison with NATO, the WEU secretariat was moved from London to Brussels in January 1993.

Much like the EU, the Western European Union has a presidency that rotates among the ten member states, and it has a Council of Ministers – made up of the foreign and defence ministers of the member states – that meets biannually in the capital city of the presidency to discuss policy. A Permanent Council of ambassadors meets weekly in Brussels to direct the activities of WEU working groups, while a Parliamentary Assembly drawn from national legislatures meets twice a year in Paris, providing the kind of link with elected representatives that might eventually be taken over by the European Parliament.

As a possible foundation for the development of a real European defence capability, the WEU has one critical handicap: it has no troops of its own. Its ministers can reach decisions, but they can only put words into effect if the WEU member states are prepared to contribute the necessary men and matériel. An embryonic WEU defence force exists in the form of the Eurocorps and the various other specialist units that answer to the WEU (Box 8.2), but much work remains to be done. On the other hand the WEU has several advantages:

- It already exists and the work of its governing bodies has been refined over several decades, so no new organizational machinery is needed.
- It could be used by the EU to develop its own defence policy independent of the United States, while at the same time continuing to work closely with NATO.
- It can operate outside its member states (unlike NATO, which is technically limited to the territory of its member states).
- It provides a useful means of building bridges between the EU and its neighbours.
- Not all EU member states are full members of the WEU, so the EU can develop its defence capability through the WEU while respecting the neutrality of Ireland, Finland and Sweden.

Despite these advantages, opinion is divided on what to do with the WEU. Its secretary-general in 1991, Willem van Eekelen, felt in the long term that it was destined to be absorbed into the EU (*The Economist*, 2 February 1991). Speaking in 1997, his successor José Cutileiro said that the job of the

Box 8.2 Eurocorps and the development of a European army

Talk of the development of a European army started in the late 1940s and early 1950s, when the idea was mooted in Germany and France. These discussions died with the end of the European Defence Community, however, and it has only been since the Petersberg Declaration that several experimental military units have encouraged joint operations among EU member states. Known collectively as the Forces Answerable to WEU (FAWEU), they include a British–Dutch amphibious force and two bodies consisting of personnel from France, Italy, Spain and Portugal: a 20 000-strong Rapid Deployment Force (EUROFOR) headquartered in Florence and designed for humanitarian or peacekeeping operations in the Mediterranean area, and a non-permanent European Maritime Force (EUROMARFOR). The WEU also runs a 50-person planning cell with representatives from 12 countries, which is charged with providing rules for engagement, designing operational procedures and planning exercises.

The most likely candidate for a European army, though, may be Eurocorps, created in May 1992 by Germany and France to replace an experimental Franco-German brigade set up in 1990. Headquartered in Strasbourg, the 50 000-member Eurocorps has been operational since November 1995 and has been joined by contingents from Belgium, Spain and Luxembourg. It was conceived as a step towards the development of a European army that would give substance to the CFSP, give the EU an independent defence capability and provide insurance for Europe should the United States decide to withdraw its forces from Europe.

Germany insists that the Eurocorps would complement NATO, and that it would be placed under NATO 'operational command' in the event of a threat to western European security, but Britain, the Netherlands and the United States suspect that France's objective – as it has been since the time of de Gaulle – is to displace the US dominance of NATO. Britain would prefer Eurocorps to operate under the auspices of the WEU, while France apparently prefers to see the WEU and Eurocorps as the basis of an EU defence wing, and for the WEU eventually to merge with the EU.

WEU was to prepare its member nations 'to run military operations on behalf of the European Union, following a distinctly European line. We are after all the only military organization that could act on behalf of the European Union' (Heyman, 1997). Some European leaders argue that it should be given more powers and might eventually become the defence arm of the EU, while others argue that it should be a European pillar of NATO rather than a replacement for NATO. Much depends on a 50-year review of the WEU that began in 1998 as one of the requirements of the Treaty of Brussels.

For now, the work of the WEU is limited mainly to the jobs outlined in a declaration agreed by the WEU Council of Minister in June 1992 at Petersberg, near Bonn; under the 'Petersberg tasks', military units from member states, acting under the authority of the WEU, can be used for humanitarian, rescue, peacekeeping and other crisis management tasks, including peacemaking, in cooperation with the CSCE and the UN Security Council. Hence the WEU worked with NATO in monitoring the UN embargo on Serbia and Montenegro in 1993–96, helped set up a unified Croat–Muslim police force to support the administration of the city of Mostar in Bosnia in 1994–96, and helped restructure and train the Albanian police force in 1997.

Meanwhile the United States has been concerned about the implications for NATO (Menon *et al.*, 1992), and sees the WEU as complicating the attempt to set up trans-European security arrangements. NATO itself has been going through something of an identity crisis, since its original mission – to protect western Europe against the threat of Soviet attack – has apparently been completed. It began trying to build closer links with Russia in 1994 through its Partnership for Peace programme, under which military exchanges, training and joint exercises between the two sides would take place. It has also been trying to transform itself into an organization responsible for collective security both inside and outside Europe.

A symbolic change came in 1994 when NATO warplanes bombed Serbian positions in Bosnia, the first 'out of area' operation ever under-taken by NATO. This was followed by the NATO-led peacekeeping operations in Bosnia (Intervention Force, or IFOR, and its successor, Stabilization Force, or SFOR). Whether NATO will move even further 'out of area', and – for example, become involved in removing threats to Persian Gulf oil supplies – is debatable. The United States has expressed concern about the proposal for a 'Combined Joint Task Force', which might cause its Europe-based forces to become involved in European military ventures (Barber, 1997). There has also been a certain amount of concern in Russia since 1997 as NATO has begun to consider expanding its membership eastward, bringing in former Warsaw Pact countries such as the Czech Republic, Hungary and Poland, thus expanding its territory to the borders of the former USSR.

Europe as an economic superpower

While the prospect of the EU becoming a major military power is uncertain, its status as an economic superpower is no longer in doubt. The common external tariff is in place, the single market is all but complete, the Commission has new powers to represent the governments of all the member states in negotiations on global trade, and it is now well understood by everyone that the EU is the most powerful actor in those negotiations. There has also been rapid economic growth in most parts of the EU over the last twenty years, with even some of the poorer parts catching up as a result of the opportunities opened up by the single market and investments made under the structural funds. The conversion to the euro is likely to add to the economic power of Europe by giving it a currency that can stand alongside the US dollar and the Japanese yen in terms of power and influence.

The economic significance of the EU is clearly reflected in the statistics:

- It is the world's largest economic bloc. With just 6.4 per cent of the world's population, it accounts for 28 per cent of global GNP (Table 8.1).
- It is the world's biggest trader, accounting for nearly 37 per cent of world exports, compared with nearly 20 per cent for NAFTA and 5.9 per cent for Japan (Table 8.2). Six of the EU member states rank among the world's ten largest importers and exporters.
- The EU is the biggest market in the industrialized world (with a population of more than 370 million), and one of the most open. Just as multinational corporations have found it essential since the Second World War to sell to the US market in order to maximize their profits, so the European market is becoming increasingly important, and increasingly accessible thanks to the removal of internal trade barriers under the single market programme.
- Intra-EU trade has grown and now accounts for 62 per cent of all EU trade.
- The EU has a close relationship with Russia and eastern Europe, which already account for about 7 per cent of EU imports and exports, and offer enormous potential for the growth of trade.
- Asia, Africa and Latin America account for one third of EU trade (Table 8.3), and the rise of newly industrializing countries will increase that proportion.

The removal of trade restrictions and the lowering of customs barriers has been a goal of the EU since the Treaty of Rome. Article 110 outlined a Common Commercial Policy (CCP), stating that the Community would contribute 'to the harmonious development of world trade, the progressive abolition of restrictions on international trade, and the lowering of customs barriers'. To this end the EU has built up a complex network of multilateral and bilateral trading networks and agreements. Some of these are based on proximity (agreements with eastern Europe and Mediterranean states), some on former colonial ties (see the section on the

Table 8.1   *The EU in the global economy*

	Population 1997 (million)	Share of world population	GNP 1995 ($US billion)	Share of world GNP (%)
Germany	82.2	1.4	2252	8.0
France	58.5	1.0	1451	5.1
Britain	58.2	1.0	1095	3.9
Italy	57.2	1.0	1088	3.9
Spain	39.7	0.7	532	1.9
Netherlands	15.7	0.3	371	1.3
Belgium	10.2	0.2	250	0.9
Austria	8.2	0.1	216	0.8
Sweden	8.8	0.1	210	0.7
Denmark	5.2	0.1	156	0.6
Finland	5.1	0.1	105	0.4
Portugal	9.8	0.2	97	0.3
Greece	10.5	0.2	86	0.3
Ireland	3.6	0.06	53	0.2
Luxembourg	0.4	0.006	17	0.06
EU total	373.3	6.40	7979	28.3
United States	272.0	4.7	7100	25.2
Canada	30.3	0.5	574	2.0
Mexico	97.6	1.7	305	1.1
NAFTA total	399.9	6.8	7979	28.3
Japan	126.0	2.2	4963	17.6
China	1221.6	20.1	745	2.6
Russia	147.7	2.5	332	1.2
WORLD total	5848.7	100.00	28183	100.00

Sources: GNP figures from World Bank, *World Bank Atlas 1996* (Washington, DC: World Bank, 1997); population figures from UN Population Fund, *The State of the World Population* (1997).

Lomé Conventions below) and some on expediency (agreements with the United States and Japan).

The economic power of the EU has been helped by an institutional structure that promotes common positions among the member states. The Council of Ministers is responsible for making the final decisions, but it uses qualified majority voting, and the Commission plays an active role at every level: it generates policy initiatives, is responsible for investigating and taking action against unfair trading practices, and makes suggestions

Table 8.2 *The EU share of world trade, 1996*

	Share of imports (%)	Share of exports (%)
European Union*	36.2	36.7
NAFTA	18.5	19.6
Japan	8.4	5.9
ASEAN	6.3	6.7
China and Hong Kong	5.8	6.2
Other Asia	5.9	5.6
Eastern Europe and former USSR	4.9	5.5
Others	14.0	13.8

Source: International Monetary Fund, *Direction of Trade Statistics* (Washington, DC: IMF (March 1998), pp. 2–5.

Table 8.3 *EU trade with the rest of the world, 1996 (per cent)*

	Share of EU exports	Share of EU imports
United States	19.7	19.4
Non-Soviet eastern Europe	9.2	7.6
Japan	5.6	10.5
Non-EU Mediterranean	11.1	8.6
Asian tigers*	8.5	7.0
OPEC	7.5	8.2
Latin America	5.9	5.6
ACP states	3.0	3.7
Other	29.5	29.4

* Hong Kong, Singapore, South Korea, Taiwan.
Source: Economist Intelligence Unit, European Union report, 1st quarter 1998.

to the Council of Ministers when it thinks that agreements need to be negotiated with other countries or international organizations. Most importantly, once the member states have agreed a position among themselves, they leave it up to the Commission to negotiate almost all external trade agreements on behalf of the EU as a whole. So if anyone was to ask to whom they should speak in Europe regarding trade matters, the clear answer would be the European Commission.

The fundamental issue in international trade is the extent to which states take action to protect their domestic industries. In good times the pressure to do so diminishes because there are fewer threats to those industries from abroad. In bad times, however, governments may be more inclined to protect their industries from cheap imports, and may either impose tariffs on imports (taxes that make imports more expensive and provide a source of government revenue) or impose non-tariff barriers such as quotas and higher technical standards.

Since the Second World War there has been a concerted programme of international negotiations aimed at removing trade restrictions and liberalizing trade. These originally took place under the auspices of the General Agreement on Tariffs and Trade (GATT), which was replaced in 1995 by the World Trade Organization (WTO). The principle underlying GATT/WTO is that economic welfare is best promoted by exploiting comparative advantage – that is, countries should specialize in what they produce best. The United States argues that trade liberalization helps consumers by opening markets to cheaper goods, taxpayers by cutting subsidies to inefficient industry, producers by giving them access to bigger markets, and workers by creating new jobs.

Negotiations under the auspices of GATT/WTO have been carried out in successive rounds lasting several years, the lengthiest and most contentious of which was the Uruguay round, which was launched in 1986 by 105 countries (there were 117 by the time it concluded in 1993). The EC had been involved in several earlier rounds of negotiations, but the Uruguay round promised to be particularly controversial because its scope was broadened to include agricultural trade, thereby posing a direct challenge to the most protectionist of all Community policy areas.

Led by the United States, the Community's major trading partners insisted on cuts of 90 per cent in EC export subsidies and 75 per cent in other farm support over a period of ten years, charging that they gave EC farmers an unfair advantage. The EC initially agreed only to a 30 per cent cut in farming subsidies and refused to reform the Common Agricultural Policy. After teetering several times on the brink of collapse, negotiations finally achieved a breakthrough in 1992 thanks in part to CAP reforms agreed by the EC, including production and price reductions and a switch away from subsidies to farmers based on production. Although the Europeans eventually made concessions on production and export subsidies, and the Uruguay round was finally concluded in December 1993, the attitude of the EU towards the negotiations underlined some of its protectionist tendencies, and some of the problems that had emerged from its focus on completing the single market without paying due attention to its global implications. At the same time, the European experience during the Uruguay round clearly showed the benefits of policy collaboration and speaking with a single voice (Woolcock and Hodges, 1996).

Despite its support for free trade, the EU's external economic policies have caused concern among some of its major trading partners. Most fundamentally, the Community was not founded until ten years after GATT came into force, and it was never formally recognized under GATT rules. A combination of the EC's position on global trade negotiations, its focus on internal economic issues and its promotion of special arrangements with ACP states (see below) subsequently led to talk about 'Fortress Europe', particularly from political and corporate leaders in the United States worried about the implications of the single market and about the EC's unwillingness to cut agricultural subsidies as part of global trade negotiations. The charges of protectionism have proved unfounded, however; not only has the creation of the single market led to the reduction of internal and external barriers to trade, but the EU has overtaken the United States as the primary champion of global trade liberalization under the auspices of the WTO.

Building on its successes to date, the EU will have to prepare itself for some substantial realignments in world trade as the new millennium proceeds:

- The United States remains the EU's largest trading partner, accounting for 19.7 per cent of exports and 19.4 per cent of imports, but these figures may fall as the United States develops economic ties with the Pacific rim.
- The Millennium round of negotiations on global trade liberalization under the auspices of the WTO is due to be launched in late 1999 or early 2000. The United States is particularly keen to see agriculture at the top of the agenda, presenting another challenge to the EU to reform the Common Agricultural Policy. At the same time though, the new role of the Commission as a negotiator will give the EU significantly more influence than it had during the Uruguay round.
- The ACP programme has invested in building trade with developing countries, but with mixed results, and together the 71 ACP states account for just over 3 per cent of EU trade.
- India, China, Japan and Australasia are more likely to strengthen the trading links among themselves than to build up their trade with the EU. The EU's relationship with Japan has been dominated for many years by a substantial trade deficit, with Japan currently exporting about 50 per cent more to the EU than it imports from the EU. The presidents of the Commission and the Council meet annually with the Japanese prime minister, and a variety of cooperative links have been established, including an executive training programme that takes European business executives to Japan for a year of in-house training. The relationship will remain unbalanced, however, as long as Japan continues to protect its domestic market.

While EU trade with the rest of the world grows, substantial new opportunities lie closer to home, most notably on the Mediterranean rim, in eastern Europe – with more than 127 million consumers and enormous productive potential – and in Russia and the former Soviet republics of eastern Europe – with about 218 million consumers and a wealth of largely untapped natural resources. The challenge for the EU is to help them continue to make the transition to free market economics, and to help Russia, Romania, Bulgaria and other troubled states in the region achieve stability.

Relations with the United States

The EU's relationship with the United States has blown hot and cold as the interests of the two sides have converged and parted. The United States was originally supportive of the idea of European integration, seeing it as a way of improving European security in the face of the Soviet threat, and as a means of assisting the rebuilding of West Germany. Transatlantic relations cooled in the early 1960s with Konrad Adenauer's antipathy towards John F. Kennedy, and Charles de Gaulle's neuroses about Anglo-American relations. They continued to cool as the Europeans fell out with the United States over Vietnam, and as German Chancellor Willy Brandt began to make diplomatic overtures to eastern Europe. Anti-Americanism grew despite the money, personnel and resources that the United States was committing to the defence of western Europe.

The collapse of the Bretton Woods system in 1971 marked the beginning of a steady withdrawal of the US responsibility for global leadership; the decision by the Nixon administration to abandon the gold standard also emphasized to many Europeans the unwillingness of the United States to take Europe's position into account. The EC economies were rapidly catching up with the United States, the EC did less trade with the United States and more with eastern Europe, and the revival of the European antinuclear movement in the early 1980s placed a further strain on US–EC relations.

The changing balance was exemplified by the growing differences of opinion on policy which had begun to emerge between the two sides; the EC was slow to criticize the 1979 Soviet invasion of Afghanistan, for example, and West Germany was the only EC member to support the US-led boycott of the 1980 Moscow Olympics. More recently, the Europeans have been much more critical than the United States of Israeli policy in the occupied territories, the United States was disappointed by the lukewarm response of some EC countries to the Gulf crisis, the two sides have disagreed over policy in the Balkans, and they disagreed over how much to cut farm subsidies during the final stages of the Uruguay round of GATT negotiations (a disagreement that was symptomatic of the growing economic power of the EC relative to the United States, see Smith and Woolcock, 1993, p. 2). None of this should come as a surprise, however, because they inevitably reflect the reassertion of European economic and military influence, the relative decline of US influence and a recalculation of the balance of power in the vacuum left by the collapse of the USSR.

Contact between the United States and the EC was formalized in 1989–90 following the call by US Secretary of State James Baker for a new 'Euro-Atlantic architecture' of cooperation. In November 1990, when the United States was becoming concerned about the growing volatility of Europe, the two sides signed a Transatlantic Declaration committing them to regular high-level meetings. In 1995 a New Transatlantic Agenda and a Joint EU–US Action Plan were adopted, whereby the two sides agreed to move from consultation to joint action aimed at promoting peace and democracy around the world, contributing to the expansion of world trade and improving transatlantic ties. Biannual meetings now take place between the presidents of the United States, the Commission and the European Council, between the US secretary of state and EU foreign ministers, and between the Commission and members of the US cabinet.

Despite policy differences and President Clinton's overtures to the Pacific rim states in the mid-1990s, the interests of the United States and western Europe continue to overlap at almost every turn. The EU remains a major US ally, the largest market for US exports, the largest destination of US foreign investment and the largest source of foreign direct investment in the United States. But as economic issues replace military security as the key element in the transatlantic relationship, and as the power of the EU grows and the US looks increasingly to Latin America and Asia, the United States will need to redefine the balance between prosperity and security, and to bring economic issues to bear in its relationship with Europe (Smith and Woolcock, 1993, p. 7).

One issue that has strained EU–US relations in recent years has been US policy towards Cuba, Libya, Iran and other so-called pariah states. The biggest controversy broke in March 1996, when President Clinton signed into law the Cuban Liberty and Democratic Solidarity Act, otherwise known – after its two principal sponsors – as the Helms–Burton Act. It was ostensibly a response to the shooting down by the Cuban government of two civilian aircraft associated with the anti-Castro movement, and its objective was to increase the economic pressure on Cuba by discouraging foreign investment in land and property expropriated by the Castro regime. Had it applied only to US companies the matter might have ended there, but it made provision for foreign companies investing in Cuba to be sued in US courts, and for executives from those companies to be refused entry into the United States.

The Act was strongly criticized by the major trading partners of the United States, notably Canada and Japan, and was met with outrage by the EU, which threatened sanctions against US firms and citizens. The passage of the Act was widely seen as a domestic political ploy by Bill Clinton as he was preparing to run for a second term of office, and courting the influential Cuban–Hispanic vote in large southern states such as Florida and Texas. It added fuel to the flames of a transatlantic dispute over another US law, which required that sanctions be imposed on foreign firms investing in the oil industries of Iran and Libya. A disputes panel was set up within the World Trade Organization to investigate the matter, and regular meetings took place between US trade representatives and the European Commission. The problem was finally resolved in May 1998 when the United States agreed to a progressive lifting of the sanctions imposed on European companies, and to waive the ban on European executives entering the United States.

Relations with eastern Europe

EU relations with central and eastern European countries (or the CEECs in Eurospeak) have strengthened so rapidly in the last few years that the EU is now the major source of Western aid for the eastern bloc, and several CEECs have signalled their hope of joining the EU. The two sides have come a long way since the initial refusal of the USSR to recognize the existence of the European Community (it finally acquiesced in the late 1970s). The possibility of trade agreements strengthened during the Gorbachev era, and the collapse of the Soviet hegemony forced a rapid reappraisal of the EU's eastern European policy in the late 1980s, raising the serious prospect (for the first time) of an eastward extension of the EU's borders.

A concerted EU response to changes in eastern Europe was agreed at the December 1988 Rhodes European Council. Within three months of taking office in January 1989, US president George Bush was describing western Europe as an economic magnet that could pull eastern Europe towards a new commonwealth of free nations, and the United States began to encourage the EC to take responsibility for coordinating Western economic aid to the east. This was formalized at the 1989 G7 meeting, and December 1989 saw the launch of the PHARE programme to help with economic restructuring in Poland and Hungary (PHARE stands for *Pologne-Hongrie: Actions pour la Reconversion Economique*, but 'phare' also means 'lighthouse' in French). PHARE has since been extended to other eastern European states and the Baltic states, and 5.3 billion ecu was channelled to the east during the period 1990–95.

Trade and cooperation agreements have been signed with almost all east European states, several billion dollars in loans have been made available by the European Investment Bank, the EU has sent food aid to the east, and several functional programmes have been launched to help east European social reform, including help to upgrade university departments in the east under the Tempus programme. The Commission now coordinates the aid efforts of the G24 countries: the EU, what remains of EFTA, and the United States, Canada, Japan, Australia, New Zealand and Turkey. The EU's leading role in this programme has not only helped define EU foreign policy, but has also made the EU a major independent actor in the economic and political future of eastern Europe.

The EU's influence was also boosted by the creation in 1990 of the European Bank for Reconstruction and Development (EBRD), which has channelled public money from the EU, the United States and Japan into development of the private sector in the east. Based in London, the EBRD is not actually part of the EU, but its foundation was an EU initiative, it derives 51 per cent of its capital from the EU, it deals in euros, and it has had a growing influence on EU decisions. Much like the International Bank for Reconstruction and Development (the World Bank), the EBRD was founded to provide loans, encourage capital investment and promote trade, but its specific focus is on helping East European countries make the transition to free-market economics. Both East and West European states are members, as are the United States and Russia.

The end of the cold war produced a growing number of eastern European requests for associate or full membership of the EU, and an irresistible moral pressure on the EU to open its doors to them. Germany (and Chancellor Helmut Kohl) was particularly active in promoting the idea, in part because of its historic links with the east, while the Major government in Britain also supported eastward expansion, but mainly to slow down the process of integration. Europe Agreements came into force in 1994 with with Hungary and Poland, with the Czech Republic, Slovakia, Bulgaria and Romania in 1995, and with the three Baltic states in 1998. The agreements are seen as a step beyond associate membership, and are designed to integrate eastern European economies with those of the EU as quickly as possible through the staged removal of barriers to trade in industrial and agricultural goods, and barriers to the movement of workers. The Treaty of Amsterdam paved the way for eastward expansion, which was confirmed in 1998 when membership negotiations began with Hungary, Poland, the Czech Republic, Slovenia, Estonia and Cyprus (Box 8.3).

Box 8.3 The implications of eastward expansion

Eleven countries are currently on the shortlist for the next round of EU expansion: Cyprus, the Czech Republic, Estonia, Hungary, Poland and Slovenia (with which negotiations began in 1998), and Bulgaria, Latvia, Lithuania, Romania and Slovakia. The general assumption is that the first wave of new members may join by 2002–4, and will probably include Poland, Hungary and the Czech Republic, and perhaps Estonia and Slovenia.

In order to prepare them for membership the EU has agreed 'pre-accession strategies' with all eleven, and is publishing reports every year on the progress each country is making towards aligning their national laws and standards with those of the EU. The Copenhagen summit of the European Council in 1993 set down three conditions they must meet before being allowed to join: they must prove their respect for democratic principles, the rule of law, human rights and the protection of minorities (all but Slovakia were doing well in this regard in late 1998), they must have functioning market economies that are able to cope with the competitive pressures and market forces of the EU (only the six countries with which negotiations have opened have met this requirement), and they must be able to take on all the obligations of membership, including incorporating into their national legal system all the laws agreed by the EU (progress in 1998 was patchy in all eleven).

Several applicant countries complained in 1998 that much more was being expected of them prior to accession than had been the case with earlier entrants. Furthermore, they are being expected to wait longer; while Greece, Spain and Portugal joined the EU seven, 11 and 12 years respectively after freeing themselves from dictatorship, the first eastern European entrants (former East Germany excepted) will have had to wait at least 12 years from the end of the cold war. The wait can be seen as commendable caution on the part of the EU, however, especially given that Poland alone – where GNP is one eighth of the EU average and one in four inhabitants make their living from agriculture – has a population that is larger than that of Spain.

There are strong political and economic arguments in favour of accepting the east European applicants: EU membership is likely to underpin the democratic transition for these states in the same way as it did for Greece, Portugal and Spain, it would open up new investment opportunities, and it would pull them into a strategic relationship with the west that could be useful if relations with Russia were to deteriorate.

The promise of eastward expansion has forced a reappraisal of the EU decision-making process, which has been adjusted regularly since 1958 but is still founded on a club of six countries. If all ten CEEC applicants were to join, they would increase the EU population by 28 per cent but its GNP by less than 4 per cent. Accession will inevitably mean a recalculation of the distribution of seats in the European Parliament, a revised weighting of votes in the Council of Ministers, a rethinking of the balance of national representation in the Commission, and a new system for rotating the presidency of the EU.

The inclusion of poorer states such as Spain, Portugal and Greece created problems enough in the 1980s – which have been partly overcome by huge EU investments in infrastructure in the three countries – but the challenge promises to be much greater with eastern Europe. Its governments and citizens are still struggling with the job of transforming their economies from central planning to the free market, and the political transition from one-party authoritarianism to multiparty democracy. Eastern Europe is also poor. While per capita GNP runs at well over $15 000 in most EU states (Greece and Portugal being notable exceptions, running at less than half the EU average), it is in the $1000–4000 range for most of eastern Europe.

In order to help these countries make the transition and prepare them for EU membership, the EU launched the Agenda 2000 programme in 1997. Essentially a working programme for the EU until 2006, it includes a list of all the measures that the Commission believes are needed to bring the 10 CEECs into the EU without risking institutional paralysis and substantially increased costs for the existing members. The measures include reform of the structural funds to ensure that they are spent in the regions of greatest need, the reduction of subsidies under CAP and a new focus for PHARE on training local specialists in fields such as law and administration. The Commission also used Agenda 2000 to make a new appeal for institutional reform, including a reweighting of votes in the Council of Ministers, a limit of one commissioner per member state and the convening of an IGC by 2002 at the latest to overhaul the EU decision-making process in preparation for enlargement.

Development cooperation

As the progenitor of and major participant in the most active and comprehensive programme of colonization in world history, Europe has long had close economic and political links with the South: Latin America, south Asia and Africa. The end of the colonial era in the 1950s coincided with the beginning of the process of European integration, so the relationship between Europe and its former colonies has been a key item on the agenda of integration almost from the beginning.

EU development aid policies are based partly on remedying quality of life issues such as poverty and hunger, but there are also less than altruistic motives: the South accounts for just over one third of EU exports (half as much again as the United States and Japan combined), more than one fifth of exports from the South go to the EU, and the EU continues to rely on the South as a source of oil and of key raw materials such as rubber, copper and uranium. Development aid now accounts for about 3 per cent of the EU budget, adding to the much larger bilateral flows of aid from each of the member states.

The EU aid programme has several different aspects. As well as allowing all Southern states to export industrial products to the EU tariff- and duty-free (subject to some limitations on volume), the EU provides food and emergency aid, and sponsors development projects undertaken by non-governmental organizations. The EU has also negotiated a series of cooperative agreements with selected former colonies (mainly non-Asian former colonies of Britain and France). These began with the 1963 and 1969 Yaoundé Conventions (named after the capital of Cameroon, where they were signed) which gave 18 former colonies of the original six EEC member states preferential access to Community markets. The 18 in turn allowed limited duty-free or quota-free access by the EC to their markets.

The provision of trade concessions was expanded by the series of Lomé Conventions (named after the capital of Togo), which together have become the single biggest aid programme in the world. The first three Conventions (signed in 1975, 1979 and 1984) each lasted five years; Lomé IV, which was signed in 1989 to cover the period 1990–2000 and was revised in 1995, does the following:

- It provides financial aid to 71 African, Caribbean and Pacific states (the ACP states – see Table 8.4) under the European Development Fund. This mainly takes the form of grants for development projects and low-interest loans. The amount available under the fund increased from 7.5 billion ecu under Lomé III to just over 14.6 billion ecu during the last five years of Lomé IV (1995–2000).
- It provides free access to the EU for products originating from ACP countries, with the exception of agricultural products covered by CAP. About 95 per cent of ACP exports enter the EU duty free; in contrast only 10 per cent of agricultural goods from other countries enter the EU duty-free, and other goods are subject to tariffs in the range of 17–23 per cent.
- It provides an insurance fund for ACP exports. Called Stabex, the purpose of the fund is to offset falls in the value of 50 specified ACP agricultural exports. If prices fall below a certain level, Stabex makes up the deficit. If they go above that level, ACP countries invest the profits in the fund for future use.

The EU has also become the single biggest source of official development assistance in the world, with its member states collectively accounting for 45–50 per cent of the total in 1998 (Europa Homepage), much more than the 20 per cent provided by the United States and the 18 per cent by Japan. Most EU aid (15 per cent of which is channelled through the EU) goes to

Table 8.4 *The ACP states*

Africa (47)		Caribbean (16)
Angola	Mali	Antigua
Benin	Mauritania	Barbados
Botswana	Mauritius	Barbuda
Burkina Faso	Mozambique	Bahamas
Burundi	Namibia	Belize
Cameroon	Niger	Dominica
Cape Verde	Nigeria	Dominican Republic
Central African	Rwanda	Grenada
Republic	Sao Tome and	Guyana
Chad	Principe	Haiti
Comoros	Senegal	Jamaica
Congo	Seychelles	St Christoper and Nevis
Djibouti	Sierra Leone	St Lucia
Equatorial Guinea	Somalia	St Vincent and Grenadines
Ethiopia	South Africa	Suriname
Gabon	Sudan	Trinidad and Tobago
Gambia	Swaziland	
Ghana	Tanzania	Pacific (8)
Guinea	Togo	Fiji
Guinea Bissau	Uganda	Kiribati
Ivory Coast	Zaire	Papua New Guinea
Kenya	Zambia	Solomon Islands
Lesotho	Zimbabwe	Tonga
Liberia		Tuvalu
Madagascar		Western Samoa
Malawi		Vanuatu

sub-Saharan Africa, but an increasing proportion is going to Latin America. At the same time the EU provides emergency humanitarian aid, much of which has gone in recent years to the victims of conflicts in Afghanistan, Armenia, Azerbaijan and Tadjikistan. It has also become the second largest provider of food aid in the world after the United States, supplying food worth about 600 million ecu per year; and it operates a Generalized System of Preferences under which Southern states are allowed to export finished and semifinished goods duty-free to the EU, and are encouraged to industrialize and to diversify their exports.

Opinions are mixed about the efficacy of the ACP programme. On the one hand, it has built closer commercial ties between the EU and the ACP states, and there has been an overall increase in ACP exports to Europe.

On the other hand, Stabex does not help countries that do not produce the specified commodities, payments from the European Development Fund are relatively small by the time the fund has been divided among 71 countries, the ACP programme excludes the larger Southern states that have negotiated separate agreements with the EU (for example India and China), too little attention has been paid to the environmental implications of the focus on cash crops for export, and the programme has neither helped deal with the ACP debt crisis nor really changed the relationship between the EU and the ACP states.

The biggest problem has been internal to the ACP countries themselves. They have failed to diversify their exports, to invest in infrastructure, to build up a more skilled labour force and to become more competitive in the world market. The EU provides them with a generous set of trade preferences, and yet ACP exports as a share of the EU market have fallen from 6.7 per cent in 1976 to less than 4 per cent today. Oil, diamonds, gold and other industrially related products account for about two thirds of ACP exports to the EU, the balance being made up by agricultural products (30 per cent) and fish (5 per cent). Four countries – Nigeria, Ivory Coast, Cameroon and Mauritius – between them account for more than 40 per cent of ACP exports.

Lomé IV included an attempt to push EU policy in a new direction by adding a structural adjustment element to ACP aid; that is, it now encourages economic diversification in the ACP states rather than simply providing project aid. This has made the EU more like the International Monetary Fund or the World Bank as a significant financial actor in international economic relations (Cosgrove and Laurent, 1992), but whether this will improve the South's prospects remains to be seen. Negotiations opened in September 1998 between the EU and the ACP states to replace the Lomé Convention with a more flexible structure based on a series of interregional free trade agreements between groups of ACP countries and the EU. The goal is to bring these into force from 2005, and to allow a further 10–15 years for full application.

Conclusions

The process of European integration was born as a way to help western Europe rebuild itself after the Second World War, and to remove the historical causes of conflict in the region. Over time the EC/EU has become increasingly extroverted, and integration now has implications not just for internal European relations, but for Europe's relations with the rest of the world. While the EEC focused on bringing down the barriers to internal trade, the EU has turned its attention to common foreign and security policies. The process has steadily acquired consistency and regularity, and the CFSP now makes up one of the three pillars that constitute the European Union. Unfortunately the EU is trying to cement its common foreign policy at a time of great change in the world.

One of the sparks that led to the creation of the EU was the obvious security threat posed by the Soviet Union, but that threat has since been replaced by less easily definable economic concerns, and by more specific regional problems such as those in the Balkans, the possible worsening of nationalist pressures in Russia, and the danger of the spread of nuclear weapons technology. Meanwhile the global economic system continues to grow under the auspices of the World Trade Organization, and the United States is slowly shifting its economic interests more towards the south and the east. Finally, the wealth and competitiveness of China, India and other newly industrializing countries continue to grow, altering the balance of global economic power.

All these changes make it essential for the EU to give its own identity clearer definition, and to build up the kind of defensive capability and credibility that it needs as a new economic superpower. While most of the questions about the economic weight of the EU have been answered, it is likely to be some time before the world wakes up to the sight of multilingual soldiers, sailors and pilots going to war under the colours of the European flag, following an agreement reached by Europe's political leaders. However, while the EU may still present a rather confused and confusing image to the outside world, the outline of that image is slowly becoming sharper.

Appendix: A Chronology of European integration, 1944–99

1944	July	Bretton Woods conference.
1945	May	Germany surrenders; European war ends.
	June	Creation of United Nations.
1947	September	Launch of Marshall Plan.
1948	January	Creation of Benelux customs union.
	April	Organization for European Economic Cooperation founded.
	May	Congress of Europe held in The Hague.
1949	April	North Atlantic Treaty signed.
	May	Council of Europe founded.
1950	May	Publication of Schuman Declaration.
1951	April	Treaty of Paris signed, creating the European Coal and Steel Community.
1952	March	Nordic Council founded.
	May	Signature of draft treaty creating the European Defence Community.
	August	ECSC comes into operation.
1953	November	Plans announced for a European Political Community.
1954	August	Plans for EDC and EPC collapse.
	October	Creation of Western European Union.
1956	October	Suez crisis.
1957	March	Treaties of Rome signed, creating Euratom and the European Economic Community.
1958	January	Euratom and EEC begin to operate.
	February	Benelux Economic Union founded.
1960	May	Creation of European Free Trade Association.
	December	OEEC becomes Organization for Economic Cooperation and Development (OECD).
1961	February	First summit of EEC heads of government.
	August	Britain, Ireland and Denmark apply for EEC membership.
1962	April	Norway applies for EEC membership.
1963	January	De Gaulle vetoes British membership of the EEC; France and Germany sign Treaty of Friendship and cooperation.
1965	April	Merger treaty signed.
1966	May	Britain, Ireland and Denmark apply for the second time for EEC membership (Norway follows in July).
1967	December	De Gaulle vetoes British membership of the Community.

1968	July	Agreement of a common external tariff completes the creation of an EEC customs union; Common Agricultural Policy agreed.
1970	June	Membership negotiations opened with Britain, Denmark, Ireland and Norway; concluded in January 1972.
1971	August	US leaves gold standard; end of the Bretton Woods system of fixed exchange rates.
1972	September	Referendum in Norway turns down EEC membership.
1973	January	Britain, Denmark and Ireland join the Community, bringing the membership to nine.
1974	January	Creation of the European Social Fund.
1975	January	Creation of the European Regional Development Fund.
	March	First meeting of the European Council in Dublin.
	June	Greece applies for Community membership; negotiations begin in July 1976.
1977	March	Portugal applies for Community membership; negotiations begin in October 1978.
	July	Spain applies for Community membership; negotiations begin in February 1979.
1979	March	European Monetary System comes into operation.
	June	First direct elections to the European Parliament.
1981	January	Greece joins the Community, bringing the membership to ten.
1984	January	Free trade area established between EFTA and the EC.
1985	June	Schengen Agreement signed by France, Germany and the Benelux states.
1986	January	Spain and Portugal join the Community, bringing the membership to 12.
	February	Single European Act signed in Luxembourg.
1987	June	Turkey applies to join the Community.
	July	Single European Act comes into force.
1989	April	Delors report on economic and monetary union.
	July	Austria applies for Community membership.
	December	Adoption of the Social Charter by 11 EC member states; rejection of Turkish membership application.
1990	July	Cyprus and Malta apply for Community membership.
	October	German reunification brings former East Germany into the Community.
1992	February	Treaty on European Union signed.
	June	Following a popular referendum, Denmark rejects the terms of Maastricht.
1993	May	Referendum in Denmark leads to acceptance of terms of Maastricht.
	November	Treaty on European Union comes into force.
1994	January	Creation of the European Economic Area.
	March	Poland and Hungary become associate members of the EU.

1994	May	Opening of the Channel Tunnel, linking Britain and France.
	June–Nov	Referenda in Austria, Finland and Sweden go in favour of EU membership, but Norwegians say no.
1995	January	Austria, Sweden and Finland join the European Union, bringing the membership to 15.
	March	Schengen Agreement comes into force.
	July	Europol Convention signed.
1997	October	Treaty of Amsterdam signed.
1998	March	EU membership negotiations open with the Czech Republic, Cyprus, Estonia, Hungary, Poland and Slovenia.
	June	Establishment of the European Central Bank.
1999	January	Adoption of single currency by 11 EU member states.

Sources of Further Information

The literature on the European Union has grown dramatically in the last few years, with the number of new books, journal articles and Web sites increasing to match the pace of change in the EU itself, and of expanding public interest in EU affairs. The sources listed here do little more than provide a sampling of what was available as this book went to press. To keep up with developments, you might want to monitor new acquisitions at your nearest library, keep an eye out for new books from the publishers with the best lists on the European Union (including Macmillan, St. Martin's Press, Routledge, Oxford University Press, and Lynne Rienner), and search online book dealers such as Amazon.com.

Books

The best general introductions to the European Union are Archer and Butler (1996), George (1996), Dinan (1999) and Nugent (1999). Useful edited collections on recent developments in the EU include Laurent and Maresceau (1998) and Cram *et al.* (1999). For general surveys of the history of the EU, see Black *et al.* (1992), Pinder (1995), and Urwin (1995).

After a sustained dry spell, the number of books on EU institutions has grown dramatically in the last few years; the Commission in particular has become the subject of a rash of new studies, notable among which are Cini (1996), Nugent (1997, forthcoming), and Edwards and Spence (1997). The best surveys of Parliament are offered by Westlake (1994), Jacobs *et al.* (1995) and Corbett (1998), and political parties are the focus of a book by Hix and Lord (1997). Most studies of the Court of Justice are written by lawyers with their uniquely detailed legalistic style, and there are few good general introductions beyond Brown and Kennedy (1994), Lasok (1998) and Dehousse (1998).

Despite its obviously critical role in the EU, the Council of Ministers has been the subject of very little scholarly literature so far, the only recent full-length study being Hayes-Renshaw and Wallace (1997). For an assessment of the role of the presidency of the Council of Ministers, see Kirchner (1992), and for the European Council, see Johnston (1994) and Bulmer and Wessels (forthcoming).

For edited collections dealing with a variety of EU policy areas, see Richardson (1996) and Wallace and Wallace (1996). A good general survey of economic policy can be found in Tsoukalis (1997), while there are now an increasing number of studies of EU activities in many specific policy areas, including agriculture (Grant, 1997), energy (Matláry, 1997), competition (Cini and McGowan, 1998), technology (Peterson and Sharp, 1998), the environment (McCormick, forthcoming), and foreign policy (Rhodes, 1998, Whitman, 1998).

Periodicals and EU publications

The Economist. A weekly news magazine that has stories and statistics on world politics, including a section on Europe (and occasional special supplements on the EU). Selected headline stories can be found on the *Economist* Web site:

http://www.economist.com/

The Economist also publishes two series of quarterly reports that are a treasure-house of information, but they are expensive, so you will probably need to look them up in your nearest university library: *Economist Intelligence Unit Country Reports* (these cover almost every country in the world, and include a series on the European Union), and *European Policy Analyst.* Both provide detailed political and economic news and information.

Finally, *the Economist* also publishes *European Voice*, a weekly newspaper published in Brussels that is packed with all the latest news and information on the EU. Selected headline stories can be found on its Web site:

http://www.european-voice.com/

Journal of Common Market Studies. This quarterly academic journal is devoted to the EU and contains scholarly articles and book reviews. Many other academic journals include articles on the EU, but the most consistently useful are *West European Politics, International Organization* and *Parliamentary Affairs.*

Official Journal of the European Communities. Published daily, this is the official gazette of the EU and the authoritative source of information on all EU legislation, proposals by the Commission for new legislation, decisions and resolutions by the Council of Ministers, debates in the European Parliament, new actions brought before the Court of Justice, opinions of the Economic and Social Committee, the annual report of the Court of Auditors, and the EU budget. It is now available on the Web through the Europa site (see below).

General Report on the Activities of the European Union The major annual report of the EU, with a record of developments in all the key EU policy areas, and key statistical information.

Bulletin of the European Union. Published monthly, this is the official record of events in (and policies of) all the EU institutions. Contains reports on the activities of the Commission and other EU institutions, along with special feature articles. Supplements contain copies of key Commission documents, including proposed legislation.

Directorate-General Documentation. Every DG in the Commission publishes its own periodicals, reports and surveys, but these are too numerous to list here. One of the most useful of the regular publications is the series of biannual Eurobarometer opinion polls published by DGX (Information, Communication and Culture). These have been carried out in the EU since 1973, mainly to provide

EU institutions and the media with statistics on public attitudes towards European issues and European integration.

Eurostat. An acronym for the Statistical Office of the European Communities, Eurostat is based in Luxembourg and collects and collates statistical information of many different kinds from the EU member states. Much of this is available on computer online services; all of it is published in the form of yearbooks, surveys, studies and reports.

Directory of Community Legislation in Force and Other Acts of the Community Institutions. Published annually, with biannual supplements. Lists directives, regulations and other legislation, as well as internal and external agreements.

Web sites

Anyone who uses the internet knows how quickly the World Wide Web is changing, how often sites are replaced or closed down, and how regularly URLs seem to change. Instead of listing useful sites here, I have set up a series of links on my home page, which I shall do my best to keep up to date. The URL is:

http://www.iupui.edu/~jmccormi/

Meanwhile, one of the best places to start to search for information is Europa, the official EU site This offers a vast array of information on developments in the EU, although some of the pages are not always entirely up to date. The URL is:

http://europa.eu.int

Bibliography

Airbus Industrie Homepage (1998) World Wide Web < http://www.airbus.com/ >.

Allen, David (1996a) 'Cohesion and Structural Adjustment', in Helen Wallace and William Wallace (eds), *Policy-Making in the European Union,* 3rd edn (Oxford: Oxford University Press).

Allen, David (1996b) 'Competition Policy: Policing the Single Market', in Helen Wallace and William Wallace (eds), *Policy-Making in the European Union,* 3rd edn (Oxford: Oxford University Press).

Anderson, Scott (1992) 'Western Europe and the Gulf War', in Reinhardt Rummel, *Toward Political Union: Planning a Common Foreign and Security Policy in the European Community* (Boulder, CO: Westview).

Archer, Clive and Fiona Butler (1996) *The European Union: Structure and Process,* 2nd edn (London: Pinter).

Armstrong, Kenneth and Simon Bulmer (1998) *The Governance of the Single European Market* (Manchester: Manchester University Press).

ASEAN Homepage (1998) World Wide Web < http://www.asean.or.id/ >.

Aspinwall, Mark and Justin Greenwood (1998) 'Conceptualising Collective Action in the European Union: An Introduction', in Mark Aspinwall and Justin Greenwood (eds), *Collective Action in the European Union: Interests and the New Politics of Associability* (London: Routledge).

Bainbridge, Timothy and Anthony Teasdale (1995) *The Penguin Companion to European Union* (London: Penguin).

Balassa, Bela (1961) *The Theory of Economic Integration* (Homewood, Ill.: Irwin).

Barber, Lionel (1997) 'NATO's New Mission', *Europe*, no. 367, pp. 12–15.

Barber, Lionel (1998) 'Sharing Common Risks: The EU View', *Europe*, no. 374, pp. 8–9.

Barnes, Ian and Pamela M. Barnes (1995) *The Enlarged European Union* (London: Longman).

Barzini, Luigi (1983) *The Europeans* (London: Penguin).

Black, Cyril E. *et al.* (1992) *Rebirth: A History of Europe Since World War II* (Boulder, CO: Westview).

Bradford, Michael (1998) 'Education and Welfare', in Tim Unwin (ed.), *A European Geography* (Harlow, Essex: Longman).

Brewin, Christopher and Richard McAllister (1991), 'Annual Review of the Activities of the European Community in 1990', *Journal of Common Market Studies*, vol. 29, no. 4 (June), pp. 385–430.

Brown, L. Neville and Tom Kennedy (1994) *The Court of Justice of the European Communities,* 4th edn (London: Sweet and Maxwell).

Bugge, Peter (1995) 'The Nation Supreme: The Idea of Europe 1914–1945', in Kevin Wilson and Jan van der Dussen (eds), *The History of the Idea of Europe* (London: Routledge).

Bulmer, Simon and Wolfgang Wessels (forthcoming) *The European Council: Decisionmaking in European Politics,* 2nd edn (Basingstoke: Macmillan).

Cecchini, Paolo (1988) *The European Challenge: 1992* (Aldershot: Wildwood House).

Cini, Michelle (1996) *The European Commission: Leadership, Organization and Culture in the EU Administration* (Manchester: Manchester University Press).

Cini, Michelle and Lee McGowan (1998) *Competition Policy in the European Union* (Basingstoke: Macmillan).

Colchester, Nicholas and David Buchan (1990) *Europower: The Essential Guide to Europe's Economic Transformation* (London: Economist Books).

Collins, Ken and David Earnshaw (1993) 'The Implementation and Enforcement of European Community Environment Legislation', in David Judge (ed.), *A Green Dimension for the European Community: Political Issues and Processes* (London: Frank Cass).

Commission of the European Communities (1973) *Report on the Regional Problems of the Enlarged Community* (The Thomson Report), COM(73)550 (Brussels: Commission of the European Communities).

Commission of the European Communities (1975) *Economic and Monetary Union 1980* (The Marjolin Report) (Brussels: Commission of the European Communities).

Commission of the European Communities (1985) *Completing the Internal Market* (The Cockfield Report), COM(85)310 (Brussels: Commission of the European Communities).

Commission of the European Communities (1993) *Youth Exchanges in the European Community* (Brussels: Commission of the European Communities).

Coombes, David and Nicholas Rees (1991) 'Regional and Social Policy', in Leon Hurwitz and Christian Lequesne (eds), *The State of the European Community* (Boulder, CO: Lynne Rienner).

Corbett, Richard (1998) *The European Parliament's Role in Closer EU Integration* (New York: St Martin's Press).

Cosgrove, Carol and Pierre-Henri Laurent (1992), 'The Unique Relationship: the European Community and the ACP', in John Redmond (ed.), *The External Relations of the European Community* (New York: St Martin's Press).

Cram, Laura, Desmond Dinan and Neill Nugent (eds) (1999) *Developments in the European Union* (Basingstoke: Macmillan).

Dahrendorf, Ralf (1988) *The Modern Social Conflict* (London: Weidenfeld and Nicolson).

Daltrop, Anne (1987) *Politics and the European Community* (London: Longman).

de Bassompierre, Guy (1988) *Changing the Guard in Brussels: An Insider's View of the EC Presidency* (New York, NY: Praeger).

Dehousse, Renaud (1998) *The European Court of Justice* (Basingstoke: Macmillan).

Delanty, Gerard (1995) *Inventing Europe: Idea, Identity, Reality* (New York: St Martin's Press).

Delors, Jacques (1991) 'European Integration and Security', *Survival*, vol. 33, no. 2 (Spring), pp. 99–109.

den Boer, Pim (1995) 'Europe to 1914: The making of an idea', in Kevin Wilson and Jan van der Dussen (eds), *The History of the Idea of Europe* (London: Routledge).

de Rougemont, Denis (1966) *The Idea of Europe* (Macmillan, London).

Dinan, Desmond (1994) *Ever Closer Union? An Introduction to European Integration*, 2nd edn (Boulder, CO: Lynne Rienner/Basingstoke: Macmillan Press).

Dougherty, James E. and Robert L. Pfaltzgraff (1990) *Contending Theories of International Relations* (New York: Harper & Row).

Edwards, Geoffrey and David Spence (eds) (1997) *The European Commission*, 2nd edn (London: Cartermill).

Elsom, Derek (1987) *Atmospheric Pollution* (Oxford: Basil Blackwell).

Europa Homepage (1988) World Wide Web < http://europa.eu.int > .

Featherstone, K. (1994) 'Jean Monnet and the "democratic deficit" in the EU', *Journal of Common Market Studies*, vol. 32, no. 20, pp. 149–70.

Fernández-Armesto, Felipe (ed.) (1997) *The Times Guide to the Peoples of Europe* (London: Times Books).

Franklin, Mark (1996) 'European Elections and the European Voter', in Jeremy Richardson (ed.), *European Union: Power and Policy-Making* (London: Routledge).

Fratianni, Michele and Jurgen von Hagen (1992) *The European Monetary System and European Monetary Union* (Boulder, CO: Westview Press).

Freestone, David (1991) 'European Community Environmental Policy and Law', in *Journal of Law and Society*, vol. 18, no. 1, pp. 135–54.

Gallagher, Michael, Michael Laver and Peter Mair (1992) *Representative Government in Modern Europe*, 2nd edn (New York: McGraw-Hill).

George, Stephen (1996) *Politics and Policy in the European Community*, 3rd edn (Oxford: Oxford University Press).

Geyer, Robert and Beverly Springer (1998) 'EU Social Policy After Maastricht: The Works Council Directive and the British Opt-Out', in Pierre-Henri Laurent and Marc Maresceau (eds), *The State of the European Union Vol. 4* (Boulder, CO: Lynne Rienner).

Gillingham, John (1991) *Coal, Steel, and the Rebirth of Europe, 1945–1955* (Cambridge: Cambridge University Press).

Grant, Wyn (1997) *The Common Agricultural Policy* (Basingstoke: Macmillan Press).

Greenwood, Justin (1997) *Representing Interests in the European Union* (Basingstoke: Macmillan).

Haas, Ernst B. (1958) 'The Challenge of Regionalism', *International Organization*, vol. 12.

Haas, Ernst B. (1964) 'Technocracy, Pluralism and the New Europe', in Stephen R. Graubard (ed.) *A New Europe?* (Boston, MA: Houghton Mifflin).

Haas, Ernst B. (1968) *The Uniting of Europe: Political, Social, and Economic Forces, 1950–57* (Stanford, CA: Stanford University Press).

Haas, Ernst B. (1975) *The Obsolescence of Regional Integration Theory* (Berkeley, CA: Institute of International Studies, University of California).

Haas, Ernst B. (1976) 'Turbulent Fields and the Theory of Regional Integration', *International Organization*, vol. 30, no. 2, pp. 173–212.

Haigh, Nigel (1990) *EEC Environmental Policy and Britain*, 2nd edn (Harlow, Essex: Longman).

Hall, Derek R. (1998) 'Tourism and Travel', in Tim Unwin (ed.) *A European Geography* (Harlow: Addison Wesley Longman).

Hardgrave, Robert L. and Stanley A. Kochanek (1993) *India: Government and Politics in a Developing Nation* (Fort Worth, TX: Harcourt Brace).

Hay, David (1957) *Europe: The Emergence of an Idea* (Edinburgh: Edinburgh University Press).

Hayes-Renshaw, Fiona and Helen Wallace (1997) *The Council of Ministers* (Basingstoke: Macmillan).

Heater, Derek (1992) *The Idea of European Unity* (New York: St Martin's Press).

Heisler, Martin O., with Robert B. Kvavik (1973) 'Patterns of European Politics: The "European Polity" Model', in Martin O. Heisler (ed.), *Politics in Europe: Structures and Processes in Some Postindustrial Democracies*(New York: David McKay).

Heyman, Charles (1997) interview with José Cutileiro in *Jane's Defence Weekly*, vol. 27 (18 May), on Jane's Homepage, <http://www.janes.com/defence/interviews>.

Hildebrand, Philipp M. (1993) 'The European Community's Environmental Policy, 1957 to "1992": From Incidental Measures to an International Regime?', in David Judge (ed.), *A Green Dimension for the European Community: Political Issues and Processes* (London: Frank Cass).

Hill, Christopher (1992) 'EPC's Performance in Crises', in Reinhardt Rummel, *Toward Political Union: Planning a Common Foreign and Security Policy in the European Community* (Boulder, CO: Westview Press).

Hix, Simon and Christopher Lord (1997) *Political Parties in the European Union* (New York: St Martin's Press).

Hobsbawm, Eric (1991) *The Age of Empire 1848–1875* (London: Cardinal).

Hogan, Michael J. (1987) *The Marshall Plan: America, Britain, and the Reconstruction of Western Europe, 1947–52* (New York: Cambridge University Press).

Hooghe, L. and M. Keating (1994) 'The Politics of European Union Regional Policy', *Journal of European Public Policy*, vol. 1, no. 3, pp. 367–93.

Ionescu, Ghita (1975) *Centripetal Politics: Government and the New Centres of Power* (London: Hart-Davis McGibbon).

Jacobs, Francis, Richhard Corbett and Michael Shackelton (1995) *The European Parliament*, 3rd edn (New York: Stockton).

Johnston, Mary Troy (1994) *The European Council: Gatekeeper of the European Community* (Boulder, CO: Westview Press).

Kaufmann, Hugo M. and Stephen Overturf (1991) 'Progress Within the European Monetary System', in Leon Hurwitz and Christian Lequesne (eds), *The State of the European Community Vol 1: Policies, Institutions and Debates in the Transition Years* (Boulder, CO: Lynne Rienner).

Keating, Michael and Liesbet Hooghe (1996) 'By-passing the Nation State? Regions and the EU Policy Process', in Jeremy Richardson (ed.) *European Union: Power and Policy-Making* (London: Routledge).

Keegan, Victor and Martin Kettle (1993) *The New Europe* (London: Fourth Estate).

Kellas, James G. (1991) 'European Integration and the Regions', in *Parliamentary Affairs*, vol. 44, no. 2, pp. 226–39.

Keohane, Robert O. and Stanley Hoffmann (1990) 'Conclusions: Community Politics and Institutional Change', in William Wallace (ed.), *The Dynamics of European Integration* (London: Royal Institute of International Affairs).

Keohane, Robert O. and Stanley Hoffmann (eds) (1991) *The New European Community: Decisionmaking and Institutional Change* (Boulder, CO: Westview Press).

Kirchner, Emil Joseph (1992) *Decision-Making in the European Community: The Council Presidency and European Integration* (Manchester: Manchester University Press).

Krause, Axel (1991) *Inside the New Europe* (New York: HarperCollins).

Lasok, K.P.E. (1984) *The European Court of Justice: Practice and Procedure* (London: Butterworths).

Lasok, Dominik (1998) *Law and Institutions of the European Communities*, 7th edn (London: Lexis Law Publishing).

Laurent, Pierre-Henri and Marc Maresceau (eds) (1998) *The State of the European Union, vol. 4: Deepening and Widening* (Boulder, CO: Lynne Rienner).

Lijphart, Arend (1968) *The Politics of Accommodation: Pluralism and Democracy in the Netherlands* (Berkeley, CA: University of California Press).

Lijphart, Arend (1979) 'Consociation and Federation: Conceptual and Empirical Links', *Canadian Journal of Political Science*, vol. 22, no. 3, pp. 499–515.

Lindberg, Leon N. (1963) *The Political Dynamics of European Economic Integration* (Stanford, CA: Stanford University Press).

Lindberg, Leon N. and Stuart A. Scheingold (1970) *Europe's Would-Be Polity: Patterns of Change in the European Community* (Englewood Cliffs, NJ: Prentice-Hall).

Lindberg, Leon N. and Stuart A. Scheingold (1971) *Regional Integration: Theory and Research* (Cambridge, MA: Harvard University Press).

Lodge, Juliet (1993) 'EC Policymaking: Institutional Dynamics', in Juliet Lodge (ed.), *The European Community and the Challenge of the Future*, 2nd edn (New York: St Martin's Press).

Loedel, Peter H. (1998) 'Enhancing Europe's International Monetary Power: The Drive Toward a Single Currency', in Pierre-Henri Laurent and Marc Maresceau (eds), *The State of the European Union Vol. 4: Deepening and Widening* (Boulder, CO: Lynne Rienner).

Lustick, Ian (1979) 'Stability in Deeply Divided Societies: Consociationalism Versus Control', *World Politics*, vol. 31, no. 3, pp. 325–44.

Macrory, Richard (1992) 'The Enforcement of Community Environmental Laws: Some Critical Issues', *Common Market Law Review*, vol. 29, pp. 347–69.

Magiera, Siegfried (1991) 'A Citizen's Europe: Personal, Political and Cultural Rights', in Leon Hurwitz and Christian Lequesne (eds), *The State of the European Community* (Boulder, CO: Lynne Rienner).

Mancini, G. Federico (1991) 'The Making of a Constitution for Europe', in Robert O. Keohane and Stanley Hoffmann (eds), *The New European Community: Decisionmaking and Institutional Change* (Boulder, CO: Westview Press).

Marks, Gary (1993) 'Structural Policy and Multilevel Governance in the EC', in Alan Cafruny and Glenda Rosenthal (eds), *The State of the European*

Community II: The Maastricht Debates and Beyond (Boulder, CO: Lynne Rienner).

Matláry, Janne Haaland (1997) *Energy Policy in the European Union* (Basingstoke: Macmillan).

Mazey, Sonia and Jeremy Richardson (1996) 'The Logic of Organisation: Interest Groups', in Jeremy Richardson (ed.), *European Union: Power and Policy-Making* (London: Routledge).

McCormick, John (1995) *The Global Environmental Movement*, 2nd edn (London: John Wiley).

McCormick, John (1997) *Acid Earth: The Politics of Acid Pollution*, 3rd edn (London: Earthscan).

McCormick, John (forthcoming) *Environmental Policy in the European Union* (Basingstoke: Macmillan).

McGrory, Daniel P. (1990) 'Air Pollution Legislation in the United States and the European Community', *European Law Review*, vol. 15, no. 4.

Menon, Anand, Anthony Forster and William Wallace (1992) 'A Common European Defense?', *Survival*, vol. 34, no. 3, pp. 98–118.

Milward, Alan S. (1984) *The Reconstruction of Western Europe, 1945–51* (Berkeley, CA: University of California Press).

Minshull, G. N. and M. J. Dawson (1996) *The New Europe Into the 21st Century*, 5th edn (London: Hodder and Stoughton).

Mitrany, David (1966) *A Working Peace System* (Chicago, Ill.: Quadrangle).

Mitrany, David (1970) 'The Functional Approach to World Organisation', in Carol A. Cosgrove and Kenneth J. Twitchett (eds), *The New International Actors: The UN and the EEC* (London: Macmillan).

Monnet, Jean (1978) *Memoirs* (Garden City, NY: Doubleday).

Nugent, Neill (ed.) (1997) *At the Heart of the Union: Studies of the European Commission* (Basingstoke: Macmillan).

Nugent, Neill (1999) *The Government and Politics of the European Union*, 4th edn (Basingstoke: Macmillan).

Nugent, Neill (forthcoming) *The European Commission* (Basingstoke: Macmillan).

Nye, Joseph S. (1971a) 'Comparing Common Markets: A Revised Neofunctionalist Model', in Leon N. Lindberg and Stuart A. Scheingold (eds), *Regional Integration: Theory and Research* (Cambridge, MA: Harvard University Press).

Nye, Joseph S. (1971b) *Peace in Parts: Integration and Conflict in Regional Organization* (Boston, MA: Little, Brown).

Orzak, Louis H. (1991) 'The General Systems Directive and the Liberal Profession', in Leon Hurwitz and Christian Lequesne (eds), *The State of the European Community* (Boulder, CO: Lynne Rienner).

Owen, Richard and Michael Dynes (1992) *The Times Guide to the Single European Market* (London: Times Books).

Palmer, Michael (1968) *European Unity: A Survey of European Organizations* (London: George Allen & Unwin).

Peterson, John and Margaret Sharp (1998) *Technology Policy in the European Union* (Basingstoke: Macmillan).

Pinder, John (1995) *European Community: The Building of a Union*, 2nd edn (Oxford: Oxford University Press).

Pye, Lucien (1966) *Aspects of Political Development* (Boston, MA: Little, Brown).

Rehbinder, Eckard and Richard Stewart (eds) (1985) *Environmental Protection Policy, Vol. 2 – Integration Through Law: Europe and the American Federal Experience* (Firenze, Italy: European University Institute).

Rhodes, Carolyn (ed.) (1998) *The European Union in the World Community* (Boulder, CO: Lynne Rienner).

Richardson, Jeremy (ed.) (1996) *European Union: Power and Policy-Making* (London and New York: Routledge).

Romero, Federico (1992) 'Cross-Border Population Movements', in William Wallace (ed.), *The Dynamics of European Integration* (London: Pinter).

Saint-Ouen, Francois (1988) 'Facing European Integration: The Case of Switzerland', in *Journal of Common Market Studies*, vol. 26, no. 3, pp. 273–85.

Salmon, Trevor and Sir William Nicol (eds) (1997) *Building European Union: A Documentary History and Analysis* (Manchester: Manchester University Press).

Schmitter, Philippe C. (1971) 'A Revised Theory of Regional Integration', in Leon N. Lindberg and Stuart A. Scheingold, *Regional Integration: Theory and Research* (Cambridge, MA: Harvard University Press).

Schultz, D. Mark (1992) 'Austria in the International Arena: Neutrality, European Integration and Consociationalism', in Kurt Richard Luther and Wolfgang C. Muller (eds), *Politics in Austria: Still a Case of Consociationalism?* (London: Frank Cass).

Shackleton, Michael (1990) *Financing the European Community* (New York: Council on Foreign Relations Press).

Smith, Michael (1998) 'What's Wrong with the CFSP? The Politics of Institutional Reform', in Pierre-Henri Laurent and Marc Maresceau (eds), *The State of the European Union*, vol. 4 (Boulder, CO: Lynne Rienner).

Smith, Michael and Stephen Woolcock (1993) *Redefining the US–EC Relationship* (New York: Council on Foreign Relations Press).

Springer, Beverly (1992) *The Social Dimension of 1992: Europe Faces a New EC* (Westport, CT: Praeger).

Streit, Clarence (1961) *Freedom's Frontier – Atlantic Union Now* (Washington, DC: Freedom and Union Press).

Taylor, Paul (1990) 'Consociationalism and Federalism as Approaches to International Integration', in A. J. R. Groom and Paul Taylor (eds), *Frameworks for International Cooperation* (New York: St Martin's Press).

Thatcher, Margaret (1993) *The Downing Street Years* (New York: HarperCollins).

Tsoukalis, Loukas (1997) *The New European Economy Revisited: The Politics and Economics of Integration*, 3rd edn (Oxford: Oxford University Press).

Union of International Associations Homepage (1998) World Wide Web < http://www.uia.org/welcome.htm >.

Urwin, Derek (1995) *The Community of Europe*, 2nd edn (London: Longman).

van Eekelen, Willem (1990) 'WEU and the Gulf Crisis', *Survival* 32:6, pp. 519–32.

von der Groeben, H. (1987) *The European Community, the Formative Years: The Struggle to Establish the Common Market and the Political Union (1958–66)* (Brussels: European Commission).

van Hamme, Alain (1991) 'The European Court of Justice: Recent Developments', in Leon Hurwitz and Christian Lequesne (eds), *The State of the European Community, Vol. 1: Policies, Institutions, and Debates in the Transition Years* (Boulder, CO: Lynne Rienner).

Wallace, Helen (1991) 'The Council and the Commission After the Single European Act', in Leon Hurwitz and Christain Lequesne (eds), *The State of the European Community: Policies, Institutions, and Debates in the Transition Years* (Boulder, CO: Lynne Rienner).

Wallace, Helen (1992), 'What Europe for Which Europeans?', in Gregory F. Treverton (ed.) *The Shape of the New Europe* (New York: Council on Foreign Relations Press).

Wallace, William (1990) *The Transformation of Western Europe* (London: Royal Institute of International Affairs).

Wallace, William (1994) *Regional Integration: The West European Experience* (Washington, DC: The Brookings Institution).

Wallace, William (1996) 'Government Without Statehood: The Unstable Equilibrium', in Helen Wallace and William Wallace (eds), *Policy-Making in the European Union*, 3rd edn (Oxford: Oxford University Press).

Weigall, David and Peter Stirk (eds) (1992) *The Origins and Development of the European Community* (London: Pinter).

Weiler, J. H. H. (1991) 'The Transformation of Europe', *Yale Law Review*, vol. 100, no. 8, pp. 2403–83.

Westlake, Martin (1994) *A Modern Guide to the European Parliament* (London: Pinter).

Wexler, Immanual (1983) *The Marshall Plan Revisited: The European Recovery Program in Economic Perspective* (Westport, CT: Greenwood).

Whitman, Richard G. (1998) *From Civilian Power to Superpower? The International Identity of the European Union* (New York: St Martin's Press).

Williams, Shirley (1991) 'Sovereignty and Accountability in the European Community', in Robert O. Keohane and Stanley Hoffmann (eds), *The New European Community: Decisionmaking and Institutional Change* (Boulder, CO: Westview Press).

Woolcock, Stephen and Michael Hodges (1996) 'EU Policy in the Uruguay Round', in Helen and William Wallace (eds), *Policy-Making in the European Union* (Oxford: Oxford University Press).

World Trade Organization (1996) *Compendium of Tourist Statistics 1989–94* (Madrid: World Trade Organization).

Zurcher, Arnold J. (1958) *The Struggle to Unite Europe, 1940–58* (New York: New York University Press).

Index